An Insider's Guide to Working in International Higher Education

This is a guide for anyone considering a move into international education. It explores the journeys and experiences of those within international higher education and offers perspectives, advice, and guidance on how to navigate issues such as partnership development, cultural interaction, international working environments, and distance.

This is both an insightful and practical book that provides a unique perspective by drawing upon international case studies and highlighting key factors and issues for navigating international higher education. The book examines the realities and lived experiences of transnational education activity through the lens of a journey. It is constructed around three key stages of travel: preparation, getting there, getting home again. The book draws on case studies and first-hand perspectives to provide the reader with guidance on how to navigate the different aspects of international higher education travel and work. A diverse group of stakeholders including students, academics, administrators, and leaders discuss their experiences and provide reflections and lessons learned.

This engaging book will be of interest to anyone considering embarking on a transnational education journey, as a practitioner, a policy maker, as well as university leaders and prospective international students.

Christopher Hill is Vice President Research and Innovation at the Canadian University Dubai. He has worked in international higher education in Asia and the Middle East since 2008, publishing and presenting widely on transnational education. He hosts the Think Education podcast.

Judith Lamie is the Pro Vice-Chancellor for International Engagement at Swansea University, United Kingdom. She has published and presented widely in the fields of applied linguistics, change management, and international higher education for over 30 years.

"*An Insider's Guide to Working in International Higher Education* offers an insightful perspective on partnership development, cultural interactions, leadership, and international working environments. It is a must-read for practitioners, policymakers, university leaders, researchers, and students."

Janet Ilieva, Director and Founder, Education Insight

"Transnational Education (TNE) is now part of the mainstream of international higher education. The field is in need of professionalisation, and *An Insider's Guide to Working in International Higher Education* by experts Christopher Hill and Judith Lamie distils decades of experience in an essential set of tools for international educators both experienced and new. A must-read."

Eduardo Ramos, Head of Higher Education Systems & Internationalisation, Going Global Partnership Programme | Cultural Engagement, British Council

"Through the lens of a journey, this insightful book provides both practical guidance and a deep understanding of the realities of working in international higher education; essential reading for those starting out or looking to deepen their engagement."

Sirin Myles, Co-founder and Director, The IC Global Partnership

CHRISTOPHER HILL AND JUDITH LAMIE

An Insider's Guide to Working in International Higher Education

LONDON AND NEW YORK

Designed cover image: Kinga Krzeminska/Getty Images

First published 2026
by Routledge
4 Park Square, Milton Park, Abingdon, Oxon, OX14 4RN

and by Routledge
605 Third Avenue, New York, NY 10158

Routledge is an imprint of the Taylor & Francis Group, an informa business

© 2026 Christopher Hill and Judith Lamie

The right of Christopher Hill and Judith Lamie to be identified as authors of this work has been asserted in accordance with sections 77 and 78 of the Copyright, Designs and Patents Act 1988.

All rights reserved. No part of this book may be reprinted or reproduced or utilised in any form or by any electronic, mechanical, or other means, now known or hereafter invented, including photocopying and recording, or in any information storage or retrieval system, without permission in writing from the publishers.

Trademark notice: Product or corporate names may be trademarks or registered trademarks, and are used only for identification and explanation without intent to infringe.

British Library Cataloguing-in-Publication Data
A catalogue record for this book is available from the British Library

Library of Congress Cataloging-in-Publication Data
Names: Hill, Christopher, 1978- author | Lamie, Judith author
Title: An insider's guide to working in international higher education / Christopher Hill, and Judith Lamie.
Description: Abingdon, Oxon ; New York, NY : Routledge, 2026. | Includes bibliographical references and index.
Identifiers: LCCN 2025020718 (print) | LCCN 2025020719 (ebook) | ISBN 9781041093374 hardback | ISBN 9781041093367 paperback | ISBN 9781003649571 ebook
Subjects: LCSH: Transnational education | Educational exchanges | Education, Higher--International cooperation
Classification: LCC LC1095 .H55 2026 (print) | LCC LC1095 (ebook) | DDC 378.0023--dc23/eng/20250621
LC record available at https://lccn.loc.gov/2025020718
LC ebook record available at https://lccn.loc.gov/2025020719

ISBN: 9781041093374 (hbk)
ISBN: 9781041093367 (pbk)
ISBN: 9781003649571 (ebk)

DOI: 10.4324/9781003649571

Typeset in Joanna
by KnowledgeWorks Global Ltd.

Contents

List of Figures	vii
List of Tables	viii
List of Case Studies	ix

Introduction   1
Christopher Hill and Judith Lamie

The Accidental TNE Practitioner – Routes into International Higher Education   **One**   4
Judith Lamie and Christopher Hill

Starting Out – A Few Practicalities   **Two**   24
Christopher Hill and Judith Lamie

Broadening Horizons and Making Us Kinder – The Impact of Early Opportunities for Student Mobility   **Three**   38
Judith Lamie and Christopher Hill

I'm a Stranger Here Myself – The Joys of International Education Travel   **Four**   58
Christopher Hill and Judith Lamie

Developing TNE Partnerships – The Beginning – Deciding Where to Go and Who to Partner With   **Five**   78
Judith Lamie and Christopher Hill

The Role of Language and Cultural Responsiveness in Promoting Diversity, Equity, and Accessibility in Transnational Education   **Six**   100
Stephanie Martin

Conversation Not Confrontation – Women in Leadership in TNE **Seven** 123
Judith Lamie

Lost in Translation – Culture, Community, and Communication on Our International Travels **Eight** 144
Judith Lamie and Christopher Hill

Managing Transnational Education Partnerships – An Evolving Journey **Nine** 161
Nigel Healey and Rob Hickey

Developing TNE Partnerships – The End – Planning or an Amicable Separation **Ten** 192
Judith Lamie and Christopher Hill

Responding to the Student Voice – Reflections on Journeys in International Education – Into the Mist and Heading for the First Tree **Eleven** 209
Christopher Hill

Conclusion 226
Christopher Hill and Judith Lamie

Index 229

List of Figures

2.1	Word Cloud – First Time TNE Experience	26
3.1	The Benefits of Language Learning	39
3.2	How Can We Help Protect Language Learning?	56
5.1	Weighing Risk and Market Opportunity (Ilieva et al., 2023)	83
5.2	TNE Regulatory Environment (Ilieva et al., 2023)	85
5.3	Seven-Stage Partnership Process Model (Bryan and Henry, 2012)	94
5.4	It's Who You Know "and" What You Know (Hands, 2005)	94
9.1	World Gross Tertiary Enrolment Ratio (%)	162
9.2	Top 15 Home Countries of International Branch Campuses 2023	180
10.1	Red Lines of Partnership	197
10.2	Example University Governance Structure: Regent's University London, UK	202

List of Tables

9.1	Gross Tertiary Enrolment Ratios for Selected Anglophone Countries	163
9.2	International Enrolments	164
9.3	Global Enrolments	164
9.4	Students Studying Wholly Offshore at UK Universities	167
9.5	The TNE Spectrum of Control	167

List of Case Studies

1.1	Judith's Story: Leaving on a JET Plane	7
1.2	Christopher's Story: Go East Young Man	14
2.1	Vicky Lewis's Story: Barefoot in Sri Lanka	31
3.1	Amy's Story: A Tale of Two International Education Journeys	47
4.1	UK TNE Programmes: The Balkans: Bulgaria and Romania	61
4.2	UK-China Higher Education Mission 2023	68
5.1	The British University in Dubai (BUiD) and Its UK Alliance Partnership	87
5.2	Global Regional Engagement Groups	89
5.3	Université Grenoble Alpes and Swansea University and the Joint Doctoral Degree	96
8.1	Sharon Davies-Smith's Story: "Are We There Yet?"	144
8.2	Andrew Disbury's Story: "I Put a Spell on You"	151
10.1	YALE-NUS	198
10.2	Exploring the Opportunity to Establish a Campus in South Korea	203

Introduction
Christopher Hill and Judith Lamie

This, the third book in our trilogy (until the fourth comes out and we produce a quadrology) picks up, in many ways, where the second book left off. Our work on the second book, and in no small part the contribution of guests on our Think Education podcast, prompted and deepened our ongoing interest in the journeys and stories of those involved in international higher education. We wanted to place the individual at the heart of the narrative; to learn from experiences, successes, failures, and stories told. We wanted, in essence, to bring the human back into the discussion. So, we asked some people. We listened to what they had to say and learned from their experiences, and in so doing, we saw quite a bit of ourselves reflected back.

TAKING THE JOURNEY

We fashioned this book on the notion of a journey. We start at the beginning, when things are unknown and when the planning begins. We moved through the process of packing a metaphorical suitcase, getting on the plane and getting off in a new place. We thought about the first day in the new office or environment, the first interactions with new colleagues, cultures, and food. We observed our travellers as they navigated new languages and systems, when they felt lost and confused, and when they experienced small victories. We watched them integrate and learn from those around them. We watched them develop and grow.

Then we put them on a plane again and sent them home. We watched to see what happened when they got back, how much of the new experiences they took with them, and what they were able to achieve. And then, like any good Euripidean hero, we threw rocks at them. We observed what happens when the international experiment fails and the partnership needs (or has) to end. We asked questions about navigating this process, how to plan for it, and how to manage the aftermath. An ending does not have to mean failure and can, at times, be in the best interests of all parties involved.

DOI: 10.4324/9781003649571-1

VOICES

Over the course of thinking about and writing this book, we discussed engagement, culture, language, governance, control, risk management, preparation, success, and failure. We thought about our own backgrounds and origin stories, and this prompted us to ask others about theirs. We were interested in the why behind the what of international engagement.

The book includes in-depth case studies and personal journeys. The balance of institutional and personal serves to highlight on the ground realities and discuss actual reactions and responses to them. We wanted to learn from real examples and to provide, you the reader, with a more layered and nuanced view of the inner workings of international and transnational higher education.

As with the two previous books, we have a chapter on the student voice where we learn about perspectives from around the world – and at differing levels of study – regarding motivation, mobility and integration. As always, this chapter provides a much-needed glimpse into the emerging trends and realities that face international students today as they navigate their world of study, work and life.

This book also contains a chapter on the female voice that includes women from South Africa, Venezuela, Türkiye, the UK, Uzbekistan, Canada, and Taiwan and highlights their experiences in the world of international higher education, the role of mentors in their development, and their advice to their younger selves.

SHARED EXPERIENCES

Beneath the theoretical rests the actual. We have both read, written, and presented on the theoretical in multiple formats and locations. We have also both lived and experienced the actual in multiple formats and locations, and wanted to voice more of this perspective – hence this book.

We, as we have done in previous books, turned to learned and international colleagues to hear from them and to learn from their experiences and ideas. We have been able to include examples of student mobility and exchange, international travel, and working abroad for both short and long periods. In all cases, we encountered the notion of community and the value of human engagement. This book firmly acknowledges the challenges and obstacles that can be ever present in the world of international education but time and time again, we came back to the "kindness of strangers" and the clear resolution that we depend on each other and are stronger when we engage, collaborate, and learn from each other.

We hope that you enjoy this book, and we thank you for taking this journey with us and our collaborators. Now please, make sure your seatbelts are securely fastened, your seat backs and tray tables are in the upright position, and all carry-on luggage is safely stowed beneath your seat in front of you or in the overhead bins.

If you are sitting comfortably, let's begin.

The Accidental TNE Practitioner – Routes into
International Higher Education
Judith Lamie and Christopher Hill

One

INTRODUCTION

I was itching to get back to university life in Swansea and was so happy when I could finally do that. It's been a wonderful academic journey since then, and I've made some great friends and got to really settle down in the city. Everyday gives me a new experience I can learn from. I graduate this year and I am excited by the new opportunities that lie ahead of me.[1]

(Jason Makwabarara)

In *The Evolving Nature of Universities* (Lamie and Hill, 2023), we explored what shapes and influences identity in International Higher Education (IHE). We critically reflected on the role of IHE and how it impacts a sense of place, identity, and engagement within the communities it serves. We looked at this through the lens of the university, the academic, the student and their parents, and the transnational education (TNE) professional and, in doing so, studied their motivations for programme development and delivery, for research and enterprise, and for study.

In this book we trace the origins back further. Following a brief sojourn into the dreams, aims, and ambitions of some of the younger inhabitants of our planet, this chapter explores the very nature of IHE, what it is, and why we might be drawn to it. The authors share their personal stories and reflect on what they have learned as they have arrived at their respective places in their careers. The chapter then introduces a number of the key themes that the book will examine in more detail, such as engagement and culture, leading to the inevitable question, does the destination even really matter, isn't it the journey that is important?

This book is about journeys. Journeys we take as people, as families, and as individuals. In our lives we will take many journeys; they don't all begin when we are young or when we are about to leave school, but some of them do. This is where we will begin.

DOI: 10.4324/9781003649571-2

THE BEGINNING

What Do You Want to Be When You Grow Up?

How many times were we asked the question, "what do you want to be when you grow up", when we were children? We asked a small group of school pupils (and two past students) what they wanted to be when they grow up:

Sprout (aged 7):	An author. A ballet dancer. A baseball player. An actor. So many things really.
Mason (aged 9):	I don't know. I am open to see what happens.
Jihu (aged 7):	A professional baseball player.
Jed (aged 9):	A policeman. In Cheshire.
Quinn (aged 7):	An illustrator or a photographer.
Chris (when aged around 8):	A footballer
Judith (when aged around 8):	A truck driver

In many ways these reflect realities inhabited, by the children, at the time of asking. Our perception, and indeed conception, of the future is more often than not dictated by the present. By what we see around us. Some are fixed in place. Some are completely open. Some are about how they see the world, or their own place within it. Some may seem ambitious, others practical, many are associated with the hobbies that the children, or members of their family have, or the current and past occupations of parents, siblings, friends, or people they've seen on television. Occasionally, they are wild and wacky, other times intriguingly specific; a policeman, in Cheshire?

Of course, we enter different areas in the world of work at various times in our careers. When viewed from a distance, these can indeed appear to form a cohesive pattern, one that demonstrates design. In reality, this is often not the case, and we stumble from one opportunity to the next and retroactively make sense of things by establishing connections where there had previously merely been individual things in a list. We clearly have the ability and capacity to learn along the way, to pick up new skills, new interests, and these in turn shape the next stages to come. And so, a pattern does emerge over time. Those of us involved in IHE tend to remain involved in IHE – in one capacity or another. We may drift from institution to institution, from country to country, but we often become lifers of one sort or another.

> **Did You Know?**
>
> The most popular jobs over the decades in the United States[2] have been:
>
> 1950s: Secretary, farmer, teacher, nurse, salesperson
> 1960s: Secretary, teacher, nurse, bookkeeper, salesperson
> 1970s: Secretary, teacher, nurse, bookkeeper, cashier
> 1980s: Secretary, teacher, nurse, manager, salesperson
> 1990s: Secretary, teacher, nurse, manager, salesperson
> 2000s: Teacher, nurse, manager, salesperson, cashier
> 2010s: Nurse, manager, teacher, salesperson, cashier

INTERNATIONAL HIGHER EDUCATION: WHAT IS IT AND WHY ARE WE DRAWN TO IT?

The last decade saw an explosion in the flows of knowledge, resources and people around the broad topic of what we can call international education.

(Knight, 2023)

Definitions and Motivations

IHE is a complex beast. Is it a network of educational stakeholders and policymakers coming together to debate current global challenges? Is it an interrelated system of academic institutions working in collaboration to provide solutions to those challenges? Is it a career choice, a series of activities, or an academic discipline? For a faculty member, IHE could be viewed as a vehicle for research, or an escape from the humdrum of the home department.

"We tell students that when they study abroad or engage in international programmes, they are exposed to new ideas, perspectives and ways of life" (Knight, 2023). If you are a student IHE may be a gateway to a world of opportunity, the final destination unknown, but the promise of broadening horizons, building new relationships and connections, and opening new doors. In 2024 ISCResearch[3] reported that there were over 14,000 international schools, an increase of 49% since 2014, "664,645 staff and 6.9m students, contributing a global fee income of $60.9bn". IHE is also a prominent and profitable global business.

For the TNE practitioner, IHE might be seen as an extension of existing activity. Teaching and learning across borders, in many ways the same activity, but in a different environment and with students who come from differing backgrounds; practically therefore less of a challenge, perhaps. In all of this, it is also useful to be mindful of how these definitions, and the motivations aligned to them, may shift from expectation to reality once involvement has occurred. The speculative escape from the humdrum and monotonous, to the exciting and innovative, the lure of travel, opportunity to learn a new language, the excitement of new countries and new cultures, develop cross-cultural skills, and the opportunity to build new networks.

IHE offers tremendous opportunities, but these are set within an environment (culturally, organisationally, practically) unlike the "home" situation, and it is often tricky to integrate effectively and smoothly, even if the willingness and the support locally are there. It is then, ironically, challenging to reintegrate when you do, if you do, eventually return home. Not that you might ever call it home again. This is illustrated in the following two case studies of the authors' journeys into the world of IHE.

> There is no real going back. Though I may come to the Shire, it will not seem the same; for I shall not be the same.
> (The Return of the King, J.R.R. Tolkien, 1955)

Case Study 1.1: Judith's Story: Leaving on a JET Plane
Context

Having abandoned the childhood ambition of being a truck driver and travelling the open road eating Yorkie bars I settled, on graduation from the University of Warwick, on a career as a teacher. A colleague suggested I look at a recent advertisement for English teachers in Japan, posted by the Japanese Ministry of Education (MoE): The recently established Japan Exchange and Teaching (JET) Programme. I applied largely due to curiosity and certain in the knowledge that I would be unlikely to succeed as I had been no further than France on my travels and didn't speak a word of Japanese. Following an interview at the Japanese Embassy in London (which we thought would be the highlight as we rarely had the opportunity to go to London), I was successful and found myself heading to Tokyo and then my posting in Naha, Okinawa.

Teaching English in Japan

The Japanese first encountered the English language when William Adams[4] landed in Kyushu, southern Japan, in 1600 on a trading ship called De Liefde. Japan was a closed society and the authorities did not allow Adams, and his second mate Jan Joosten, to leave. The two became among the first to receive the dignity of samurai, and Adams became a key adviser to the shogun Tokugawa Ieyasu, particularly due to his skills in shipbuilding, navigation, and mathematics. Although they were eventually given permission to leave, they decided to stay.

It was to be as late as 1872 that Japan started a national education system, which included foreign language education. One aspect of the society that existed and was reinforced during the period of self-assumed isolation of the seventeenth and eighteenth centuries was its hierarchical structure. Japan remains intensely hierarchical, and this is apparent when one examines the educational system, from curriculum structure and content to the roles and responsibilities of its staff and students.

Schools and the curriculum underwent a series of significant reforms in Japan in the 1980s and 1990s, and one principal target was the teaching of English. In 1987, in response to a government commission which stated that the education system in Japan was "outdated, uncreative, rigid and inhibiting" (Japanese Ministry of Education, 1985: 9) the Japanese MoE proposed a curriculum innovation which would radically refocus English teaching in junior and senior high schools. The proposal was for a shift from the long-established grammar-translation method towards teaching for communication and communicative competence. The official documentary outcome of the proposal was the New Revised Course of Study: Emphasis on Oral Communication, which passed through the Japanese Parliament in March 1989.

The JET Programme is a programme sponsored by the Japanese MoE. It "seeks to improve foreign language education in Japan and to enhance internationalisation by helping promote international exchange at the local level and mutual understanding between Japan and other countries" (Japanese Ministry of Education, 1994: 6). JET programme participants are divided into two groups according to their job duties: Assistant Language Teachers (ALTs) and Co-ordinators for International Relations (CIRs). The former are expected to assist in the improvement of foreign language education at school and the latter to help promote international exchange at the prefectural level. The programme was launched in 1987 with 848 participants[5] from four countries, the United States, Australia, New Zealand, and the United Kingdom. Canada and Ireland joined in 1988, Germany and France (with German and French included in the target languages) in 1989, and China in 1992. Additional countries were added, and the programme reached a record high in 2002 with 6,273 participants coming from 40 countries. By 2023 this had reached 50 countries with approximately 1,000 local government organisations, including 46 prefectures and 18 designated cities hosting the new JET participants.

Stages in the Journey

i) The Preparation

In the 1980s, there was no internet, no opportunities for extensive Google searches, and no Wikipedia to rely on for some basic facts. There were books, there were libraries, and there were people that could help you with some of the many questions you were bound to have. Beyond the obvious and the stereotypes my family, friends, and colleagues could provide little by way of preparatory support. They bought me chopsticks, which I soon discovered were impossible to use with the rice we could buy at the supermarket in the 1980s, and they bought me books about Japan, its geography, and its history. They were relatively content that it was by reputation a safe environment, and the people were polite and welcoming, if perhaps a little aloof. But it was literally on the other side of the world (we had a 20cm metal globe in our living room) and that made it both exciting and scary.

The JET programme provided participants with a short pre-departure residential to introduce them to each other, and to the language and the culture of Japan. This was a useful taster weekend, which led to more questions than it gave answers, but it was welcomed by all and did enough to settle a few nerves. Preparation is key to so many things, but when you are faced by something completely unfamiliar, then the best thing that you can do is try and prepare yourself psychologically for what is to come. You will never know how you are going to respond until you are placed in the new environment.

ii) The Arrival

It's a long way from the UK to Japan now, it was a VERY long way then. The participants all travelled together on the same plane. Some were loud, brash, and seemingly brimming with confidence; others were quieter and more reflective. The arrival was predictably exciting and daunting in equal measure. We were captivated by the shop fronts of local restaurants that had astonishingly realistic plastic creations of their menus in the windows. We swooned in the sweltering temperatures and, in my case, tried to cope with a new weather phenomenon, humidity. The first orientation week in Tokyo disappeared in a blur of new information and jetlag. The participants who were loud on the plane had quietened down a bit, and the more hesitant ones were a little less reluctant to interact. We had begun our adventure in earnest, and there was, at least for me, no turning back. Next stop, Okinawa.

iii) The First Six Months

The initial period in any new environment is often exciting. It is when the reality of you remaining kicks in that issues begin to emerge. Personally, communication back home was to be a particular challenge. With no internet, no zoom calls, and even the now redundant Skype a distant vision, it was down to telephone calls and letters. I would call my family once a month. It was wonderful to be able to hear voices and connect with them once more, but the resulting bout of homesickness was intense. An advantage was to be somewhere where others were experiencing the same thing, and the JET network was active and supportive, especially in these initial phases.

Professionally, the daily visits to the local schools and the weekly catch-up at the prefectural Board of Education added a routine, albeit an unfamiliar one. School pupils were fascinated by the new *gaijin sensei* (foreign teacher), and the constant attention was occasionally overwhelming. Teachers of English were polite, although those who struggled with English themselves found the presence of a native English speaker at one and the same time a help and a hindrance. Navigating the culture of the classroom environment proved to be an interesting experiment in negotiation and diplomacy. The teachers I worked with in Japan were committed to delivering the new curriculum; there was no choice not to be, but there were challenges associated with practice and capability, attitude and behaviour, and fundamentally I realised the process of change.

Of course, the first six months also give you an opportunity to lay solid foundations, build relationships and begin to understand the history and the culture. Japanese colleagues were fully aware that you were away from your family, so there was no excuse to refuse the invitations that would come to be taken to local tourist spots or historical sites (Okinawa has an absorbing history). Everyone knew where you lived, there would be regular knocks at the door, and welcome pots of Okinawan Soba (noodles). I am a vegetarian and that was a little puzzling for most of my new colleagues, but the fresh fruit and vegetables were wonderful and the first opportunity I had to sample *yasai* (vegetable) *tempura* would prove to be one I would never forget and gave me one of my most favourite foods.

The first six months are a seesaw of emotions, but perseverance, patience, and a willingness to engage and learn begin to see things settle.

iv) The Intervening Period

The problem with the new approach proposed by the curriculum reform in Japan was that it demanded a language emphasis, a resource utilisation, and a classroom teaching style which were all in diametric opposition to those used before it. Coupled with a lack of additional training for the Japanese teachers of English, this made the role of the JET programme participant not only an important one but also one that had to cope with the hierarchical nature of the school and the classroom from a position significantly below that of the Japanese teacher. Pupils in the schools had an impact on the teaching as well. Teaching is a highly regarded profession in Japan, and teachers are given and demand great respect. Traditionally, students have been regarded as little more than passive receivers of knowledge. This does not align well with communicative language teaching methodology. As a result of this situation, there were natural tensions in the classroom setting. One way of managing this tension is to study it.

During my time in Japan, I not only took professional qualifications, such as the Japanese Language Proficiency Tests, but also embarked on an MA by research. These not only helped me practically when it came to assisting with communication (language) but also provided me with a platform to reflect, academically, on my current environment. I was part of the change process, but was interrogating and analysing it at the same time, which provided an outlet for some of the challenges and frustrations. In addition, it resulted in some thought-provoking research and drove me academically to want to be involved in and study the IHE landscape more fully.

v) The End

Participants on the JET programme are only able to stay for a maximum of three years. One thing was very clear to me, nothing would ever be the same again. Even though my school in the UK had held my position open for me to return to, I had had a taste of IHE and I wanted to experience more. I had at the beginning expected to return home to the role I had held, but I had been given an opportunity to look towards a different direction and I took it.

Home might be home, especially if you still have family there, but, if you have had a predominantly successful time when you have been away, then you will always miss the place and the people. Homesickness that we experience when we leave is replaced by away-longing (or possibly more generically *wanderlust*) when you return. There were the inevitable questions when I got back: How was it, why do you keep taking your shoes off and leaving them at the front door, can you stop bowing? But gradually people tired of the stories, anecdotes, and pictures. I had been away, they hadn't. It wouldn't be long before the lure of overseas work and travel took me away again.

Key Themes

- **Challenge and change:** In principle the changing of practice is comparatively straightforward, the challenging of values and beliefs, however, is a completely different matter. Changing attitudes might mean the uprooting and replanting of an entire landscape of long-established assumptions; assumptions you might not know you even have until they are challenged. Organisations are made up of individuals, not things, and change evokes a variety of emotions. Common sense may prevail at times of relative stability, but at times of major change, our overriding fear of the unknown may result in us behaving irrationally. We can be afraid that the change may involve loss: loss of power, loss of position, and loss of control. This can result in us wanting to return to the comfort of the pre-change environment. Of course, if you have just travelled halfway around to begin a new job, then that may be rather difficult. If we can devise mechanisms to help us cope with the change, then we may be able to navigate our way through the process.

- **Culture:** There are several cultural networks at play when you enter the IHE world: national, regional, and school cultures. The school culture is a complex make-up of occupational, institutional, and personal influences. It can be influenced by teacher cultures and career experiences and by the occupational culture of teaching, which represents attributes of the teaching profession as a whole. Ideas and approaches that are created in one culture (such as communicative language teaching) cannot simply be transferred across cultures, particularly when different value systems apply.
- **Engaging with others:** It is vital, for your own mental health as well as for the opportunity to make new friends and build strong relationships, that you engage with those that are from the country you are living in. It can be tempting to stay with the expat community, eat cheese and pickle sandwiches and talk about your favourite television programmes and that is fine occasionally, but you have a whole new world in front of you full of people who are keen to get to know you and things you have never seen and may never see again. Don't miss the chance to step outside your comfort zone and in doing so widen it.
- **Roles and responsibilities:** Teachers appear to regard the actual job of teaching in Japan as attractive and less demanding than their own situations. Whilst there is a certain mythology around the role of the teacher in Japan, there remains the reality that it is a profession that is highly respected and that teachers are viewed as important and influential members of their local communities. The classrooms may be environments where there are few, if any, issues with discipline, but the schools demand a great deal of their teachers in terms of time and the management of what, continues to this day, to be a highly bureaucratic situation.

Lessons Learned

- If your initial reaction to an opportunity is to say no (especially if it is outside your comfort zone), then at least say maybe, if not yes. It would have been very easy for me to say no to an invitation to apply for another job on the other side of the world, safe and secure with the one I had on my own doorstep. This new opportunity immediately widened my comfort zone and set me on a path to over three decades in IHE.
- You are fully part of the change (agent) process and that brings with it both advantages and disadvantages. Try to make the most of the advantages.
- Being called an "honorary man" can be meant as high praise, even if at the time it didn't feel like it.
- Things do get easier, but it is a rollercoaster at the beginning and some days you feel as though you have just stepped off the plane.
- In travelling overseas and experiencing different countries and cultures, you learn a lot more about yourself and you own values and beliefs. Ideas and thoughts that you had previously taken for granted are challenged, often quite gently, but suddenly you are thinking about them explicitly. It is a rewarding experience, but at times quite unsettling.
- Even if you are the teacher, you are also a student. Never miss an opportunity to listen and learn.

Case Study 1.2: Christopher's Story: Go East Young Man
Context

I wanted to be a diplomat. After I gave up the dream of wanting to be a professional footballer, and then of playing professional basketball. I went to an international high school in Madrid, Spain, where (in memory at least) it seemed that this was a potential career path to consider. I liked languages and travel and so this seemed, dare I say, possible. I did Classics at university (which I loved) but wasn't sure where it would lead in terms of employment and so did a Masters in International Relations – figuring this would be a great launching pad for diplomacy.

Halfway through the masters, I was approached to see if I would be interested in doing a Phd. Flattered (as this was never something I had considered) I said yes. Early on in my PhD journey, I was approached to ask if I would be interested in teaching some undergraduate modules. Flattered, I said yes. Turns out, I loved teaching. And clearly have an ego that appreciates validation.

I was all set, therefore, for a career as an academic when the REF reared its head – as it does from time to time. Those of us in junior positions were much less secure in our long-term prospects, and our contracts were offered on a ten-month provisional basis. An opportunity came up – from within my university – to head up the graduate school on the Malaysian campus.

Stages in the Journey

i) The Preparation

I had an interview, which turned out to be with somebody I knew from within the university and I thought it went fairly well. I stressed the need for somebody internal to the university to be hired in order to ensure a strong connection between the two campuses. I think back on this now and am not sure where this came from. Turns out I was right. Got a call a few weeks later – may have been less time but the memory is a bit fuzzy – to offer me the job and that was that. The fact that it was so far away and so different was part of the appeal but I think, largely left as an unknown.

The opportunity to visit the Malaysia campus was provided and so we flew out for a week to experience considerable jet lag, humidity, and the joy of house hunting.

ii) The Arrival

We arrived on December 28th with all our luggage and broken foot in tow (toe). We stayed the first few nights in a hotel and then moved into our house. It was January but hot and humid. This is the default in Malaysia – being so close to the Equator – and, while we came to get used to it, it was a significant change. The previous visit we had been in a sort of holiday mode, now we needed to get things done and set up a life.

iii) The First Six Months

We settled in fairly quickly, thanks to the amount of work there was to do. My wife and I were both working on the campus and so spent an hour each way on the drive talking about work. Work effectively consumed our day-to-day life. We were of course able to experience some of the culture and the city but our days were spent travelling to and from campus, and on campus of course. The fact that we had each other was a safety net and comfort that not all are afforded. It was a small campus in terms of staff numbers and so you quickly got to know people. This was a real advantage, from a work perspective, and also helped to develop friendships. It also meant that everything was personal. You didn't deal with a department to get something done (or complain when it wasn't) you were talking to, and about, an individual directly. This often led to friction, sometimes as a result of miscommunication across cultures, and sometimes just people being people.

iv) The Intervening Period

Over time, we built up trust with colleagues and became more familiar with "the way things worked". This did not always align with expectations from the home campus and therefore took some adjustment. The time difference between Malaysia and the UK was often frustrating and often advantageous. You often found yourself waiting for responses from the UK (for longer than you expected) and often receiving requests well after working hours (there is an eight-hour time difference) from the UK with expectations of an immediate response. You got more adept, and more confident, in your ability to communicate and to manage communications. Clear lines and expectations were essential, and this was supported by the twice annual visits I made back to the UK. This, I would come to realise, gave me a distinct advantage over other colleagues in Malaysia. People in the UK (at least in departments with which I worked) knew who I was and saw me on a semi-regular basis. I was able to build up relationships with them over coffee. There was a connection that is far from evident when factoring in the time difference and sheer distance between an office in England and one in Malaysia.

v) The End

The end was abrupt. I had been with the same institution, in one guise or another, since I was 18 years old. It was part of my identity and I genuinely thought I would work there for ever. Due to changes made nationally (and their subsequent impact on the recruitment cycles), many of the international posts within the institution were simply not renewed. And just like that, it was over. We had spent eight years in Malaysia, instead of the originally planned three. We were at a bit of a loss as to what was next as there was no post waiting for me at the home campus (a fact that had always been clear). I don't think a return to the UK was ever a primary consideration. The eight years had given us a new world of possibilities and simply going home again felt strange. And so we looked elsewhere.

Key Themes

- **Challenge and Change:** The challenges are almost too many to list. Some are personal, some are situational, some are professional, some are bizarre and some are mundane. It is important to not get too caught up in the sense of how things should be but rather to focus on maintaining quality and integrity within the context of the possible. Communication is important here. Talk to your team and learn from colleagues about how things work (or don't) and try to get a better understanding of your context. Talk to colleagues across the institution and keep open lines of dialogue with those "back home". There can often be the sense of out of sight out of mind. This is all well and good until something goes wrong, and then we are all too visible once more.
- **Culture:** This is a curious one as it relates not just to the culture of the country but also, and very specifically, to the culture of the organisation or institution. In many ways, you can be forgiven for expecting the branch campus to be an extension of the home campus. This is how it is billed after all. It is the same thing in a different place. A lot of the quality assurance and branding rest on this very premise. The reality is of course that this is not true. The very place and location of the campus change its identity. The weather, the people, the food, the surroundings. All these factors, and many more, actively shape and reshape the identity and reality of the campus (in both locations). There is often a degree of culture shock when we travel but the reality that the institution itself is not the same can be quite jarring – at least at the outset. This is not a weakness, nor should it be seen as such, but is instead part of the opportunity to learn and engage across

communities and perspectives and in so doing, reinvigorate and reinforce the centre.
- **Engaging with Others:** Once you have taken the step to move outside your comfort zone, it is often natural to look for ways to slide back into it when you are abroad. This is perhaps natural and can be a very useful, and often necessary, safety net. The opportunity to engage across experiences and cultures should not be missed. There is often a sense of freedom and separation when you are away from "home" that allows, and even encourages, us to try new things and learn more about our place and our self.
- **Management Styles:** The lack of training and preparation provided to staff and leaders in IHE can often be glaring. This, coupled with the international and cultural diversity can overwhelm the best intentions and have significant ramifications throughout the institution. If training is provided then, quite rightly, colleagues employed in the region and by the campus usually have priority. Those who come from the home campus and/or are placed into management positions are frequently less supported.

Lessons Learned

- Things will go wrong. There will be, often sustained, periods where you have no real clue as to what you are doing. This is normal.
- People are important.
- Connections are important.
- There is no real stability in TNE. You are a guest in another country, often without access to things like a pension or a job to return to, and things can change very quickly.

ROUTES INTO INTERNATIONAL HIGHER EDUCATION: PERCEPTION VERSUS REALITY

As with many unknowns, it is often difficult to balance expectations against reality after the fact. For those of us who have worked in IHE for a number of years, the second time around is somewhat (perhaps inevitably) shaped by the first and so our expectations can be tempered by experience. This can, of course, be both a good and bad thing.

There can be a tendency to assume a level of similarity in the IHE world. After all, the programmes are the same; the quality assurance processes (at least at home) are the same; the qualifications are the same; the campus/provider/product are the same. But of course, everything is in fact different and must be approached accordingly. What we obtain over time is the ability to adapt more quickly, adapt more flexibility, and adapt more. The longer we work in IHE, the more comfortable we become with chaos and uncertainty. This does not mean we become less concerned with quality but we become more adept at "getting things done".

Communication
Communication can be difficult at times. It is impacted by time differences, distance, technology (with the home campus) and culture, understanding and power dynamics (on branch campus or in the classroom). Good lines of communication are essential, but they often take time to build and effort to sustain. Communication means different things to different people and it is much subtler than the simple sending and receiving of information. There is verbal and non-verbal communication and in the international space the differences in interpretation of non-verbal communication can be stark. Consider the following for example:

- Eye contact: Can be viewed as a positive gesture, displaying respect, honesty and trust, but may be viewed as intrusive, presumptive and even offensive.
- Hand and arm gestures: Pointing at someone may seem like the most natural thing in the world, but could be perceived as rude and aggressive.
- Head movements: Nodding can mean yes, or no.
- Physical space: How close is too close? In some cultures, close physical contact between strangers can be acceptable and hugging is part of the norm. In others, you would hesitate to do this with someone you have known for years.

Awareness, sensitivity, and empathy, however, are always pivotal. It is a difficult job to balance quality assurance expectations with capabilities across locations and so clear communication and training are required. Training itself also needs to be considered through the lens of behaviour, attitudes, and culture.

Culture, Attitudes, and Values: Understanding Not Assimilation

Communication is inextricably bound up with culture. We live in an increasingly connected world that demands the appreciation and understanding of other cultures and countries. To articulate, analyse or learn from our experience, to evaluate our effectiveness and to compare and contrast what we have learned from our experience requires identifying what our intentions and expectations are and an awareness of what the setting is. In his interrogation of teacher development and training, Allwright (1999: 4) developed a procedure which doesn't focus on change as the outcome of a situation, but rather on "understanding":

> I am using the term "understanding" in a relativistic sense, meaning something like having an adequate sense of how things work for the purpose of making practical decisions about how to proceed.
>
> I am using the term "change" in a fairly narrow sense, to capture something different, and less cerebral, from the necessary change that any reaching of an "understanding" must bring. I am talking more of observable situational change (e.g. the establishment of different ways of working in the language classroom).

Using the Friends of the Earth slogan – think globally, act locally – as a starting point, Allwright sees teacher training and development as cyclical, beginning and thinking globally, then applying this thinking to the local context (act locally), before returning to the principles and thinking locally.

In order to develop our understanding of sometimes quite basic social activities, in an unfamiliar setting, we can seek to analyse them, almost as though we are observing them from above. This lessens the challenge we might feel in unusual situations, even if that situation is as simple as going into someone's home and taking your shoes off, or eating a bowl of noodles and being aware (eventually) that slurping is a sign of contentment and not bad manners. In this way, the IHE professional and TNE practitioner can become an accidental ethno-methodologist (Garfinkel, 1967), by studying the practices of a set of actions of a specific sociocultural group, whilst not letting the group know that it is taking place. This distancing technique can not only help with understanding, but can also provide a detachment between the activity taking place and the reaction, providing an opportunity to reflect rather than criticise.

In IHE, there are lots of opportunities for misinterpretations and misunderstandings, but these may lessen if we concentrate on enhancing engagement.

Engagement: Individual and Institutional

Engagement can be looked at in a variety of ways. It is about how we engage with the community in which we are placed, if in the process of delivering TNE overseas. It is also about how we engage those on, for example, the branch campus, with those back at home base; this means those that have decided to work there on secondment as well as those that have been recruited solely for the purpose of working on the branch campus.

In the 1980s, when technology was in its infancy and the Sony Walkman was seen as cutting edge and the height of sophistication, it was less easy to avoid, if for some reason you wanted to, the new international environment in which you were placed. In some major cities, there were thriving expat communities of course, but this was not the case further afield, and although that may have seemed a significant challenge early on in the process, it proved to be a major boon when trying to build new relationships with colleagues and those within the local communities. In the age of zoom, teams, blackboard, and a wealth of social media, it is much easier to route yourself more in the virtual world that you are comfortable with and less in the real one that it just outside your door. But that is a great loss, for all of those involved.

There are numerous studies that purport the success or otherwise of the international branch campus (IBC). Many refer to the financials, student numbers and student recruitment, brand, and organisational culture and the need to liaise closely and develop strong relationships with local and regional governments. Relatively few explore in detail the importance and critical role of those that work on the IBC, the academic and administrative staff, except perhaps to criticise their commitment, but commitment works both ways. Healey (2022) refers to a number of characteristics that universities should pay attention to if they wish to expand their footprint overseas. These include: Developing an honest and robust business case, aligning core objectives, and demonstrating long-term commitment to the venture. Long-term commitment comes in many shapes and sizes. Staff support is key at all levels within the organisation.

We often talk about the need to engage more fully across locations in IHE as if we do this perfectly within the home campus, or even within single departments. Clear missions, goals, and expectations help to set the context within which we all operate and when these are supported by training and sustained engagement, the chances of success are increased. Leadership, resourcing, and ongoing support make this possible. It isn't easy, and it often isn't cheap, but it is worth it.

> **Top Tips When Entering IHE**
>
> **DO**
> - Embrace change.
> - Step outside your comfort zone.
> - Have patience.
> - Nurture relationships.
> - Keep your sense of humour.
>
> **DON'T**
> - Take offence at everything.
> - Worry when things go wrong.
> - Forget that people are people.
> - Expect no surprises.
> - Stop giving yourself the opportunity to learn.

CONCLUSION

Though here at journey's end I lie in darkness buried deep, beyond all towers strong and high, beyond all mountains steep, above all shadows rides the sun and stars for ever dwell: I will not say the day is done, nor bid the stars farewell.

(The Return of the King, J.R.R. Tolkien, 1955)

Literature abounds with the notion that it is the journey that is meaningful and not arriving at a destination. That's not to say that the destination isn't important, that goals, and outcomes aren't important, but it is equally, if not more important, to ensure that you enjoy and learn from the process of getting there, not least because you may want to go somewhere else at some stage and it is always useful to have learned from past experience. A similar point can be made when we consider whether we ever actually arrive home, once our home has been elsewhere? Is there even an actual home anymore? Are TNE practitioners destined to be perpetual travellers, missing the place(s) that they have left behind, perhaps even leaving a little of themselves in each of those places?

You can't cross the same river twice and you can't ever really go home again. We take on bits and pieces of the places we visit and the places we work in. These might be mannerisms, expressions, new foods, or new cultural constructs. We pick up new ways of doing things. New ways of viewing power and potential. New ways of understanding. We have been on the move, and it is often strange to come to a standstill once more, which is why in the weird and wonderful world of IHE we rarely do.

NOTES

1. Jason Makwabarara from Zimbabwe, and his mother Florence, told their story of why he decided to study at Swansea University at the height of the global health crisis, in Lamie and Hill (2023: 155).
2. Source: The US Census Bureau.
3. https://iscresearch.com/data/
4. Said to be the inspiration for the character of John Blackthorne in James Clavell's best-selling novel *Shogun* (1975).
5. www.jetprogramme.org/en/history

REFERENCES

Allwright, D. (1999) Processes of Language Teacher Education: three major processes and the appropriate design criteria for developing and using them. Plenary given at the International Conference on Language Teacher Education, University of Minnesota, USA

Clavell, J. (1975) Shogun. Hodder & Stoughton, London, UK

Garfinkel, H. (1967) Studies in Ethnomethodology. Englewood Cliffs, NJ: Prentice Hall

Healey, N. (2022) What Determines the Success of an International Branch Campus. https://www.timeshighereducation.com/campus/what-determines-success-international-branch-campus

Japanese Ministry of Education (1985) Report from the Ad hoc Council on Education. Tokyo: Rinkyoushin

Japanese Ministry of Education (1994) Handbook for Team Teaching. Tokyo: Gyosei Corporation

Knight, C. (2023) International Higher Education Blog. https://advance-he.ac.uk/news-and-views/international-higher-education?_ga=2.128201608.583701895.1705065676-1781623286.1705065676 (20 March 2023)

Lamie, J. and Hill, C. (2023) The Evolving Nature of Universities: What Shapes and Influences Identity in International Higher Education. London: Routledge

Tolkien, J.R.R. (1955) The Lord of the Rings: The Return of the King. London: George Allen and Unwin

Starting Out – A Few Practicalities

Christopher Hill and Judith Lamie

Two

INTRODUCTION

How do we prepare for a career, or study opportunity, in international higher education? What do we need to know before we leave? Who do we need to talk to? Who do we believe? What will it be like when we get there? Will I be ready? These are all valid questions that, at one time or other, we have probably all asked ourselves. As with most things, we go through the experience and then we get the understanding. The second foray into international higher education is often much less daunting, but this can be born out of a sense of (at times misplaced) confidence that this has been survived once and can be survived again. It also might mean that you think through things more than you did previously, when you knew and had experienced very little, leading to more excitement but more anxiety, and possibly overthinking, too.

International higher education is vastly diverse and yet has some core realities and experiences that are largely applicable to all. Those of us who have lived in this world recognise our own experiences in those of other colleagues; however, far removed the two experiences may have been. We can learn from each other's mistakes, demonstrate sympathy, and laugh in equal measure. The wonderfully weird world of international higher education is an environment of constant and ongoing learning, but it isn't always what you expect.

You usually need less than you think when planning to travel. There can be a temptation to try and predict all types of weather and entertainment scenarios, but if you are not careful, you really will be trying to pack the kitchen sink. With reference to some real-life examples from our professional TNE guides, this chapter provides some simple tips for the first and second time TNE traveller, as well as drawing some more abstract conclusions: travel light, in terms of possessions and preconceptions, take the occasional guide book with you if you want to, but be ready

DOI: 10.4324/9781003649571-3

to open yourself up to the experience, and don't always feel the need to stick to pizza and chips.

THE FIRST TIME

If you don't know where you are going, you will end up someplace else.

(Yogi Berra)

International higher education offers a world (literally) of opportunities. Partnerships and programmes are delivered across the globe, and mobility is built into the heart of everything that happens. There is a sense of adventure, of exploration, and of opportunity. There is also cost and sacrifice, departure and distance, and change. For those of us, students and staff alike, who have experienced international higher education in one form or other, there is a bond and a shared experience. While we may have been to different places and seen different things, we have walked a similar pathway. We all have stories; some good and some bad. We have all been changed by the experience; some good and some bad. We have expanded our comfort zone, or left it behind completely in some cases. We have made new friends (and maybe encountered a nemesis along the way), and we have expanded our world. In almost all cases, however, where we ended up was not where we thought we were going.

However old we are, the first time we go somewhere we cannot help but have an idea about what we might find or experience a feeling. Sometimes these are positive, and sometimes they are negative. If you are going somewhere new and are planning to stay there for more than a "holiday period" then you will naturally have a different reaction to what might be about to happen, than if you are only leaving home for a couple of weeks or so. Most of us can cope with any (non-emergency) situation if we know it is for a short amount of time. We may download favourite programmes onto our iPads, or surreptitiously squirrel away a few chocolate bars or packets of biscuits into our bulging suitcases. Longer stays, however, whether you are on your own or are taking your family with you (both of which have their advantages and their disadvantages) are a different matter.

We asked fifteen of our professional experts, with good memories, what they thought of when they remembered the first time they launched themselves into the IHE space (see Figure 2.1). The responses were a mixture of looking forward and glancing back. Of wondering

Figure 2.1 Word Cloud – First Time TNE Experience

what the future will hold and being excited yet nervous about it, whilst at the same time, a concern that friends and family will be left behind, and what that might mean. In a couple of follow-up discussions, experts shared their memories of what it was like decades ago leaving the shores of their homes for the first time, for a prolonged period of time. With no internet, no ability to zoom call or facetime, the reality was starker. The excitement was possibly greater, but the unknown would loom a lot larger.

Not Quite What You Were Expecting

There is a very real need to manage our expectations in the world of international higher education. This is true of expected levels of success and outcomes of new TNE programmes, and it is true of personal experiences and realities. There is perhaps a disconnect here between theory and practice, between the strategy and management of international higher education. There is absolutely a "way things should be done" top-down approach. This is driven by strategic goals, quality assurance benchmarks, and institutional branding. There is also an on the ground reality that supports the strategic vision, even if at times running counter to expectations.

Over time and with more experience, this process becomes almost second nature. We expect the unexpected, and we, quite often, relish the challenge. We will adapt to the situation as it arises because this is what we did in the last iteration of our TNE journey. This is a difficult thing to do, however, when we have no real basis upon which to base these expectations. For the first-time traveller, this process is considerably more alien and unsettling. In these cases, our expectations are driven by our understanding of the current: current place, current reality, current needs. To assume that this will apply in another context is folly. An understandable folly, perhaps and one driven by a need to make sense of the unknown. But folly all the same. We can take this sense of understanding with us as it constitutes a lifeline back to the home campus or operation. This lifeline is comforting and can be of immense value in terms of communication, support, and quality assurance, but it cannot represent the entirety of our experience, nor get in the way of our ability to learn and adapt within context.

This changes over time.

First Time Out – You Aren't in Kansas Anymore

Everything is new, and we often try to make sense of it by way of comparison. "It isn't done like this at home", is a familiar refrain. Countered by "you aren't at home any more". Countered in turn by, "but it is the same university, shouldn't it be the same"? This statement is both true and false and represents the learning curve we follow on our initial journey into the TNE world. There is a degree to which we can expect a sense of similarity in our TNE travels, but this will not apply to all things we encounter. Quality assurance and professional integrity to the educational offering should remain a fixed point but the manner in which it is approached, delivered, or even understood, will change.

The teaching material will be familiar; the university branding will be the same; the buildings will be familiar; there may be some familiar faces. The world outside the window will be vastly different, however, and this will have an impact on the day-to-day life and realities of your colleagues, the students, and indeed, yourself.

PREPARATION

Give me six hours to chop down a tree and I will spend the first four sharpening the axe.

(Abraham Lincoln)

We used to read guidebooks about places we wanted to/were going to visit and from these pages, plan our trip, flesh out our understanding, and create our sense of reality and expectations. This approach works well, in as far as it goes, but needs more substance and nuance when it comes to working abroad and "engaging" with the local systems and reality.

When we travel to work, we are no longer tourists – although we often may appear to be so – and should treat the experience accordingly. And in turn, expect to be treated differently by those we end up working with.

When preparing for your trip, talk to as many people as you can and ask questions. If possible, talk to people on the ground, and those who have been on the ground and are maybe now back. Take what you hear with a pinch of salt and apply the necessary filters. We do this when we read reviews regarding travel or purchases as who is saying what and why is important for context. Try to get a picture of how things actually are; who you need to talk to; what is what; and if possible, what to avoid. You won't have it all figured out but making an effort will be appreciated. Colleagues working in international higher education, particularly in TNE programmes are used to "international" colleagues flying in to "fix something", "check-up on something", or "launch something new". They have, in essence, heard this before and are often not all that impressed. Distance is not just physical, and any attempts to breach these gaps and build engagement will most likely pay off in the end.

There is also a tendency to presume that the programmes delivered on the home campus, the buildings and the infrastructure, or the student experience is, of course, going to be better than the one delivered on the branch campus, or with the university partner if it is a franchise agreement. This assumption, inevitably incorrect, will be held frequently by those who haven't even visited the country in question. Before you wax lyrical about how wonderful the home campus is, wait until you arrive at your new destination. You may not only save your blushes, but may learn a little something in the process.

Ask questions about the job but also ask questions about the context and the world in which you will be living and working. Ask about the weather – moving from one climate to another can significantly impact comfort levels and ability to function – at least at the outset. Time difference and temperature are not to be trifled with. Time difference can be overcome, with time ironically, to the point whereby your natural rhythms adapt to the place, even if the expectations and time management of the home campus colleagues do not. Temperature is a little trickier, and some of us simply never adapt fully to the change in climate.

Packing

Next comes the thorny issue of what to pack. The seasoned traveller usually fits into one of two camps: The never-take-anything-more-than-carry-on or the I-might-need-it-so-it's-going-in. On the one hand, it's useful for both to travel together, the latter with inevitably have anything that is required, but the former will get endlessly frustrated at having to hang around at airport carousels waiting for the largest suitcase in the world to emerge.

There is a real difference when travelling alone or as part of a group (even if a group of two). Both can have their ups and downs. There is of course security in travelling with others, in multiple senses of the word. There can also be frustrations too – often a strange reality as you work together at home – born out of the wonders that come with travel, time zones, long days, and picking somewhere to eat that suits all!

A conversation in advance about what is needed (and who will be carrying it) can be more than helpful. Depending on the nature of your trip, there will likely be corporate gifts to carry and, if you are really unlucky, a banner or pull-up stand. Try to keep these to a minimum but do expect to receive gifts while abroad and factor this into your luggage capacity. We all have offices full of mugs after all, and the occasional glass bowl.

Our packing, both actual and metaphorical, changes over time, and our second trip will be more efficient (or at least targeted) than the first one. While we cannot fully prepare for every eventuality, we can take a universal adaptor. We might not be able to fully immerse ourselves wherever we go but our technology should not face similar constraints.

Top Tips for Packing

Short Trip

- Use your itinerary to write what you might wear each day. You don't need to stick to it, but it will give you a realistic sense of what you need.
- Check out the mini-toiletries section of your local supermarket. You really don't need a 500ml bottle of shampoo for three days.
- Invest in a good, lightweight carry-on suitcase.

Long Stay
- If you need check-in luggage, then take a spare set of clothes in your carry-on.
- Take a universal adaptor.
- Establish a pattern/process for communication with work back home.

Arriving

TNE is a transient reality. It is fundamentally about movement after all. Movement of ideas. Movement of people. In many ways, the place you were expecting to find when you boarded the plane, is not the place you find upon arrival. We tend to fall back on expectations once more and this can naturally create a sense of unease, even tension, when the reality inevitably does not match anticipation. Does this then mean that something is wrong? If it is not the same and not what was expected, then perhaps there is something wrong. Perhaps that something is us? There is nothing wrong with being prepared, and there is nothing wrong with having expectations – this is somewhat natural after all – but these need to be tempered by the realisation that they are a loose guide and not a fixed set of rules.

Christopher Hill: Reflections on arriving in KL

My flight to KL, all fourteen hours of it, was spent watching movies in a state of nervous excitement. My life was about to change dramatically and in practically every way possible. While I had been out on an orientation visit to KL a few months prior, this was the real thing and there was no turning back.

We arrived tired and excited and after navigating the airport and the long drive to the hotel, even more tired and slightly less excited. Time difference and fatigue won out and after a short walk around, we fell asleep in the middle of the afternoon. To wake up in the middle of the night. We were the first in the queue for breakfast, ate far too much and then had a few hours to kill before we were met by our new boss. Who took us on a long hot drive, that we could have done without, for a large meal, that we really did not need.

Heat, fatigue and overindulgence meant for a rough start to the journey. Every subsequent flight for international higher education work (conferences, workshops, etc.) has been spent mostly in slumber.

Sleep is your friend.

THE SECOND TIME

What we have done up to now is nothing to what we will do. We've only just started. Just opened the door. Now is the time to go through that door and find what lies beyond it.

(Baron Victor Frankenstein[1])

Just as there is a first time for everything, there is a second (and a third, and a fourth) too. Each new venture is a new venture. The venue is different; the expectations are different; the culture is different; we are different. It is important to draw upon our experiences of the first (or indeed second) trip to support our ability to adapt but not to be constrained by them, or by our associated expectations. To do so would be to fall back into the habit of the first-time traveller (not to be confused with an actual time traveller) expecting to find home abroad.

Travel broadens the mind and increases our ability to be flexible. This is the skill set, and indeed mindset, that we need to take with us on our ongoing journey in international higher education. For many of us, once we are on this journey – once we have walked through Frankenstein's door – we never really look back. For this reason, many of us never really go home again. We wander and we learn.

Case Study 2.1: Vicky Lewis's Story: Barefoot in Sri Lanka

Context

When I was eighteen, I spent three months as a volunteer carer in a children's home in Sri Lanka. This took me well away from my comfort zone and had an enduring influence on me. Before that, the only place outside the UK where I had spent an extended period was Germany. As a 16-year-old A-level student, I spent a full term on exchange at a school in Bad Homburg, near Frankfurt. This gave me the idea of taking a year off between school and university – to improve my German and earn enough money to travel further afield and experience a completely different culture.

The impetus to travel was probably in my blood. I was the only child of older parents, and both my parents had lived abroad before they met each other. My dad had been in the army in China and the Middle East. My mum had worked as a secretary in pre-independence Nigeria. During my teens (by which time my dad had died), we often had international students to stay through the Host scheme. I was intrigued by the photos and traditions they shared with us.

Stages in the Journey

i) The Preparation

My former host family in Germany had found me a job as secretary, translator, and general dogsbody at a German company, starting in the September after my A-levels. I taught myself to touch-type over the summer and headed back to Bad Homburg for four months, where the pay was about double what I could have hoped to earn in the UK. During that time, I finalised arrangements (involving lots of blue airmail letters) to go to Sri Lanka with my friend Claire, who was also keen to volunteer abroad.

The choice of destination was, thanks to my mum. She spotted an article about a children's home in Sri Lanka which mentioned a British volunteer helper. I wrote to the man who ran the home asking if Claire and I could come and work there – and he said yes!

I remember being incredibly excited at the prospect of going somewhere so different - and doing work that didn't involve typing up Dictaphone recordings in German. I read up a bit about Sri Lanka and was aware that there was civil war affecting the north and east of the island (not where we were going) but, looking back, I made no real attempt to prepare myself psychologically. I wouldn't have known where to start.

ii) The Arrival

We flew from Heathrow to Colombo in late February. Arriving at the airport, I remember being taken aback by the huge cockroaches running all over the luggage conveyor belt. We waited for ages – in the sort of heat and humidity I'd never before experienced. Claire's luggage arrived. Mine did not. This was my first experience of filling in a lost luggage form.

Bryan (the white-haired man of Dutch Burgher descent who founded the children's home) collected us in a red van. We had what I described in my diary as a hair-raising ride through palm trees to Prithipura Infant Home, just outside Colombo. The setting was idyllic. It was right on the coast, separated by a small lake (which could be crossed using a rowing boat) from a golden beach. We met Bryan's wife Thilaka and their three teenage sons, all of whom lived at Prithipura, along with a number of dedicated care workers, known as akkas (meaning elder sisters), and around 60 children, all living with some form of disability.

iii) The First Month

I'd never worked as hard in my life. We got up soon after 5 a.m. most mornings and worked seven days a week. Work consisted of washing cloth nappies in the lake and laying them out to dry on the grass, washing and dressing the children, making their meals, playing games with them, and sometimes taking them on outings.

The akkas and volunteers took turns making the evening meal, which we ate together at a long table. Having never eaten anything stronger than a mild "English" curry, I found it way too hot and spent the first weeks living off bread and marmalade (and I don't even like marmalade). By the end of the month, I was starting to add a small amount of curry to some rice.

There were no showers, so we washed at an outdoor well, bringing water up with a bucket and keeping our sarongs on while washing. We quickly adapted to going barefoot all the time.

iv) The Rest

Our stay in Sri Lanka coincided with both Sinhalese New Year and the Buddhist Vesak Festival, with its lanterns and pandal decorations.

Every three weeks or so we were allowed to go off travelling for a few days. We had a habit of running out of money and getting stranded. Somehow, we always made it home, often thanks to the kindness of strangers.

My mum must have been in a constant state of anxiety. There were regular news reports of bombings in Sri Lanka. Once, she gritted her teeth and made a long-distance phone call to Prithipura to speak to me, but we were away travelling.

By mid-April, we'd decided we wanted to stay for six months instead of three. We wrote to the airline (that's what you did in the 1980s) to ask if we could delay our return flight – but they wouldn't allow it.

We were in floods of tears when we had to leave at the end of May. Back in the UK, I missed the spicy food, refreshing washes by the well at the end of a hot day's work, and, most of all, the wonderful akkas and children.

Key Themes

- **Compassion:** the affection of the akkas for the children was palpable.
- **Commitment:** so many examples of hard graft and dedication.
- **Community:** Prithipura was a haven of harmony amid the political tensions.

Lessons Learned

- Write a diary. It captures first impressions and is a snapshot of the person you were when it all started.
- Reverse culture shock is real: be prepared for it.
- Always pack a spare set of clothes in your hand luggage.
- If you're going to go barefoot for three months, the dog hookworm you pick up may end up being a case study at the London School of Hygiene and Tropical Medicine!

Did You Know?

Writing a **diary** can have lots of benefits. It

- Helps you organise your thoughts.
- Improves your writing.
- Enables you to self-reflect.
- Is cathartic.
- Reduces stress.
- Gives you something to laugh and cry about many years later.

LESSONS LEARNED

Be prepared but don't be driven by expectations. They will almost always let you down and increase levels of frustration. Be open and engage where you can.

Compassion

Enter your new world with a sense of openness, a willingness to learn, and to engage. Listen more than you talk. Although you are coming from the home campus, you are not always going to be right. Assuming that you are always right creates tension, reinforces a sense of distance and power imbalance and will almost always, make your job harder than it needs to be.

There will be occasions where your way is the best way, and there will be occasions where your way would land you in significant trouble and lead to failure. There is value in understanding context and constraints and sharing war stories from both sides.

What will no doubt strike you, as it did with Vicky in Sri Lanka, is the kindness, generosity, and compassion of those that you will meet on your journey. If you are a relatively inexperienced traveller, or a first-timer to a country, then you will undoubtedly be taken care of and even welcomed into people's homes. This is of course a thoughtful act, but there may be times when you are exhausted and would probably prefer to stay on your own. Don't feel guilty about that, but at the same time don't take it out on those that are trying to be considerate. If in doubt, be honest and upfront, in a gentle way.

Judith Lamie: Reflections on the dangers of salads

I've visited Africa many times over the years.

Several years ago, I was involved in a programme that worked with schools and colleges in Kenya. But this brief reflection is less about my time in Kenya and more about the run-up to it and the aftermath. Like every sensible traveller I am always keen to have all the inoculations going that I can. I headed off to my doctor's several months prior to the visit to go through the long list of what may be required. There were the usual suspects, tetanus, cholera, and rabies, and several others too such as yellow fever. Some were your standard clear liquid, others quite a fetching bright pink colour.

Suitably stocked up (or whatever the appropriate verb is) I went on my merry way. The first two weeks went smoothly, I took heed of the various recommendations, including the mosquito bite avoidance measures, stayed out of the sun, and resisted the urge to pat stray dogs on the head. By week three, however, I knew something was up. Without going into the details, clearly something wasn't agreeing with me. With only a week to go I kept myself hydrated and could eat once back at the camp at the end of the day, but no other time.

On my return, and slightly slimmer, I headed back to the doctor's. The culprit? A tiny bug I'd caught (or rather, who'd hitched a lift) most likely from a freshly washed salad that I'd eaten.

At least of course I hadn't caught anything else, and it has made me steer clear of salads on some of my travels. Take heed fellow travellers, get yourself jabbed and stick to chocolate bars.

Commitment

Be prepared to work and not coast. There is often a sense of tension felt towards those flying out as if they are experts come to audit, or instruct, or show the right way to do things. This is often absent context and understanding. We can cite frequent examples of colleagues having flown out from the home campus (usually in business class) feeling tired at work, not necessarily working a full day and having to leave early due to fatigue. This is of course a very real state to be in but the more that we can demonstrate to colleagues that we are here to learn and to engage and not simply to instruct, the greater the chances of developing sustainable working relationships and solutions.

Demonstrating a strong level of commitment to where you are and what you are doing will help you to start to become one of the team. This is important for both short and long stays. Bonds will be made that frequently last a long time. You will have had shared experiences and learned from each other. This is never a waste.

Community

Relationships are built through engagement and interaction. These networks can help you get your job done more easily and efficiently but they can also be so much more. Connections and even friendships increase our awareness and understanding of others. They broaden our world and stretch our horizons. They lead to interesting conversations, travel opportunities, even new job offers.

Those of us in the world of international higher education share a bond of sorts, despite how disparate and diverse the experiences may be. Why not take every opportunity to strengthen this community?

Culture Shock: Back Home

When travelling overseas, we brace ourselves for the experience of culture shock. What we can forget is that reverse culture shock can be equally if not more unsettling, largely because you aren't expecting it. You may not have realised how much you had adapted to your new culture, particularly if you have been there for some time (although the intensity of the experience can make one or two months seem like one or two years). You invest a great deal emotionally in the place that you are living and working, even if you don't realise that you are doing it. Having been initially destabilised, you have adjusted, therefore your return home once again creates a level of instability and uncertainty. This does get better and you will once again adjust and settle but it will take time, and those that are surrounding you at home may not be as alive to the issue as those you met, and supported you, overseas. We will delve more deeply into culture, community, and communication in Chapter 8.

CONCLUSION

Practically, travelling is quite a simple endeavour. You decide where you want to go and what you want to do, which will no doubt be related to why you are travelling in the first place, and then you plan accordingly. You book trains, planes, and maybe even automobiles and cross your fingers that your flight isn't cancelled or diverted, and that the weather behaves itself (although you pack an umbrella anyway, even if you are going somewhere where it hasn't rained in August for the past 150 years). All the preparation you do is of course useful, whether for work, where you want to make the most of what might be a short business trip, or for pleasure.

The act of travel may be simple, the reality of the journey is less straightforward. We need to be ready and willing to expect the unexpected and to be open and receptive to change. It is probably useful for us to not be too forensic when we start out. You don't want to be naïve, that could lead to any number of issues, but if you pour over every detail, then there is a danger you will never leave your home (and your personal comfort zone) at all. That isn't a disaster in itself, but it is a missed opportunity. Life is out there and should be explored where and when possible.

NOTE

1 Peter Cushing as Baron Victor Frankenstein in *The Curse of Frankenstein*, Hammer Film productions 1957.

REFERENCE

The Curse of Frankenstein, Hammer Film productions 1957

Three

Broadening Horizons and Making Us Kinder – The Impact of Early Opportunities for Student Mobility

Judith Lamie and Christopher Hill

INTRODUCTION

Many of us who have found ourselves in this wonderful world of international higher education have been lucky enough to have had an experience, when we were younger, either at school or at university, of language learning coupled with travel, work, or study abroad. Drawing upon some real-life experiences, in this chapter, we explore the changes in early opportunities for student mobility and language learning, highlight some of the benefits and challenges and pose the question, particularly to those who have the power and influence to change our curricula, if learning languages and experiencing different cultures is so educationally rewarding, then why isn't this a priority for many of our countries, particularly those who have English as their primary language?

LANGUAGE LEARNING

The Importance of Languages

In 2020, the British Academy, American Academy of Arts and Sciences, the Royal Society of Canada, and the Academy of Social Sciences in Australia joined forces to release a joint statement[1] on the importance of languages and issued a call to action to our governments, our policy makers, educators, business and industry, and the wider community. They acknowledged the vital role that language learning plays in helping us bridge cultural divides and solve the major challenges that we are faced with:

> We must increase our capacity to speak with each other as part of a global community. Language instruction to enhance literacy and fluency, including knowledge of multiple languages, is crucial to creating future 'global citizens' who can respond to these challenges and support positive impacts on our own domestic politics.

DOI: 10.4324/9781003649571-4

During the global health pandemic, people came together from across the world to try to combat one of the deadliest foes we have encountered. They worked together within the confines of their countries and their laboratories, across boundaries, across barriers, and across languages to enable us to once again resume a life that is approximating normal. But this is not the kind of collaboration that will take place, thankfully in many ways, on a day-to-day basis. It was a collective response to a collective emergency.

Learning a language teaches us so much more than simply a new set of vocabulary. It teaches us about ways of lives, it helps us to understand and appreciate situations that are different from our own, it helps us to be tolerant, curious, and reflective. It helps us to learn more about ourselves as well as others.

According to the philosopher Roger Bacon, "knowledges of languages is the doorway to wisdom". Lewis (2023), in an informal gathering of feedback from members of the international higher education community, highlighted a number of skills and attributes that can be derived from language learning, as illustrated in Figure 3.1. Skills that

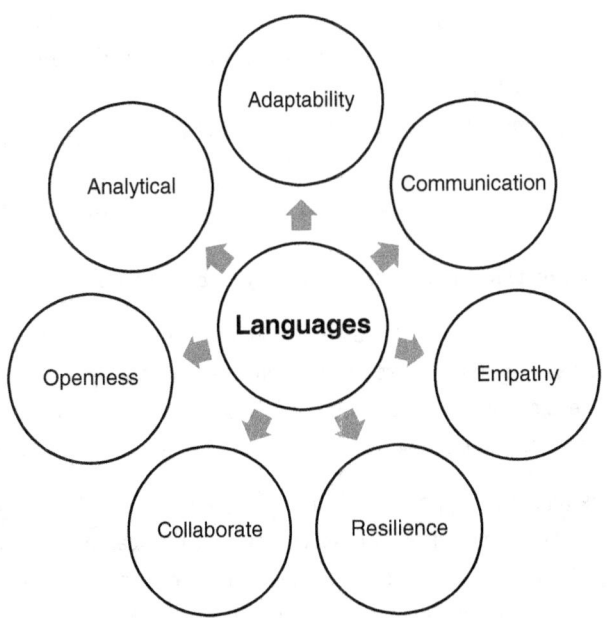

Figure 3.1 The Benefits of Language Learning
Source: Lewis (2023).

were mentioned included those anticipated when thinking of language study, such as improved communication skills, the ability to build cross-cultural relationships and the opportunity to expand your horizons, but other areas included the enhancement of problem-solving, analytical skills (you may have to piece together an understanding of a situation from limited vocabulary) as well as patience and empathy, that can in turn make us better teachers if we are ourselves to return to the lecture room and realise what it is like for our students to have to communicate in a second or third language.

With all of these positive benefits of language learning, you would presume that it would form the bedrock of our school and university curricula and that language learning and teaching over the years would have gone from strength to strength. Sadly, you would, in many cases, be wrong.

> **Did You Know?**
> - One language dies every 14 days.
> - There are approximately 7,000 languages spoken on Earth. It is predicted that by the beginning of the next century less than 3,500 will remain, with English, Mandarin, Spanish, and Hindi dominating the global language stage.
> - What stories and what historical knowledge will be lost along the way?

Cheryl Yu: Reflections on study in the UK: Part 1 – Try before you buy

My journey in pursuing a degree in the UK differs greatly from the majority of Chinese students, as I eventually ended up completing a part-time research degree instead of a full-time taught degree. This offers me quite a unique experience and learning journey.

As part of my staff development opportunity at the University of Central Lancashire in 2010, I was offered a 1-month trial period to visit the campus and to attend various lectures on business and management, and translation and interpretation courses. For the learning experience, I enjoyed all the group work of the business programme, and I felt it was so much easier and more interesting compared to the educational experience I had in China. On the contrary, I found it quite challenging and boring for the simultaneous translation course. In the end, I decided to opt for the Translation and Interpretation programme so that I could further challenge myself and grow.

The social activities in the evenings or weekends played an equally significant and memorable role, if not more, retrospectively, in the study experience. I was lucky to have made new friends easily and quickly from France, compared to some of my Chinese classmates who did not speak English well and found it difficult to adjust, being shy or linguistically finding it challenging to communicate comfortably. I did not waste my time, and I embraced all the new and different things, like anyone who goes to a new country for the first time, new friends, clubs, cultural activities, shopping, and visiting different places.

The other significant emotion that I felt was the "freedom of being myself" by speaking out my views and opinions in the classroom; whereas in the comparable Chinese context, students' active participation in class would be typically viewed as "showing off", which, subsequently, invisibly, pressurised Chinese students to form a habit of shunning away from active participation. International education is for us to be exposed to, to experience or sometimes even to form new social norms and perspectives.

Language Teaching and Learning
The decision to limit language learning in schools by making GCSE languages voluntary is probably the single most damaging education policy implemented in England so far this century.

(Nick Hillman, HEPI, 2020)

With its indigenous Celtic languages, multilingual history, and the languages of empire and migration, the status of language learning in Britain, although formally recorded as beginning around 1000 A.D. in the form of English-Latin dialogues for young monks, would have taken place informally much earlier. After the Norman Conquest in 1066, French, albeit the language of the conquerors, became the first foreign language and "language of prestige" for those outside of the clerical system (McLelland, 2018).

The popularity of learning Italian, Spanish, and German ebbed and flowed as the relations with the home countries of those languages fluctuated. Britian's continuing, if turbulent, relationship with France, however, and France's cultural dominance in Europe, kept French as the first foreign language for most of those engaged with education in Britain.

When the national curriculum was introduced in the UK in 1988, the vast majority of pupils learned a language. This was at its peak in 1997 when 82% of girls and 73% of boys were entered for a modern language at GCSE. The requirement for pupils to take a language at GCSE (beyond the age of 14) ended in 2004 and by 2007 the proportion of pupils taking a modern language fell dramatically to 47%. The government noted the trend and in 2011, in an attempt to combat the fall in the number of students studying foreign languages (and science) introduced a new performance indicator called the English Baccalaureate (EBacc). The EBacc was designed to enable students to keep their options open when it came to further study and included: English language and literature, mathematics, the sciences, geography or history, and a language. The government's ambition is to see 90% of pupils studying the EBacc combination by 2025. In 2019 40% of pupils were entered for the EBacc. A failure to secure a good GCSE grade in a language is by far the most significant obstacle to achieving the EBacc. In 2019, of those that had entered subjects in four of the five required components, 80% were missing the language element. The teaching and learning of foreign languages in Britain continues to struggle.

Language Trends, which began in 2002, is an annual survey of primary and secondary schools in England created to gather information about the situation of language teaching and learning. In 2019 the survey noted that the long decline on language teaching at primary school and leading into secondary school was having a lasting effect on numbers of students choosing to study languages and also on their performance once they did; it also highlighted the challenges that teachers had in delivering the subjects given the deficit in knowledge in initial teacher training and in professional development programmes and the reduction in the numbers of Foreign Language Assistants employed by schools to help teach in the classroom.

This is only one example of a country's struggles with language teaching and learning, but it is not unique, and many of the challenges are replicated particularly in other English-speaking nations. In 2021 a study of Australian students revealed that only 8% of Australian students are learning two or more foreign languages compared to 50% of students across OECD countries (Richardson, 2021): "while being aware of intercultural communication is certainly useful, being able to communicate with people from different countries in their own languages is even better". A further 64% of students said that they did not study a language at all. As with Britain, teacher training and support was also flagged as an issue, as was the fact that language learning is patchy across states, with some having no language policy at all.

If Britain and Australia are at the less positive end of the multilingual, language learning scale, then a country firmly at the other is Luxembourg. Multiple languages are spoken on a daily basis in Luxembourg. Landlocked in Europe, Luxembourg is bordered by Belgium to the west and north, Germany to the east, and France to the south. It is Europe's seventh smallest country with a population of 660,800 (50% coming from outside Luxembourg itself). The Luxembourg education system is mainly based on German and French. German is the language of instruction at primary school and for the first years of secondary school, while French is used to teach most subjects in the upper years of secondary school. But Luxembourg is also pursuing a policy to diversify its school options, offering international French- and English-speaking classes, welcome classes, and a system of intercultural mediators. The curriculum also places strong emphasis on learning Luxembourgish. Multiculturalism is one of the key principles of the University of Luxembourg.

Maybe this is to be expected. Around 400,000 people in the world speak Luxembourgish, 1.35 billion people (out of a population of 7.8 billion) speak English. There is a simple excuse for those in the governments of English-speaking nations that other languages are more of a luxury than a necessity. However, we are all aware that the study of languages offers us so much more. If we bring together language study with the opportunity to visit the country of the language in question, then the benefits increase at least twofold.

> Twenty years from now, you will be more disappointed by the things you didn't do than by the ones you did. So throw off the bowlines. Sail away from the safe harbor. Catch the trade winds in your sails. Explore. Dream. Discover.
>
> (Mark Twain)

TYPES OF STUDENT MOBILITY

School Exchanges

In the 1980s and 1990s, it was a regular occurrence in the UK to see coachloads of school pupils heading off to Calais to take the ferry or, for those with better sea legs, a hovercraft, to Europe. For many, this was to be their first experience of travelling abroad, their first chance to test out their language study on unsuspecting locals and to taste the delights, or otherwise, of a different cuisine. Importantly, these were exchanges, which meant that a few weeks later a corresponding set of students would travel back to the UK, accompanied by their teachers, to stay with host families and to experience the UK in all its glory, from mushy peas to a strong brummie accent.

These exchanges would have been prepared for in a number of ways. This being pre-internet school, children were paired with each other and would write to each other to start to learn a little about their counterparts, their hobbies, and their ambitions, and were encouraged to write where possible in the foreign language, or at least partly in it. That way when you eventually met your new pen pal you would already know something about them and their family, making the transition into meeting each other smoother.

There were lots of advantages to such schemes. You could practise language skills (written and then spoken), enhance intercultural skills, develop confidence, learn about another country and culture, and very often meet a new friend that you will have for the rest of your life. For some of it was the first opportunity to taste chocolate spread, that you could put in a sandwich, which seemed in the 1980s to be decadent and heavenly (the corresponding introduction to Irn Bru and a Scots pie wasn't as well received).

But as the century drew to a close these programmes were on the decline. Languages were taught less in schools, taking pupils out of the school during term-time was viewed with unease, and there were safety concerns. Prompted by the decline, in 2014 the British Council launched a campaign to "bring back school exchanges", and in a separate survey carried out with university language students, said that over 60% had been influenced to study a language at university as a direct result of a school exchange experience. Sadly, however, language teaching in schools has continued to decline, and those benefits of short bursts of international travel have been experienced by fewer and fewer students as the years have progressed.

There do remain opportunities, and in many ways now physical boundaries have been replaced by virtual mobility and electronic experience, but nothing can really replace the sights, and the sounds, and the smells of somewhere new and exciting.

Stephen Barry: Reflections on a first trip abroad and the wonders of garlic

My first trip abroad was in 1972 – foreign trips were usually limited to "foreign exchanges" of school students at that time. I was in the Lower Sixth studying French A Level, only four boys in what was otherwise "a girls' subject". I was lucky enough to get a place on a *Semaine Culturelle* which was intended to help A level students study our French literature set books in France and to practise speaking French in surroundings of real French people. We travelled there by coach then ferry then train. Arriving in Paris and opening the train door, I recall announcing "Cor, it smells of garlic round here" or something equally disobliging. This was my first introduction to French cuisine, and garlic was an unknown entity in our kitchen at home. The trip was over 50 years ago, so my memory of it is rather vague but I do remember that we stayed in a school in the suburb of Sceaux.

The trip was only a week long (obviously) but it certainly increased my enthusiasm for the French language and for foreign travel in general. It helped me with learning the language and French was my best grade in an admittedly poor haul of A levels. However, the Paris trip had sparked my enthusiasm for travel and a few years later I abandoned my sandwich year in UK industry in favour of working on French campsites during the legendary summer of 1976. After leaving college I went to work in the international geophysical exploration industry, so my French language skills were in demand (because real Englishmen don't speak French). A little later I even managed to get a job with a French mud-logging contractor working on oil-drilling rigs with real French speakers and later doing geophysical surveying in francophone countries.

Eventually I returned to England to settle down, but I would never have imagined that the *Semaine Culturelle* at age 16 could lead me to such an interesting and well-travelled decade in my 20s and a love of international travel to this very day.

Mobility Schemes
Erasmus+

The Erasmus (European Community Action Scheme for the Mobility of University Students) Programme is a European Union student exchange programme established in 1987. It became Erasmus Plus (+) in January 2014 when all of the programmes for education, training youth, and sport, across the EU, were combined. The programme has engaged over 13 million participants since its inception. One of the most successful programmes for Erasmus+ activity in Ireland is at the University of Limerick.

The University of Limerick (UL) located in the Wild Atlantic Gateway city of Limerick on the west coast of Ireland is committed to offering an inclusive and high-quality international educational experience to all students irrespective of their backgrounds and programmes of study. With strong links to industry and business, UL has played a crucial role in the economic and social development of the region over the past five decades. Today Limerick is a central hub for multinational companies and high-tech industries and opportunities for UL graduates. It has also led to an increased focus across all of the university's academic programmes on this transformation has brought new and exciting employment, the development of transversal, workplace skills, and the embedding of internships (known as Cooperative Education) and Erasmus mobility which have become central to the identity and mission of the university.

Students from over 95 different countries come to Limerick to experience Ireland and life at an Irish university and 17% of students at the university are from an international background. Foreign language learning and intercultural skills development lie at the heart of the University's internationalisation agenda. In addition to taught undergraduate and postgraduate degree programmes in languages including French, German, Japanese, and Spanish, all students can avail of opportunities to either begin or further their foreign language learning by enrolling in additional classes in the Language Opportunities Programme or by participating in more informal language exchange activities organised by the UL Language Learning Hub. The UL Global Lounge also offers an inclusive designated space for intercultural training and activities for students and staff alike and to celebrate the rich and growing cultural diversity of the campus community.

UL has the largest outgoing Erasmus+ mobility programme in all of Ireland in terms of outbound students, and it welcomes more incoming Erasmus students from European universities than any university in the country. UL students enrolled in language and cultural study degree programmes have the opportunity to engage in one or two semesters of Erasmus study as a core component of their course, and Erasmus is also offered as an elective on many other degree programmes across all faculties.

In Case Study 3.1, we hear first-hand from Irish undergraduate student Amy as she reflects on two memorable international education journeys she undertook while studying for a bachelor's degree in Applied Languages at UL. Amy spent one semester in Argentina teaching English as part of a cooperative education experience and then went on to study for a further semester at a university in Munich, Germany, on Erasmus. Both experiences created valuable opportunities for the young Irish student to hone her foreign language and intercultural skills and also learn a great deal about herself in the process.

Case Study 3.1: Amy's Story: A Tale of Two International Education Journeys

Context

The Cooperative Education (Coop) work placement programme at the University of Limerick (UL) is a core, accredited element of the UL student experience with all undergraduates required to undertake a six-to-eight-month placement in second or third year of their four-year degree. Coop involves a network of 4,000 employers, both national and international, and is unique in the Irish and international contexts, with students eligible for placement, regardless of discipline and vocational orientation, academic standing, and skills profile. As such, it is a tangible manifestation of the value of switching the locus of learning and knowledge between the classroom and the workplace and offers students the opportunity to develop and apply a range of understandings and competences that they could not acquire in either single context.

As an undergraduate student studying Applied Linguistics, I engaged in two study abroad opportunities. Here I reflect on some of the challenges I faced, but some of the wonderful learning experiences I had along the way.

Stages in the Journey

i) The Preparation

One of the main reasons I chose to study at UL was that it allowed me to spend a full year abroad. This was split over Years 2 and 3 of my degree programme, with a one-semester Coop placement first followed by a second semester on Erasmus. I chose to do international

Coop teaching English in Argentina and to spend my Erasmus semester studying at a university in Munich, Germany. This allowed me to develop my Spanish language proficiency and at the same time gain some useful teaching skills and then to move on to hone my German and gain insights into a different European country and culture.

What was really helpful was that there was preparation for both placements from the start of my degree programme with practical workshops provided by the UL Coop Division and UL Global Erasmus team. This included "warts and all" talks by students who had just returned from their year "out". Hearing their authentic experiences was both reassuring and daunting and it definitely motivated me to do everything possible to get the most out of my own year abroad.

ii) The Arrival

Despite being given a lot of practical information in advance, the first few weeks following my arrival in each country found me grappling with trying to find affordable accommodation and navigating my way around two unfamiliar cities. In Argentina, I got a very warm welcome from the other teachers at the secondary school where I found myself teaching conversational English to a bunch of unruly teenagers for the next six months. Meanwhile, on my arrival in Germany, I was straight into Bavarian culture with a visit to the first weekend of Oktoberfest. Then began the university's orientation week with a hectic round of meetings, tours, and schedules.

iii) The Rest

My first few weeks on Erasmus in Germany brought many challenges as university life there was so different from what I had previously experienced in Ireland. The first task I had to come to overcome was choosing my modules from a huge list of all the available courses, and the next was to try to figure out where to find the various buildings and classroom which were spread out across the city in different locations unlike in Ireland where everything was conveniently situated on one large campus. I can't remember how many times I arrived late to class because of this, and I found this very frustrating as I am usually a very punctual person.

I was also out of my comfort zone in Argentina as despite being provided with an intensive course in teaching before I had to "go solo" in the classroom, I still felt like an imposter when I realised just how little I actually knew about my own native language. Trying to settle into life in Argentina also proved difficult as I had to move between living and teaching in two different cities. But in the end, this turned out to be a blessing as it really allowed me to get to know the local culture, and I always felt very welcome in both of the cities and schools I lived and taught in.

Key Themes

- **Culture**
- **Life skills**
- **Communication**

Lessons Learned

- What struck me most culturally was that I had to learn new ways of interacting and communicating in each context as the types of engagement and norms varied a lot from Germany to Argentina. For instance, in Ireland, students on the same course tend to hang out with each other and become friends but in Germany there were less opportunities to socialise with peers as students tended to go home straight after class, and they didn't place as much emphasis on small talk and building social rapport. So, I actually spent most of my free time socialising with other Erasmus students rather than with the locals. By contrast, in Argentina, it was easier to make friends but social gatherings tended to be loud and somewhat chaotic with people constantly interrupting and talking over each other. In the end, I think I learned to adapt to both cultures and became a more confident global communicator along the way. Naturally, living in Germany and Argentina also helped me to improve my foreign language skills to the point where I have actually started to think in German and Spanish, and I can converse in both languages with greater ease and confidence.
- Both international experiences gave me so many life skills for which I am very grateful. Living abroad on my own taught me in particular to overcome my fear of failure, which had plagued

> me throughout my teenage years. Studying in Germany, getting lost on the metro, having to cook for myself and organise my own finances, and trying to navigate an unfamiliar culture, made me realise how capable I actually was, and I definitely came back more self-assured. Meanwhile, standing up in front of a class of boisterous Argentinian pupils and managing to get their attention and teach them something useful gave me a real sense of confidence and pride.

The Turing Scheme

When the UK voted for Brexit, one of the consequences was that it (England specifically) was no longer able to take part in the Erasmus exchange programme. A new scheme, Turing, was launched in September 2021 with an initial budget of £100 million for the academic year (a reduction of over £30 million when compared to the Erasmus grants of 2019). It was intended to encourage mobility globally. UK organisations with successful applications received funding towards placements and exchanges, this included providing participants with grants to help cover travel expenses and cost of living, and administrative funding for delivering the projects.

The focus of Turing was widening access, with the UK government emphasising that the scheme would target students from disadvantaged backgrounds, due to the fact that they were less likely to undertake forms of study abroad and exchange: 7.6% of non-language subject students from "more advantaged backgrounds were mobile, compared to 4.6% of students from less advantaged backgrounds".[2] A significant difference from Erasmus is that Turing only funds outwards mobility, not providing any funding to facilitate inbound student exchange. This has had its challenges and gives European partners, in particular, little incentive to partner with the UK.

Taith

> It's one of the best things I've ever done. I've got to meet so many new people from different backgrounds to mine. I've taken so many different modules I couldn't have taken at home and as cliché as it sounds I feel like a whole new person. There is not a second I have regretted taking part.
>
> (Outgoing Taith Scheme participant, Swansea University 2023)

In the UK, the situation in Wales has been slightly different from that of England. In 2022 the Welsh Government set aside £65 million to support short-term travel and study opportunities for learners and staff across Wales in every type of education, from schools and youth work to further, higher, and adult education. As with Turing, the Taith Scheme focuses on making international exchange more inclusive and accessible. Activities are different for learners and staff and include study, volunteering, job shadowing, and attending a course. Crucially, for partnership development between academic institutions, it also provides funding to bring learners and educators from around the world to Wales.

As with Turing, the administration of the scheme is complex and has its challenges for institutions, but feedback on the scheme for those that have taken part in the exchanges has been resoundingly positive. Portfield School[3] is a special school for pupils aged 3–19 who have a wide range of complex additional learning needs (ALN) such as autism spectrum condition and social, emotional, and behavioural needs. Pupils in years 8–11 are involved in a project to enable staff and pupils to visit ALN schools in Uppsala, Sweden, and Flanders, Belgium. The funding also enables pupils and staff from the partner schools to visit Wales in the summer. Many of the Portfield pupils have never been abroad. Greater levels of independence and communication skills are just some of the benefits. Ellie, one of the Portfield pupils said:

> For me it was life-changing because you actually got to see what the children did in the school. My favourite part was the art. We made cardboard Christmas trees with wool around them. I learnt you can do different things. I learnt how the children are different from us as they play different games on the playground.
>
> I would tell people to go to Bruges to see the Christmas markets. The thing that was special was how big they were and how there were loads of different stalls. It was the time of my life, it truly was.

LESSONS LEARNED

Culture and Developing Cultural Diplomacy Skills

> Simple exchanges can break walls down between us, for when people come together and speak to one another and share a common experience, then their common humanity is revealed.
>
> (Barack Obama)

Beaven et al. (2017: 137) in an analysis of the impact of language exchange programmes and their role as a potential tool for plugging the gap in formal language learning, noted that interacting with speakers of the chosen language can provide a wealth of benefits from focusing on the importance of communication rather than absolute accuracy, to providing a snapshot of into their culture, as one of the research participants stated:

> I believe I have not only met a very nice person, but I am also learning Italian. This method of improving your language skills gives you a direct glimpse into the life of your language partner, his/her culture and everyday concerns.

The participants also flagged that although they were initially concerned about meeting their exchange partner, and were worried whether they had prepared enough, or whether they would have anything to talk about, in reality that concern dissipated shortly after they met. Being face-to-face with a real person which may be different from yourself but in many ways will be the same highlighting the fact that what you have in front of you is another human being. Someone who won't correct every little grammatical error you make, someone who just wants to communicate like you do, and someone that might even have your taste in music. It's all about the people.

Learning about a country's art, learning about its language, about its culture, is a way in which we can build mutual respect and understanding. In this politically delicate and fragile world, cultural diplomacy plays a vital role in building bridges and crossing divides. It will not solve all of the world's problems, it will not stop disagreements, or wars, but it can only help combat some of the problems and lessen the likelihood of conflict.

Compassion and Kindness

A word that is mentioned frequently when those that have experienced language exchange abroad are surveyed is compassion. Vicky Lewis referred to this when describing her experience in Sri Lanka (see Chapter 2). Whether you are school pupil taking part in an exchange programme and staying with a host family, who will have welcomed you into their home, or a university student teaching in Argentina being welcomed by school teachers you are going to be working with for the coming weeks, there is a thoughtfulness that those you are visiting will often display. This is good for the spirit, good for the mind, and good for the soul, and gives us hope that eventually all in the world will be well.

Cheryl Yu: Reflections on study in the UK: Part 2 – Be Kind.

Do we all need external validation- yes!

In our educational experience, we all need encouragement from our parents, our tutors or classmates. This cannot be separated from the conditioned psychological reaction from our childhood being the 'good girl' or 'good boy' expectation from our parents. At work, we aspire that our efforts and achievements are acknowledged by our line managers and colleagues.

Being proud of our progress does not come from ourselves easily. It originates from the acknowledgement of our PhD supervisors. I was lucky enough to have had a PhD supervisor who was extremely supportive, sympathetic, and compassionate often in his approach in working with me. Looking back the outputs that I produced in my first year were significantly lower quality compared to the last two years. However, throughout the whole journey, I only received positive feedback about my efforts, commitment and progress from my supervisor. So, most of the time, I was a very happy and content student working independently and confidently.

Positive psychology works in education.

Be kind.

Engaging with Others and Developing a Global Mindset

If you talk to a man in a language he understands, that goes to his head. If you talk to him in his language, that goes to his heart.

(Nelson Mandela)

Engaging with others and developing a global mindset is increasingly important in our interconnected world. What has been evident in the examples we have seen in this chapter, and throughout the book, is that having these international experiences provides you with an invaluable lesson in being able to navigate the complexities of the global marketplace and differing cultures. They provide you with an opportunity to learn about something new, but also to learn something new about yourself. These opportunities for understanding and self-reflection can only be of benefit as you seek to work and to live on the international stage. You become more open, more willing to listen, more practised at interacting with others. Your global mindset is not entirely altruistic. You benefit as much as those around you.

Present and future generations will be responsible for the health of our planet, they will be responsible for building collaborations, locally, nationally, and internationally, and they will be responsible for fostering harmony and well-being. They need to be able to communicate with each other, and they need to be able to engage.

> **Top Tips for Gaining the Most From International Exchange**
>
> **DO**
> - Reflect on your experience.
> - Do your homework.
> - Budget carefully.
> - Immerse yourself in the culture.
> - Record your learnings for your CV.
>
> **DON'T**
> - Only stick with people from your own country.
> - Underestimate yourself – be positive!
> - Be afraid to try new things such as the local food dishes.
> - Worry if you feel homesick.
> - Forget to actually study.

THE FUTURE – WHERE WILL OUR LANGUAGE LEARNING JOURNEY GO FROM HERE?

Just as we need to devote time and energy to save the plants and animals that are unique to our earth, we should work towards preserving our uniquely human way of describing and understanding ourselves through language.

(The Great Gathering: One Voice, One People, One Earth)

AI: The Digital Babel Fish

If you stick a babel fish in your ear you can instantly understand anything said to you in any form of language.

(The Hitchhiker's Guide to the Galaxy, Douglas Adams, 1979)

When the computer was invented, there was a concern that this would spell the end for teachers. That did not happen. When the handheld calculator entered the classrooms, that was to be the end of our ability to do mental arithmetic. That did not happen either. There is a similar narrative emerging around artificial intelligence (AI) and language learning. Will we still need to learn languages if there are universal language translators there at our disposal (although not as fish popped into our ears)?

There are huge advantages to the existence of universal translators, particularly for the written word, but in some shape or form, this has existed for a number of years, albeit providing translation at a more sedate pace. Where AI may add benefit is in potentially preserving some of the languages we are set to lose over the next 50 years, as well as, more fundamentally, enhance the language learning process itself, from helping provide feedback on students written work, to producing interactive content that is personalised to an individual's ability and need. This facilitation of a personalised learning experience can foster independent learning skills and self-regulation, as well as supporting students in identifying resources to practise their language skills independently. To an extent, some of the techniques that have been developed over the years with data-driven learning and the use of language corpora have done this, but possibly in a less interactive or entertaining way.

New technologies, from AI to social media, do not have to be seen as a threat, but can enable learners to expand and even personalise their learning environment. As with online learning and face-to-face teaching, it does not have to be an either/or. With a positive mindset, there can be a place for both.

Far from making language learning obsolete, AI may even encourage more people to engage. According to Hua and Wang (2023), "by simulating a strong illusion of presence, VR has great potential to be incorporated in language education to promote contextualised and interactive learning experiences". By simulating real-life experiences that would be difficult to replicate in the traditional classroom environment virtual reality-assisted language learning has the opportunity to help prepare students more comprehensively for any future real interaction that may take place. Therefore, as a preparatory tool, it can take away some of the anxiety and replace it with confidence as well as enthusiasm. AI may even help us protect our language learning. There are other ways we can do this too.

What Can We Do to Protect Our Language Learning?

How can governments, universities and colleges, and individuals reverse what appears to be a downwards trend for language teaching and learning? In Luxembourg,[4] 100% of children start learning foreign languages in primary school, compared to 94% in Sweden and 10% in the UK. Governments need to bring back (if it isn't there) language study to the primary school classroom and to secondary schools, making its study compulsory. They also need to communicate and value the benefits. This will then have a positive effect on the study of languages at universities and colleges.

Language skills have become increasingly important in the workplace as the world becomes more globally connected. Employers are looked for well-rounded individuals, with a global mindset. To be able to communicate effectively, have strong analytical skills, have patience and empathy with others, and be understanding and open are all skills that benefit the employer as well as the individual. Further suggestions for protecting our language learning can be found in Figure 3.2.

> The study of languages opens pupils' minds and opens doors of opportunity. It develops a deep cultural awareness that is difficult to grasp without an understanding of the linguistic heritage of countries. The goals of wanting pupils to broaden their horizons, converse with others, explore cultures and strengthen their economic prospects will only be reached when we build firm foundations of language learning.
>
> (Ofsted, 2021)

Governments	Universities	Individuals
• Bring compulsory language study back to primary and secondary school classrooms • Provide government funded projects to support language study • Value and communicate the benefits that language study and exchanges bring	• Connect international students with local schools • Provide opportunities for short term mobility for all students • Embed language learning activities and measure into International Strategies	• Embrace the positives of enhanced technologies • If you've has an experience communicate how positivew this was and pay it forward • Volunteer as a mentor • Study a language - you are never too old!

Figure 3.2 How Can We Help Protect Language Learning?

THE FINAL WORD

The final word goes to Amy from the University of Limerick:

So what next? What both experiences have shown me is that this is just the beginning of my international journey and I am already planning my next overseas adventure after I graduate next year!

NOTES

1 Joint Statement on Languages - Draft (thebritishacademy.ac.uk)
2 Widening access - Turing Scheme (turing-scheme.org.uk)
3 https://portfield-special-school.j2bloggy.com
4 The Worldwide Language Index | Preply

REFERENCES

Adams, D. (1979) The Hitchhikers Guide to the Galaxy. Pan: London

Beaven, T. Motzo, A. and Gutiérrez, M. (2017) The Language Exchange Programme: Plugging the Gap in Formal Learning, in Q. Kan and S. Bax (Eds) Beyond the Language Classroom: Researching MOOCs and other innovations: 127–140

HEPI (2020) Action Needed to Avert the Growing Crisis in Language Learning. Available at Action needed to avert the growing crisis in language learning - HEPI

Hua, C. and Wang, J. (2023) Virtual Reality-Assisted Language Learning: A Follow-up Review (2018-2022), in *Frontiers in Psychology*, March 2023. Available at Frontiers | Virtual reality-assisted language learning: A follow-up review (2018–2022) (frontiersin.org)

Lewis, V. (2023) Reflections on the Benefits of Language Learning. Blog available at Reflections on the benefits of language learning - Vicky Lewis Consulting

McLelland, N. (2018) The History of Language Learning and Teaching in Britain. The Language Learning Journal, 46(1), 6–16

Ofsted (2021) Research Review Series: Languages. Crown: London

Richardson, S. (2021) Australian Students Say They Understand Global Issues, But Few Are Learning Another Language, in The Conversation, September 2021. Available at https://theconversation.com/

I'm a Stranger Here Myself – The Joys of International Education Travel

Christopher Hill and Judith Lamie

Four

INTRODUCTION

While conversations regarding travel have, rightly so, focused on sustainability and necessity, there is still tremendous value in meeting in person and building trust through engagement. In this chapter we look at how best we can prepare for travel, such that we maximise the return for the cost and impact. Work travel is about work but there should be time to look around and learn more about where we are and who we are meeting. International higher education is not merely transactional and is, at its heart, about people.

Christopher Hill: Reflections on a trip to Taiwan

A common reality of international higher education travel is a packed agenda, resulting from a short trip. We frequently justify this in light of demonstrating value for travel, the need to return and not waste expense while there. This is frequently a reality of travel and, while economical, it does often prevent engagement. In the case of my recent trip to Taiwan, it was arranged over a weekend and in between work commitments at home. This ensured minimum disruption to my work requirements but did not afford much time while there and ensured relatively 'healthy' levels of fatigue.

Thankfully, my recent trip was all in one place and this cut down on the logistics of having to move from one building to the other. It is always interesting, however, when you first see your itinerary and realise that you have been booked for back to back meetings from 9 am until 3 pm without a lunch, or even toilet break! This is not unique to Taiwan of course and I have experienced this in many places I have worked. The reality is that meetings run over. Frequently. Building in a little flexibility can be very helpful.

DOI: 10.4324/9781003649571-5

Travel is tiring. Not just the physical act of moving around the world, but the need to focus and be present, even though your body clock and the local time zone are competing for attention. It is important to be prepared but also to realise that there will often be that point (usually towards the end of the day) when our mind starts to wander a little bit and fatigue begins to nudge ahead of caffeine.

Trips back to familiar locations are always easier than those to new places. The familiarity and consistency can really help to reduce stress and unnecessary hassle. In some cases, as with Taiwan, I was staying in the same hotel. This was the international house attached to the university and houses international students and guests. It was within walking distance to the campus and a few streets away from supermarkets, eateries and a bus stop.

Ask questions and engage with colleagues as best you can. If you are lucky enough to go out to eat with colleagues (either during the day or in the evening) then try to take advantage of the opportunity to learn more about their context and experiences. This will help you to form a more in-depth understanding and awareness and provide you with insight that can help shape future interactions. Don't be afraid to ask questions about the food either. As we travel, we are often exposed to food we haven't tried before, and in some cases, don't recognise. If you have doubts or concerns, then ask. Guest friendship is a wonderful thing and travel in international education often exposes us to the very best of humanity. People are welcoming and supportive and not there to catch us out or expose our possible cultural ignorance.

PREPARATION

What to Pack?

Frequent travellers often get quite good at packing and are able to do so economically. Those of us who have experienced challenges with lost luggage, delayed luggage, or simple time implications of waiting for luggage – sufficient to miss the last bus connection to our hotel – are often proponents of hand luggage only. There is a certain freedom (and perceived superiority) in being able to exit the airport immediately. This does of course mean that we have to exercise restraint in what we pack and make do with what we have. This is a good metaphor for internationalisation as we don't always have access to everything we would "at home" and yet we still have a job to do.

Take an umbrella (unless you are travelling to Wales, where it can be very, very windy, the same may of course be said of Chicago). This is both literal and metaphorical advice. Be prepared for adverse weather. If you have presentations you are going to give, or files you are going to need, have them on a pen drive/USB stick and don't rely on being able to connect to your home server. The frustration of not being able to do something so taken for granted can throw us off, make us feel stressed and worried that we don't look as professional or prepared as we are. Have the material on your laptop. Have the material on a USB stick as a back-up. Have the material in your head (as best you can) as a back-up back-up. You could even keep notes using a pen and paper, if you are old enough to remember what they are.

What to Expect?

The more you travel, the easier it becomes. This is the theory of course. It isn't always easy but it is often easier with time and experience. There are always trips where things go wrong; where we lose luggage; where we have packed the wrong items; where we don't have enough time; where we have too much time and not enough to do (these are pretty rare); where the weather is not at all what was expected, which was certainly the case with Romania (see Case Study 4.1), although with all the apps and websites available to tell you what the weather is like pretty much anywhere in the world, there really is no excuse for packing snow boots and a winter trapper when it's sunny, with no wind and a balmy 19°C.

There is also the likelihood that something at home will require our immediate attention – usually at some inopportune moment. This is a balancing act we have to accommodate when we travel in international higher education. We have travelled for a specific purpose, and this requires our attention, energy, and focus. At the same time, however, our day job doesn't simply disappear. It is important to be able to focus on one thing at once and to build in time during the day to accommodate home issues where and when necessary. We can of course plan in advance to ameliorate this reality, but this will only take us so far. The typical impact of this is even longer days when travelling with our downtime in the evenings, if we have any, and if we are not having dinners, meeting with prospective students, or meeting with alumni, is taken up with work at home.

Case Study 4.1: UK TNE Programmes: The Balkans: Bulgaria[1] and Romania

Context

The British Council has developed a suite of TNE programmes with key countries in order to forge new partnerships, maximise bilateral engagement across various agencies and governments, and support best practice. Two such programmes took place in October 2023 and February 2024; the first was to Bulgaria and the second to Romania.

Trip 1: Bulgaria

At its peak Bulgaria had a population of nearly 9 million, now it is around 6.4. The largest city with a population of over 1.2 million is the capital, Sofia. The UK-Bulgaria TNE programme was hosted at the Residence of the British Ambassador in Sofia. There are 200,000 students in Higher Education in Bulgaria, including 16,500 international students. Due to its location, a significant number of students come from Greece (4,000), and due to its history and reputation, the UK (approximately 5,000). There is an extensive history of students studying Dentistry and Medicine in Bulgaria.

Trip 2: Romania

With fewer than one thousand students studying on UK courses, Romania is not currently among the countries where UK institutions undertake extensive TNE. However, this has an opportunity to change. European students have historically made up around a third of all international students in the UK. This changed when the UK left the European Union. However, the appetite for a UK degree and the desire to come to the UK for a period of study remains.

There has always been a strong bond between the UK and Romania. There is a diaspora of 1.3 million in the UK. Prior to Brexit Romanian students were the third most popular group of students to come to the UK, it was also the country that had made the most dramatic increase in sending students over the previous six years.[2] Therefore, the appetite is there, and crucially now there has been a new Education Law passed in Romania that supports TNE initiatives. The trend is positive.

Stages in the Journey

i) The Preparation

There is a great deal of time dedicated, by the organisers in preparing for programmes such as the ones set by the British Council. Often multiple agencies may be involved including in the UK, Universities UK International (UUKi), the Quality Assurance Agency (QAA), and the Office for Students (OFS). When trying to bring together the timetables for the events the coordination and the content can be something of a logistical challenge, particularly when you add 10 to 20 universities into the mix. This can mean that information you receive is quite late in the day.

It is important if at all possible to do your preparation ahead of the visit. What is the education landscape like, what historical factors may impact future plans, what regulatory framework is used, what is the market demand and market opportunity and what might you already be doing within the country with the academic institutions that will be attending the programme. The latter is particularly useful as it can be difficult to map activity that you have in your own institution, and this gives you an opportunity to at least do this on a focused country level.

For the Romania delegation, we learned from the previous experience in Bulgaria and had some virtual group matchmaking sessions ahead of the programme. This served to break the ice and enable us to start to build up relations.

ii) The Programme

Trip 1: Bulgaria

The participants comprised the British Embassy and the British Council, including the Science and Innovation network, Education Insight (who facilitated the event), the Ministry of Higher Education, the Directorate for Academic Recognition, the QAA, nine representatives from Bulgarian HE institutions, and eight from the UK.

The Bulgaria programme began, for the governmental institution on the afternoon of Day 1, with the participants coming from the academic institutions joining at the networking dinner in the evening. Day 2 began with presentations on the education and regulatory landscape and focused on financial and HR matters, capacity building, language requirements, accreditation, and quality assurance and suggestions on how to choose the right partner. This was delivered lecture style with Q&A from the floor. The afternoon was then dedicated to matchmaking sessions delivered on a one-to-one/two basis.

The evening saw an opportunity to meet with alumni, which was, as it always is, extremely valuable. They shared their thoughts on studying at the university and the support they had received once they had graduated. Most mentioned that they would be happy to provide the university with more support themselves but where not often asked. This is a learning point for all of us. Ask your alumni, learn from them, and enable them to share their experiences with current and prospective students. Employability was a key topic and one that they felt they could also assist with more, particularly those alumni in more senior positions. As we are preparing students for the global marketplace, it is worth reflecting on how alumni can actively assist in the employability space.

Trip 2: Romania

The participants of the UK-Romania HE Partnerships Forum were the British Council and the British Ambassador, the Romanian Ministry of Education, Education Insight (once again facilitating the event), senior representatives from the QAA, the OfS, the Romanian Agency for Quality Assurance in Higher Education (ARACIS), the national Agency for Community Programmes in the Field of Education and Training (ANPCDEFP), UUKi, the National Council of Rectors (NCoR), Ecctis, the National Centre for Recognition and Equivalency of Diplomas (CNRED), and 29 institutions/organisations.

Learning from the experience in Bulgaria, the British Council extended the invitation in Romania to the academic institutions to join the entire event. Day 1, set in a world café style, was launched by a welcome from the British Council, the Embassy, and the Ministry of Education (who stayed for the entire day). This was followed by:

- Highlights of the research on the Romania TNE landscape.
- Setting the policy scene: the new Education Law, provision for joint, double and multiple degree programmes as well as microcredentials, and market demand in Romania.

- Quality oversight and regulations: joint presentations and discussion with ARACIS and QAA.
- Roundtable introductions of all institutions and organisations at the event and their aims and objectives.

The day concluded with a guided tour of Bucharest ahead of a networking reception and buffet dinner.

Day 2 was an opportunity to drill down further into the detail and to match institutions together:

- The NCoR and UUK (the sister organisation) shared their objectives and suggested some areas of focus for activity.
- Ecctis and CNRED shed light on the work in the TNE quality benchmarking area, drawing on broader strategic engagement with national authorities, regulators, and recognition bodies.
- Various case studies were presented and discussed (with a rule of no more than four slides) from Envisia's executive education partnership with Henley Business School to the short courses in Law provided by the University of Bucharest.
- The afternoon comprised matchmaking sessions between institutions and a final roundup of the achievements and actions arising.

An additional purpose of the day was to provide the Ministry and the regulatory agencies with any major issues that would appear to be arising as the TNE activities are taken further. To that end, an outcome was the setting up of a Community of Practice from the participants of the event so that information can be exchanged swiftly and acted upon.

This was the end of the formal programme, but most institutions stayed for a further day to conduct follow-up meetings, visit prospective new partner universities, and engage with alumni in the country.

iii) The Follow-up

Trip reports can be prepared and circulated, but it is the action plan, and how that is implemented, that is pivotal. Draft the action plan template ahead of going and fill it in as you are going through the days. Leaving to memory afterwards is unwise. This can seem like the less joyous part of international travel, possibly along with the unpacking, washing, and ironing. But you do need to demonstrate worth and value, and the best way to do that is to achieve something.

If you are travelling as a couple or a group, this is even better as you can schedule in time when you get back to follow up and share out the actions. If you have deliberative structures that you can feed into, such as an International Board, or a Faculty Internationalisation Committee, then do that, and promise a follow-up report too. Essay deadlines work whether you are a school pupil or a senior manager at a university.

Key Themes

- **Engaging with others:** If you have the right people in the room, you can get answers to questions swiftly. It's important to set the strategic context, but the devil is always in the detail and therefore to interrogate some case studies and trace through a few examples is vital to help identify any potential sticking points or areas for clarification. Make the most of the time that you have. It is tempting, when an event runs for a couple of days, to dash back to the ranch, but you are there and you have the chance to meet other people and follow up immediately with them in situ, so do that. That way you are rolling two trips into one.
- **Culture:** We learn about and experience culture in different ways. It's in the history of a place, the language, the food, and the people. The more you interact with the culture of your destination, the more you will learn and the more you will understand when situations arise where you find yourself in disagreement. It is perfectly understandable and much easier to deal with if you are open and empathetic.
- **Roles and responsibilities:** There are a lot of different players involved in International Higher Education: those that strategise, those that deliver, those that monitor quality, and those that take part. These of course are not mutually exclusive. From State Secretaries in governments to academic and professional service staff in universities, all have a vital role to play and actions and activities of one will certainly impact on another. Knowing who is involved and why and what their responsibilities and drivers are assisted in the process of developing a IHE plan that can be delivered as

effectively and efficiently as possible. It may seem sometimes that people are trying to be obstructive. More often than not, they are not. They have a job to do, and they have aims and objectives and KPIs as we all do. It is important to map and match these where possible so that you can together work towards mutual goals and ambitions.

Lessons Learned

- Involve as many of the participants as possible from the outset, including any pre-event virtual meetings. Don't presume that you know what all members are looking for or can contribute. They may surprise you.
- Be brave enough if planning the event to leave space for informal networking.
- Experienced facilitators cannot only make the event run smoothly and provide a wealth of information but can also ask those taxing and potentially delicate questions that members of universities, or agencies may not be able to.
- Schedule in time for your initial follow-up activities before you leave. Draft thank you emails on the plane, and pick one or two actions that you are going to achieve within the first couple of months, ideally agreeing on your timeframe, and how you will feedback on it, with your new partner. That way you will be supporting each other but also holding each other to account.
- If you can travel with colleagues. This is not a waste of money. Two (or three) heads can be better than one, can take up the reins when you are flagging in a meeting, and can work together to take forward the actions on return to the home base.
- Make the most of the alumni networks you have, even if there are relatively few individuals in a country or a region. The bond that international alumni have with their institutions is strong and there are multiple ways in which they would like to stay involved, from mentoring current students, to helping set up internship programmes. Your alumni network has a massive set of networks itself, and we can make the most of the links and connections and request introductions. Don't be shy to ask your alumni, they may say no for very good reasons, but they are much more likely to say yes, and of course if you don't ask, they will never be able to say yes.

- Use the opportunity to learn a little about the place you are visiting, and in doing so, the people who are living there and who you may be working with in the future. This is one of the true joys of international travel. The walking tour of Bucharest that took place at the end of Day 1, after the sessions finished (at 6pm) and before the buffet-style dinner (7.45pm) was an inspired idea. Not only did we learn from the guide on the tour, but from the Romanian colleagues that joined us. The conversations weren't always about what was taking pace on the tour (especially if you were at the back of a long crocodile of people), but that didn't matter. Developing partnerships involves developing relationships. Relationships involve people. It's all about the people.

Did You Know?

Romania isn't just famous for Dracula. It:

is home to the world's heaviest building *The Palace of Parliament*.
has a perfectly round-shaped village, *Charlottenburg*.
was the first European city to have electric street lights.
has more than 60% of the brown bear population of Europe.
boasts a host of inventions including the jet engine.
is one of the best places to go for a good bowl of soup!

THE PROGRAMME: AGENDAS

How to Cope?

In the post-pandemic era, there is a very real need to demonstrate value and return for travel, and this can put a lot of pressure on international trips. Agendas are full, as we can see particularly with the UK-China Higher Education Mission (Case Study 4.2); travel can be taxing; and there are often simply too many cups of coffee and not enough opportunities for the coach to make the necessary stops!

Make sure you take the time – or ensure that it is built into your schedule – to be able to step away from the desk or meeting, if even for only a few meetings. Weather permitting, being able to wander around the campus or area you are visiting can provide an insight into the context and reality of colleagues you are working with, or may be working with in the future. There is not always time for a grand tour but a simple walk around can be of real benefit, as was demonstrated in Romania. Take the time to sit and experience the campus from a different perspective. Look at the posters and flyers in the corridors. Get a sense of what the university is like for the students studying there. Take note of the facilities that support the people working there. A university is a community and an ecosystem that reaches far beyond the office you are likely to be working from.

> ## Case Study 4.2: UK-China Higher Education Mission 2023[3]
>
> **Context**
>
> China remains a top market for UK student recruitment. Despite the challenges of the global health pandemic, Chinese students continue to be attracted by the prospect of overseas travel and of studying in the UK, although competition from Australian and other anglophone countries is strong. Rankings continue to be a key driver for Chinese students' destination choice, but employability is also gaining in value. Postgraduate enrolments far outnumber undergraduate and the gap is growing larger every year. From roughly half of all new enrolments from China one decade ago, postgraduate students now make up over 70% of all new students joining UK Higher Education Institutions. Student flows are popular in both directions; however, with China hosting the largest number of transnational education students (71,000), this is continuing to rise. There are over 200 UK-China joint education programmes at the undergraduate level in China and over 40 Joint Education Institutes, which are predominantly undergraduate but can include postgraduate teaching, PhDs, and research.
>
> Quality higher education in China continues to increase at pace. From 2018 to 2022, the number of top 500 universities in China doubled. Chinese academics now produce nearly a quarter of all global research output, and between 2018 and 2021, UK-China co-authored research increased by 35%.
>
> For both higher education systems, the importance of developing partnerships with universities, schools, and agents is pivotal, and whereas digital innovations have helped keep that going during the health crisis, the vital role of face-to-face interaction cannot be underestimated.

Stages in the Journey

i) The Preparation

The UK-China Higher Education Mission was the first major educational delegation to visit China since the onset of the pandemic. Senior representatives from across twenty universities visited Beijing, Shanghai, and Suzhou and were joined by UUKi, UK Research and Innovation (UKRI), with the programme being led by the British Council China. The purpose was to scope research and educational partnerships, engage with alumni, hold policy dialogues, and build an understanding within the UK sector of the latest developments within the HE landscape in China. The mission had significant engagement across a wide range of both UK and Chinese stakeholders, including Chinese policymakers, senior representatives from the British Embassy and Consulates, businesses in China, and international schools.

Preparation for the British Council and UUKi who were leading the programme was extensive. The mission had been informed by the relevant resources available to manage and mitigate any risks that may arise, and to maximise the opportunities both at a policy dialogue and a practical, partnership-building level. At an institutional level, we prepared a number of briefing documents that provided information on: current students, demographic and popular areas of study; student exchange; agent activity; articulation and recruitment links; scholars; and research connections, citations, funding, and projects. Pre-mission meetings discussed where there may be the prospect of collaboration with new partners taking part in the programme, as well as further development of established partnerships in meetings around the mission schedule.

ii) The Programme

The programme was a mixture of networking events, formal education fora, including lectures and seminars, visits to academic institutions and research centres, roundtables with agents and international schools, and a lot of travelling in coaches (and occasionally trains).

The four-day agenda began in Beijing with a detailed briefing for the UK participants and an exchange of aims and objectives.

Delegations such as these can prove to be as beneficial a networking opportunity for those that you have travelled with as well as those in the destination country. It was important therefore to devote enough time to this series of sessions so that we could all be clear what the opportunities and challenges might be. A stakeholder reception then took place at the Ambassador's Residence which gave all involved an opportunity to interact with each other in a more relaxed and informal, if grand, situation.

Day 2 involved the main policy dialogue, the UK-China Higher Education forum. This five-hour morning event was jointly organised by the British Council and China Education Association of International Exchange (CEAIE) and supported by UKRI and UUKi. The forum aimed to rebuild connections and dialogue between UK and Chinese universities. In addition, it sought to improve understanding of the Chinese Ministry of Education's policies and to identify opportunities for transnational education and research collaboration. This was the first formal face-to-face higher education forum between the UK and China following China's re-opening in early 2023.

The afternoon was split into two roundtable activities. A meeting with the National Natural Science Foundation of China (NSFC) and a recruitment roundtable with key agents and international schools. The focus of the former was to provide an overview of China's research landscape and funding system and to understand how bilateral funding mechanisms might work, with the latter providing the participants with insights into the current environment for student mobility, the decision making process for students and their parents, and some thoughts on how the relationships between universities, schools, agents, and students could be improved.

The delegation then moved onto Beijing train station for the five-hour journey to Shanghai. Those who were still able spent quite a lot of the journey introducing themselves and sharing their thoughts with each other, but by the time we reached Shanghai, most were asleep.

Day 3 began with a visit to Shanghai Jiao Tong University, which included the opportunity to hear from members of SJTU about their global collaborations and partnerships, meet some students, and visit their Joint Education Institute with Michigan, the Michigan College and Innovation Centre. The second half of the morning was spent at the Shanghai Theatre Academy. Over the past six years, UKRI-AHRC (Arts and Humanities Research Council) has developed a wide-ranging portfolio of activity aimed at building new research and innovation partnerships in the arts and humanities between the UK and China. STA is one of the best higher education art institutions in China and has been a key stakeholder for AHRC's engagement with China. This session gave an overview of UK's research collaboration with Shanghai in arts and creatives and the plan of establishing a UK-China Creative Industries Research and Innovation Hub.

The penultimate activity of the day was a senior stakeholder dialogue at the Consul-General Residence. A presentation on China's social, political, and economic outlook, and the implications for educational exchange, was followed by full and frank discussion. The final event was a large alumni reception which included a three-course meal, interspersed with panel discussions by delegates, businesses, and alumni and cultural performances. It is a testament to the excellence of the latter that everyone stayed and talked and took lots of photographs.

The Oxford Suzhou Centre for Advanced Research (OSCAR) was the location for the final day in the morning. The centre is the University of Oxford's only engineering and physical sciences research institute outside of the UK. Officially inaugurated in 2018, the Centre is a partnership between the University of Oxford and the Suzhou Industrial Park (SIP). OSCAR led a tour of their research laboratories where the delegation was able to get an overview of their research work with China. Followed by a meeting with their Deputy Director to hear insights into their experience in China.

The final formal event was a debriefing held at a Suzhou Tea House during which participants reflected on the mission, shared their initial thoughts on follow-up actions and provided an evaluation of the activities that had taken place. Then there was the inevitable parting as newfound friends and colleagues made their way onto other engagements across China, or returned home.

iii) The Follow-up

A meeting for the UK delegation participants was set to take place at the British Council Going Global Conference in Edinburgh in

November. This timeframe meant that members were able to return to their respective institutions, communicate the outcomes of the visit, and develop action plans ready to give feedback two months later.

Key Themes

- **Communication:** Frank and informed dialogue is crucial across all forms of engagement. We are all aware of the geopolitical tensions. Use this as an opportunity to work together, discuss the challenges, potentially find solutions, but also if required be clear about which might not be possible. Better to be open about what you might not be able to do than promise something that you cannot deliver.
- **Developing partnerships and managing risk:** There can be some challenging matters that have to be discussed with partners overseas, such as the management of risk. All international activity comes with some risk attached and increasingly academic institutions have focused on trying to minimise that risk. UUKi (2020) has produced guidelines[4] on managing risk in internationalisation, and this covers a number of topics such as protecting reputation, people, campuses, and partnerships. Dimensions of risk have changed over the years, from a focus on operational legal and regulatory compliance to a greater consideration of reputation and values. The more open your conversations are with your partners around risk, the more stable the partnership is likely to be.
- **Strategy and insight:** It became ever more apparent on the mission that most institutions from the UK had a great deal of activity within China, but that much of it was undertaken with an absence of clear strategic direction. There are student recruitment activities, events with alumni, TNE programmes, multiple research collaborations, and business partnerships, but no thread to run through all of them. This would be the case with a number of countries. The development of an up-to-date China strategy across the spectrum of activity, which would include the collating and communicating of market intelligence and insight, enables an institution to build on that activity, share best practice and knowledge and expertise, manage risk, and ultimately deliver a more sophisticated approach to international activity.

Lessons Learned

- Factor in time where possible for discussion when visiting other institutions or organisations. It can be tempting to fill a programme with presentations and events, but it will be chance missed if we are not able to follow up and ask questions there and then. If visiting a university, it is ideal to meet both staff and students.
- Rankings and league tables may be important, but on the ground interaction and engagement will always add at least 50 places to your ranking.
- Appreciate meeting people in person. We could not do that for months/years. Don't forget that we were unable to travel and therefore do not stop valuing the fact that now we can.
- Be an active participant, if possible present during the sessions or chair panels. This will put both you and your institution front and centre.
- Take lots of pictures, you will never remember all of the faces, places, and names.
- Life moves pretty fast, like a Chinese train, if you don't stop and look around once in a while you could miss it.

Teamwork Makes the Dream Work

Just as there is a tendency to ram full schedules so that you have no time to reflect or fit in on-the-spot follow-up meetings, there can also be a challenge in persuading your institution, your colleagues, and even yourself that you don't have to go have to go it alone. There is a huge amount of benefit in travelling with colleagues. You can:

- Prepare together ahead of the event and divide up sessions if there are multiple activities taking place at once.
- Cover each other in meetings, and even networking events, when the days are long and the need to stay on the ball and engaging runs into several hours without a break, you are bound to tire. Having someone else there to cover at those times is essential.
- Pool your ideas as well as your resources. Two heads really are better than one.
- Make sure you glean as much from the meetings and events as possible. Taking notes and being an active participant is not easy. You

may even be presenting, then it is impossible. Having colleagues there to note down key points when you can't is beneficial.
- Learn from them about your own institution. Whatever your role in an institution you will never be able to cover everything, either from the academic perspective or the professional services. There is an opportunity to learn about the country you are visiting, from others on the programme from your own country, but not your own organisation and an opportunity to learn more about your institution itself.
- Work together on your return to follow up on actions and keep the momentum going.

Christopher Hill: Reflections on a whistlestop trip to Uzbekistan

If Taiwan was a short trip, Uzbekistan was a micro trip. The opportunity arose recently, to present at an international conference in Tashkent – sponsored and hosted by the Ministry of Higher Education, Science and Innovation of the Republic of Uzbekistan. The trip was in association with Westminster International University in Tashkent – an institution with which I have a long-standing relationship – and I was more than happy to agree to participate.

When asked to participate I was offered the chance to spend three days in Tashkent and take full advantage of the social programme that accompanied the conference. Unfortunately, as much as I would have thoroughly enjoyed this, my work situation prevented it as I had work commitments on the Thursday and Saturday, leaving only the Friday conference day free. I was able to attend, and present a keynote on the Friday but this required me to depart my home airport at 10 pm and arrive in Tashkent at 3 am the following morning. I checked into my hotel by 4 am and was at the welcome session and registration by 0830 am that same morning. The conference lasted a full day and we were then taken to a banquet. I arrived back at the hotel at 9 pm, managed to sleep until midnight and was then taken to the airport for a 4 am flight. I landed at 7 am and was at my office for a 9 am student conference.

I agreed to undertake this trip for several reasons. A keynote, especially sponsored at ministerial level, is an ideal opportunity to network and to learn from colleagues. I know many colleagues working in Tashkent and the opportunity to meet up and engage with them helps to keep professional, institutional and personal relationships ticking over. The importance of the trip had value to my institution and they were happy to approve my travel.

The trip was tiring however. I travelled with hand luggage only and my presentation had already been sent ahead so my only job was to stay awake long enough to deliver my talk and answer any subsequent questions. Trips like this have value but they also come with a cost. We don't have to accept every trip we are offered and we need to make a rational decision based on what we can get out of the experience versus what it will cost us in time away from family and work. As your career progresses, you develop the ability to say no a little more and this means that when you do say yes, you need to commit to the experience and do all you can to ensure you are representing yourself and your institution to the best of your ability.

Culture, Communication and Engagement

There are ways of doing things. There are our ways and there are other ways. Both of these are of course right and both are wrong depending on the context. When it comes to the etiquette of trips, we are guests and therefore should follow accordingly. Conferences and events are planned and structured. We fit within this structure and adapt as necessary. Sometimes the structure might appear unusual to us but it is there nonetheless and the easier path is to smile pitch in where you can, go where they ask you to, and speak when it is your turn. We are just one of many, many moving parts in events and often the best advice is simply to roll with it. Show up, be prepared, and be flexible.

Quite often speeches will be given in languages other than your own. Introductions and formalities will likely take much longer than seem necessary, or even possible. You will feel displaced and sometimes a little lost during the proceedings, particularly if you've just arrived after a ten-hour flight and have the time difference to contend with as well.

Even on short trips, like the one above, there are opportunities to learn and to engage. Yes, you will be tired but you need to remember you are there for a reason. As events move away from the traditional institutional spiel speeches, one after another to a more interactive and reflective discourse, there is tremendous value in being present. In all senses of the word, this is something that is reflected in all of our case studies. The more exposure we have in international higher education, the more we come to realise that difference in what we see and experience should not be judged by "how we do things at home" but rather accepted for how things are.

BACK HOME

Time spent away is valuable but is also time spent away from your day to day. If you are lucky, the day to day has waited for you – and allowed you to focus on the travel agenda you have recently been living. If you have been so blessed, there will be work for you when you get home. If you haven't been so lucky, you will have been doing work while away. And there will be work waiting for you when you get home.

The day job naturally takes over your time and energy and does so immediately. Unless you can build in a series of checkpoints that enable you to both follow up on events from the recent trip, and to ensure that the value of the trip and its potential outcomes are more closely aligned to internal objectives or strategy. This provides you with an opportunity to both capitalise on your time spent away and to further demonstrate the value of said trip, and indeed, of your recent absence.

It is worth remembering that everyone else back home hasn't been on the trip. An obvious point, but one worth bearing in mind. When you do return, potentially full of enthusiasm if a bit jet-lagged, you can get a little deflated that everyone else may not be as keen as you are to follow up on what might be some joint actions, but in reality are yours. Take the time to brief people in person, and don't just send them a 25-page report to illustrate how busy you were. This is also when taking pictures can help; it brings it alive for people, especially if they have never been to where you have just visited. They will be interested, but they have their own day jobs, so try and link what you have been doing to theirs, to show how it may benefit them personally, or their teams. It may seem obvious to you, but don't presume that it is for them. Sharing with your colleagues will help you to follow up, and some may in the future have an opportunity to undertake a similar visit, or in the act of sharing, you may have given them the idea that they would like to take part in one, and they might not have considered that before.

Top Tips

DO

- Pack well, pack wisely, and avoid check-in luggage.
- Prepare, but keep your mind and agenda open.
- Take the time to take in the cultural scene.
- Take notes and fill in draft action plans.
- Share your experiences and follow-up.

DON'T

- Jump on a plane and dash back immediately.
- Be disheartened if the challenges seem vast.
- Forget that travel is tiring. Take care of yourself.
- Try to do it all yourself. Travel as a (small) pack.
- Be afraid to ask. There is no such thing as a stupid question!

CONCLUSION

Travel has changed in the post-pandemic period. Thankfully, the restrictions and associated considerations have returned, largely, to pre-pandemic levels, and travel is "more or less" back to normal. While the journey itself may be familiar, the purpose and justification of travel remain impacted. Increased awareness and conversations regarding climate change and value are, rightfully so, more commonplace now and so our approach to travel has, and should, likewise take a new direction and focus.

The value of being somewhere else, interacting with somebody else, and learning from them, cannot be underestimated or overstated. This is how relationships are formed and become sustainable partnerships. They are invaluable but need to be understood as such. Demonstrating value can be a long-term proposition as success rarely manifests overnight. There is value for the individual, for the institution, for staff and for students, and it is to how we might use the lessons of travel to help students integrate into their new communities that this book now turns.

NOTES

1. You can hear more about the UK-Bulgaria TNE Programme and the Romania visit on the Think Education podcast
2. See Studyportals Report: International Student Recruitment from Europe: the Road to Recovery (UUKi, 2022): www.universitiesuk.ac.uk/universities-uk-international/insights-and-publications
3. You can hear more about the UK-China Mission on the Think Education podcast
4. Managing risks in Internationalisation: Security related issues (universitiesuk.ac.uk)

REFERENCES

UUKi (2020) Managing Risks in Internationalisation: Security Related Issues. London: UUK

UUKi (2022) International Student Recruitment from Europe: The Road to Recovery. London: UUK

Developing TNE Partnerships – The Beginning – Deciding Where to Go and Who to Partner With

Judith Lamie and Christopher Hill

Five

INTRODUCTION

In this chapter, we explore the intersection between the theory and the practical of partnership development. This is not a short process, nor is it one that guarantees success. There are of course clear steps that can be taken; precautions and pitfalls to be mindful of; lessons that can be learned from others. What is evident, however, is that partnerships – while following formulaic structures and processes – are individual and specific to those within them. As a result, a clear sense of self and objectives are critical for any semblance of success.

Jazreel Goh: Reflections on deciding where to go and who to partner with in TNE partnerships

Setting up a Transnational Education Partnership (TNE) involves a complex interplay of *organisational strategy*, *business objectives*, *educational ambitions*, *cultural* and even *personal factors*. It requires a multifaceted approach, including legal, people, technological, and financial considerations.

Reflecting on my personal experience of working with many institutions in setting up TNE partnerships, the decision on where to go and who to partner is often a combination of opportunistic and strategic followed by extensive market scoping and due diligence. At times when the right opportunity presents itself, I noted that all that was needed then was to seek advice from professional individuals with relevant market expertise to further endorse and enhance the quality of the decision-making.

However, in most circumstances, deciding where to and whom to partner with requires careful consideration of various factors. In my opinion, once institutions are clear on their own objectives and outcomes vis-à-vis establishing TNE, then the most important starting point is assessment of market demand, the competitive landscape and the market potential. Even with an enabling regulatory environment and the best partner, there are limits to the success of any TNE operations unless there are clear demands from students and the potential for sustainable growth in the specific market under investigation.

The second important factor is identification and evaluation of potential partners. Many may place regulatory environment as the top consideration, but I would argue that the right partner is more important. They are key to success in not only setting up TNE, but will contribute to long term sustainability and growth of any TNE initiatives.

The right partner would have a deep understanding of the regulatory environment in the host country. Navigating through application, accreditation, quality assurance, and other legal requirements is easier with a partner familiar with local regulations. The right partner understands the local culture, education system, and societal norms. This cultural competence is vital for tailoring educational programmes to meet the needs and expectations of students in the host country. The right partner would want to commit and invest for long term growth, align with your goals, and ensure relevance of the TNE initiatives.

The right partner will not only provide access to necessary infrastructure, which can significantly reduce the upfront investment and logistical challenges for the home institution, but will also bring in established relationships with relevant local stakeholders, including educational institutions, government bodies, and organisations to provide further (funding) support for wider academic and research collaborations.

Finally, the right partner will have ambitions and want to build a good reputation which enhances the credibility and image of your institution. This creates a strong eco-system to recruit and attract qualified faculty that would ensure effective teaching in diverse environments.

In summary, once we have decided on where to set up TNE, identifying the right partner who can bring local expertise, cultural understanding, regulatory knowledge, and valuable connections would be absolutely crucial, as that would significantly contribute to the success and sustainability of any TNE initiative.

WHERE SHALL WE GO?
Strategic Direction

International strategies at educational institutions have matured over the years. From documents that focused almost exclusively on international student recruitment, they have shifted to encompass internationalisation at home, research collaborations, partnership development, and transnational education.

There are several strategic questions we need to ask ourselves before we embark on developing TNE partnerships:

- *Where?* Concentrated or geographic spread? Near or far? Emerging or established markets? Political and cultural environments? Stability?
- *How?* Target markets or opportunism? Volume or niche provision? Teaching and research?
- *What?* Which model? Campus, franchise, validation? Flying faculty? Matching the curricula? Language of delivery?
- *Why?* Altruism? Internationalisation? Income generation? Brand enhancement?

There are a variety of reasons why universities engage with TNE. It can, for example: assist in communicating the university's brand overseas; help diversify international activity and access a different group of students who are unable to travel abroad; enable a swift response to changing market dynamics; maximise the benefit of international partnerships, current and future; provide support for financial sustainability; and develop profile, presence and reputation. There are, of course, significant challenges:

- Completing demands on resource and opportunity costs.
- Strong competition.
- Quality assurance.
- Multiple barriers to entry.
- Questions around equity, a recognition of the student voice and parity of provision.
- Managing relationships between home and overseas.

However, there are pathways to success including:

- Investing in learning and teaching products and support systems.
- Being aware of local regulations.
- Working with in-country experts, agencies and alumni.
- Developing in-country employability connections.

- Prioritising staff development both at home and in the TNE centre.
- Finding the right partner.

The bedrock of all TNE strategies and plans is the partnership, as Jazreel mentioned. Partnerships need to be selected carefully, there must be long-term commitment from all involved, the partnerships must be sustainable and go beyond two or three individuals that are driving them forward. There needs to be shared values, goal congruence and first and foremost the entire endeavour needs to be based on solid research. Research well!

Market Intelligence

Plan A hadn't worked. Plan B had failed. Everything depended on Plan C, and there was one drawback to this: he had only ever planned as far as B.
(Pratchett, 1990)

Market selection for recruitment and partnership development is based on a number of interrelated factors. These include: GDP; size of middle class; propensity for overseas study; education system structure; lack of Higher Education capacity in-country; high quality undergraduate provision, availability of funding sources; technology infrastructure; size and accessibility of communication channels to reach appropriate market segment, British Council support, public sector engagement with TNE, size and reputation of private sector able to partner for TNE, accreditation and acceptance of TNE and preferred model, ease of travel and business culture and so on. Such market intelligence can be gained from sources including:

- HESA data (where available).
- British Council.
- UK HE International Unit.
- Government/embassies.
- Agents.
- Overseas contacts.
- Expertise within the central teams and knowledge of country experts across campus.
- Internal data on applications; conversion rates; previous institutions.

An evidenced-based approach using current data and market intelligence is key.

Data-Driven Decision-Making

Data gives empirical confidence to decision-making about which TNE markets, delivery models and partnerships to focus on. Data can also help to bring about a culture change by persuading members of staff that TNE is both a viable and valuable option. In a presentation of a case study focusing on institutional TNE strategies "starting from scratch", Ilieva et al. (2023) refer to the changing nature of engagement of some Higher Education Institutions who are taking a more proactive, systematic approach to TNE, seeking to transition from "transactional gap-plugging to deeper, multi-dimensional forms of engagement", and by delivering TNE through assessing risk within a framework of due diligence using a range of tools. They put forward a risk-informed evidence-based approach, which would enable the institution to develop a process for determining which countries to focus efforts on, taking into consideration external indicators of risk level versus market potential, institutional strengths and risk appetite.

The framework utilises a composite index methodology which ranks countries' potential for TNE taking into account factors such as: national higher education capacity, maturity of the local HE system, economic wealth and the ability to access private higher education and political stability and ease of doing business. There is, in addition, a flexible approach to identifying prospective markets with the weighting of different categories being flexed to reflect institutional priorities and appetite for change and risk (see Figure 5.1). The next stage is an in-depth exploration of a small number of countries where market opportunity and demand is correlated with institutional capacity and capability.

There is a risk involved in any interaction with partners overseas, but there is similarly a risk as a result of inaction; risk of continued reliance on direct recruitment; risk of failing to diversify; and risk of remaining vulnerable to global events, government changes, sustainability, and climate change. A managed proactive approach to risk and TNE goes some way to mitigating the challenges.

Managing Risk

The question of risk will arise at every step of the partnership development process. A university's risk appetite will be determined by many

Weighing risks vs market potential

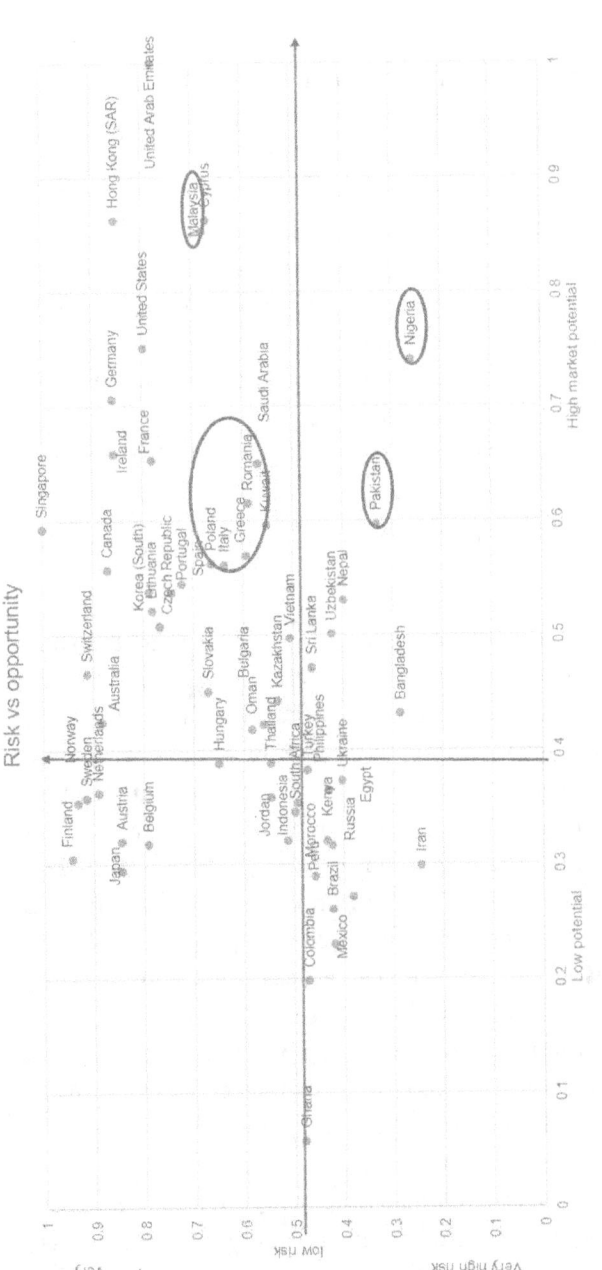

Figure 5.1 Weighing Risk and Market Opportunity (Ilieva et al., 2023)

different factors: identity, capacity, market conditions, strategic direction, previous success in engagement. Where you go, what you do when you get there, and who you do it with are all key issues that factor into any calculation of risk and engagement. An institution's identity and that of their potential partner are highly relevant as they often dictate, not just levels of capability but also aims, objectives and opportunity. There is an art to deciding what to do and where to do it. This is not always a foolproof process and is one that requires an element of faith in places.

Managing risk during the approval process is perhaps more science than art. There can be a tendency on the part of the more senior/established partner to require that their processes and documentation are used for the arrangement. If this is agreed by both parties, then there is perhaps little issue but it does need to be agreed and it does need to be transparent. Both parties will need to account for their actions and have their documents scrutinised and approved by varying levels of institutional and/or ministerial oversight.

Managing risk is essential and data are important, but it should be noted that they only tell part of the story and must therefore be understood and interpreted in context.

The Regulatory Environment

In her reflection on where to go and who to partner with Jazreel refers to the potentially challenging nature of the regulatory environment. While Jazreel states that the choice of partner is of greater importance than the choice of regulatory environment, there is little doubt from her reflections that the environment itself has a significant impact on the chances for success. Jazreel identifies the need to select the correct partner, precisely because this partner will help to navigate the environment and provide contextual and local knowledge – gained through practical experience and network building – that is largely unavailable (at least in the immediate) to the outside and international partner.

This understanding will help throughout the entire process, from application, accreditation, quality assurance and other legal requirements – some of which you may not have encountered elsewhere, or perhaps even heard of before!

In many cases, TNE operations go where TNE operations are. A welcoming regulatory environment is very attractive to new providers. Much of the work has already been done; frameworks are in place; expectations

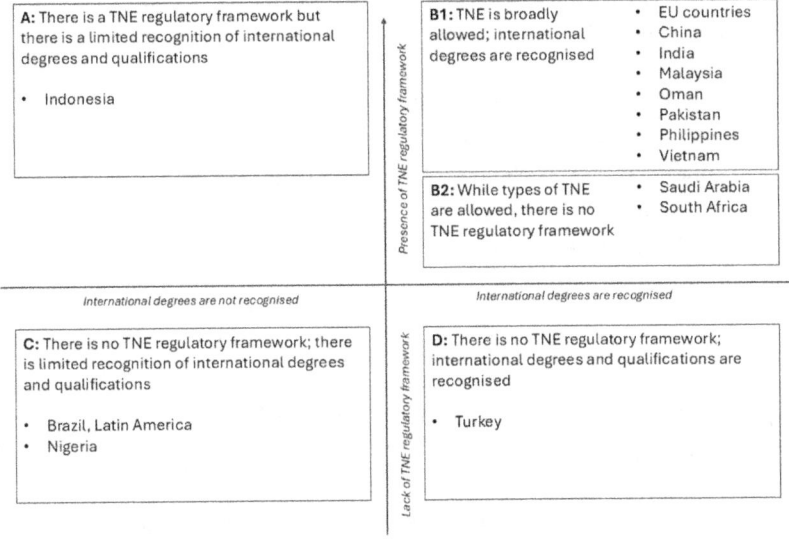

Figure 5.2 TNE Regulatory Environment (Ilieva et al., 2023)

are clearer; opportunities for success – despite a more crowded market place – are in place; risk is lower.

Changes to the regulatory environment are happening all the time (see Figure 5.2). Many of the changes have been long awaited and are welcome. Nowhere is this more relevant than India. The National Education Policy 2020 paved the way for the establishment of foreign campuses on India soil.

The aim of the NEP 2020 is that higher-ranked foreign universities will be facilitated to operate in India, thus enabling Indian students to obtain foreign degrees and qualifications domestically, with the associated cost advantage, and promote India as a global study destination.

The NEP 2020 seeks to create an educational landscape in India that supports student development with a focus on entrepreneurship. The policy is far-reaching and looks to enhance capacity at all levels of the educational structure. There will be an impact on the regulatory systems, the quality assurance, equity and inclusion and vocational training, to name but a few areas of focus.

The recent changes to policy mark a significant shift in attitude and opportunity and, while there are still areas that have yet to be fully tested, the new landscape does offer a series of interesting opportunities for partnership development and TNE growth.

Did You Know?

- India is the second largest English speaking country in the world (over 128 million speakers).
- India is home to several hundred languages.
- The National Education Policy recommends all students will learn at least three languages in their school and two of these should be native to India.

QS – Setting Up a Campus in India: The Ten-Point Plan
https://www.qs.com/india-international-branch-campus/

1. Market research and feasibility study: Undertake thorough market research to assess the demand for the programmes that the universities can offer in India, as well as the competitive landscape. Identifying potential locations and target demographics based on factors such as population density, economic development, geographic trends in education and educational infrastructure will be crucial.
2. Legal and regulatory compliance: Develop a solid understanding of the regulatory framework governing foreign educational institutions in India. International universities must be FHEI-compliant and obtain necessary approvals from regulatory bodies like the University Grants Commission (UGC) and the Ministry of Education.
3. Partnerships and collaborations: Establish partnerships with local educational institutions, government agencies, or corporate entities to navigate the regulatory environment, access resources, and gain credibility in the local market.
4. Infrastructure development: Next, identify suitable infrastructure for the campus, including classrooms, laboratories, libraries, administrative offices, and recreational facilities, while ensuring that they comply with local laws and regulations.
5. Faculty recruitment and training: Recruit qualified faculty members with expertise in relevant fields who can deliver high-quality education. They should also be provided training and support to ensure they understand local academic practices, cultural nuances, and regulatory requirements.

6. Curriculum development and adaptation: Adapting the university's curriculum to suit the needs and preferences of Indian students while maintaining the academic standards of the parent institution will be another challenge, though it can be greatly rewarding when done with care and attention. Incorporating local case studies, examples, and cultural perspectives to enhance relevance and engagement is key in this process.
7. Student recruitment and admission: Marketing strategies to attract prospective students should be geared towards an understanding of education needs and student interest.
8. Financial planning and sustainability: Develop a comprehensive financial plan that accounts for initial setup costs, ongoing operational expenses, and revenue streams such as tuition fees, grants, donations, and research collaborations. Ensure that the business model is sustainable in the long term.
9. Quality assurance and accreditation: Implement mechanisms for quality assurance and continuous improvement to maintain academic standards and credibility. Seek accreditation from relevant bodies to enhance the reputation and recognition of your programmes.
10. Community engagement and stakeholder relations: Engage with local communities, government authorities, industry stakeholders, and other relevant stakeholders to build trust, foster partnerships, and address any concerns or challenges that may arise.

Case Study 5.1: The British University in Dubai (BUiD) and Its UK Alliance Partnership

Context

The British University in Dubai (BUiD) is a private, not for profit, Emirati university that delivers a UK curriculum. It was established in 2003 by Decree Number 5/2003 by HH Sheikh Rashid Bin Saeed Al Maktoum, Ruler of Dubai, to provide British education, in the largely American market in Dubai. The University grew out of collaboration between British and Dubai Academic Government and commercial organisations to make a unique contribution to the UAE and Gulf Region.

In 2013–14, UK Universities, Glasgow, Manchester and Edinburgh, established a Concordat to provide a framework for the strategic direction of their alliance with BUiD. The UK Alliance Partners sit on the Senate and conduct quality assurance reviews. A recent change in engagement is where reviews used to be on a programme level, they are on an institutional level.

Stages in the Journey

i) The Preparation

From BUiD's perspective, the objective was to seek UK partners that would provide both a sense of credibility and critical oversight. The aim was to align with quality institutions that would support BUiD's own internal growth and provide a framework for quality assurance and development. From the UK HEI's perspective, this was an opportunity to gain a foothold in the UAE with a very low sense of risk. The levels of investment were very minor, certainly when compared to the potential opportunities.

ii) The Approval

This largely hinged on the clear articulation of intended activity and expected outcomes. Agreement to partner is one level of engagement but in order to commit resources to an endeavour, there must be a clear understanding of what this will entail, what time frame is being considered and the extent to which success will be measured and demonstrated.

iii) The First Six Months

Much of this time was spent discussing expectations and levels of engagement.

Over time, the relationship and alliance has evolved – resulting from increased trust and awareness. The initial six months were focused on laying the foundations for this eventual trust partnership; demonstrating patterns of engagement; and supporting further discussion and strategic agenda development.

Key Themes

- Agenda setting: clear aims and intentions should be outlined and agreed from the start.

- Consistent levels of communication: things evolve (often for very good reasons), and partners need to communicate and remain transparent.
- Sustained engagement: keep the partner in mind and identify and support opportunities for collaboration beyond the one-on-one arrangement.

Lessons Learned

- Be transparent and forthcoming regarding your intended objectives and expectations. It is much easier to align these as you go along rather than retroactively.
- Over time, the partnership alliance has changed with partners leaving and others joining. This is a natural evolution and should not be viewed as a failure.

WHO WILL WE PARTNER WITH AND WHAT WILL WE DO?

Universities have a wealth of international links and connections. Some of these are individual, and some of them are institutional. The challenge can be in finding out where the connections are as much as determining what can be done with them. The temptation with partnership development can be to launch yourself off into finding a new one, when you may even have the right one on your own doorstep. Therefore, finding out what you already have across your institution can be of huge benefit. This is a challenge, although focusing the effort on a particular country or region first can help to provide a structure and a framework for any future mapping exercises, as illustrated in Case Study 5.2: Global Regional Engagement Groups.

Case Study 5.2: Global Regional Engagement Groups
Context

There exists within any university a considerable body of international knowledge and expertise, much of which is untapped. The development of Global Regional/Country Engagement Groups (GREGs), which will bring together those with particular regional expertise and intelligence from across the Faculties and the Services, will enable the university to establish a platform from which they can develop collaborative activity based on clear alignment of international strengths to market opportunities.

The groups can provide a distinctive platform on which the university can take forward their International Strategy, one of the outcomes being the creation of knowledge portals through which the capability and capacity of international ambitions can be tested. The groups will:

a. Maximise the potential benefits of existing activity and add value by enabling the effective and productive management, circulation, and sharing of knowledge. This will include bringing together a body of expertise, equipped to support and advise those engaged, or planning engagement, with the region/country. Key areas include:
- Market intelligence and student recruitment.
- Collaborative provision and partnership building.
- Research links and activities.
- Corporate and agency partnerships and funding.
- Alumni networking.
- Profile raising and reputation building.

b. Help deliver a more sophisticated and strategic approach to international development activity and regional engagement, focusing on cross-institutional working to maximise resources to best grow our profile and reputation.

Description and Aims

The GREGs assist the university by making the best use of its current intelligence and existing networks to build and boost its reputation abroad and provide a platform on which to develop further strategic engagement. They also provide a forum through which potential opportunities that have arisen can be shared. The groups:

- Gain an overview of current expertise and activities across the institution.
  - Audit activity and map connections.
  - Segment alumni and key influencers.
- Collate and communicate market intelligence for opportunities including access to funding.
- Identify key opportunities for influence in the target region and align alumni engagement.

- Identify and communicate potential areas for development.
- Foster and support new initiatives, responding flexibly to new opportunities as they emerge.
- Develop a calendar of activity and coordinate joint high-level missions.
- Identify potential industry, community, and government partners and their research priorities in designated thematic areas.

Each group has an academic lead, or regional champion, with a proven track record of work associated with the region.

Benefits

Benefits include:

- Improved and targeted information sharing on activities, funding opportunities, region-specific market opportunities, links, and connections in regions.
- Increased potential for collaborative activity with international partners.
- Improved internal liaison on international activities via meetings and regional websites.
- Improved awareness of individual faculty emphasis and priority; enhanced opportunities for alignment across faculties.
- Identification of potential strategic partners and focus on developing multi-layered partnerships.
- Enhanced leverage of current external relationships and contacts including key alumni relations.
- Greater success in leveraging funding from external bodies with a regional focus.
- Improved opportunities for student and staff mobility.
- Providing high-profile, sustainable, interlocking collaborations which raise profile in target markets.

Outputs and Measures

Outputs include

- A dynamic database of staff with interest and expertise in the area.
- An intranet website that staff can access where information can be updated and opportunities shared. The site will facilitate the

> exchange of regional information, internally publicise members' regional activities, identify alumni and key influencers, promote external funding opportunities, and so on.
> - Internal fact sheets for each region/country.
> - Marketing collateral including themed fliers (country-specific) for external use.
>
> Progress is charted through monitoring a range of measures and activities. These include
>
> - Number of strategic partnerships.
> - Alumni engagement.
> - Media instances.
> - Recruitment numbers and training programmes.
> - Funding secured to support teaching, scholarships, research, and mobility.
> - Number of internationally funded projects.
> - Analysis of publication output.
> - Number of student and staff exchanges.

Activities and Approaches

Deciding what to do and determining who to partner with will normally come about in that order. You may, for example, decide that you want to establish a Joint Education Institute in China. The template for the creation of the institutes is quite clearly set out, and there are numerous examples to refer to (the UK has over 40 joint institutes with Chinese universities, and a UK China Joint Institute Alliance, set up in 2017, works to boost their development and management) and learn from. Alternatively, it may be that you already have a partner (an established one, or one that you discovered during your mapping activities for the Global Regional Engagement Groups) and you are either seeking to develop the relationship further or take the relationship in a new direction. However, the situation has been brought about initial decisions:

- What do you want to do?
- Why do you want to do it?
- Where do you want to do it?
- Who do you want to do it with and why?

- What are you prepared to commit to this endeavour?
- What are you prepared to have it cost you?
- How long are you prepared to sustain this endeavour?
- What will success look like for you?

Once these questions have been answered, there is the relative luxury of being able to follow a pre-existing framework for engagement. Partnerships are individual but they are also formulaic to an extent. There are models that can followed, or at least consulted, and this provides a form of shorthand for engagement. In many cases, of course, institutions will already have partnerships in place and offices dedicated to their production and monitoring.

1. Decide what you want to do.
2. Decide who you want to do it with or where you want to do it – and then find a partner.
3. Perform your due diligence.
4. Ensure internal capacity is there.
5. Engage with the potential partner.
6. Follow up with the potential partner.
7. Establish parameters for engagement and outline/agree intended objectives.
8. Internal approval process.
9. External approval process.
10. Agreement.
11. Activity and monitoring.

The Partnership Approval Process

The process of partnership approval is, not unsurprisingly, not a short one. It is, we are sure you will be amazed to learn, sometimes quite challenging. The process is relatively straightforward to understand but the realities, the challenges, and most obviously the time involved can create obstacles and increase the risk factor significantly.

The starting point of this process should really be the endpoint. Have a clear understanding of where you want to get to; what you want to achieve along the way; and how you will recognise and measure success. With these in mind, supported by an institutional awareness and acceptance of risk, go out to the playground of life and make a friend (Figures 5.3 and 5.4).

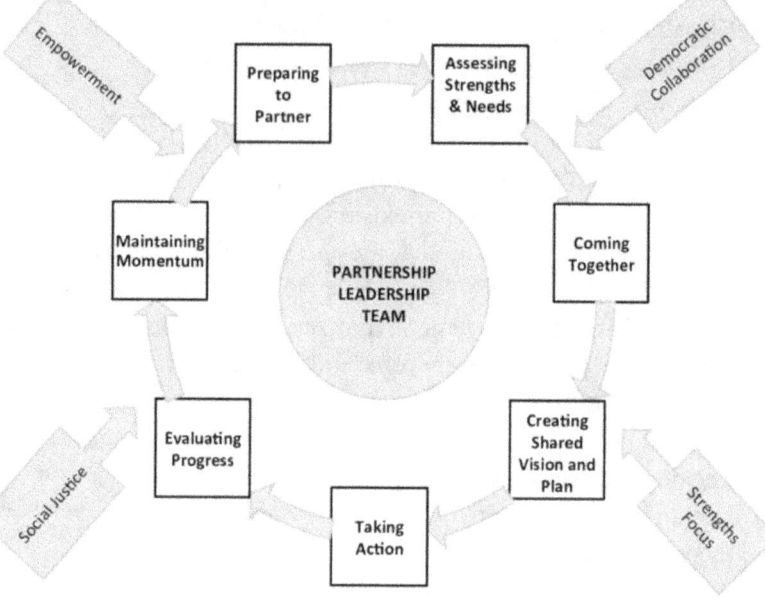

Figure 5.3 Seven-Stage Partnership Process Model (Bryan and Henry, 2012)

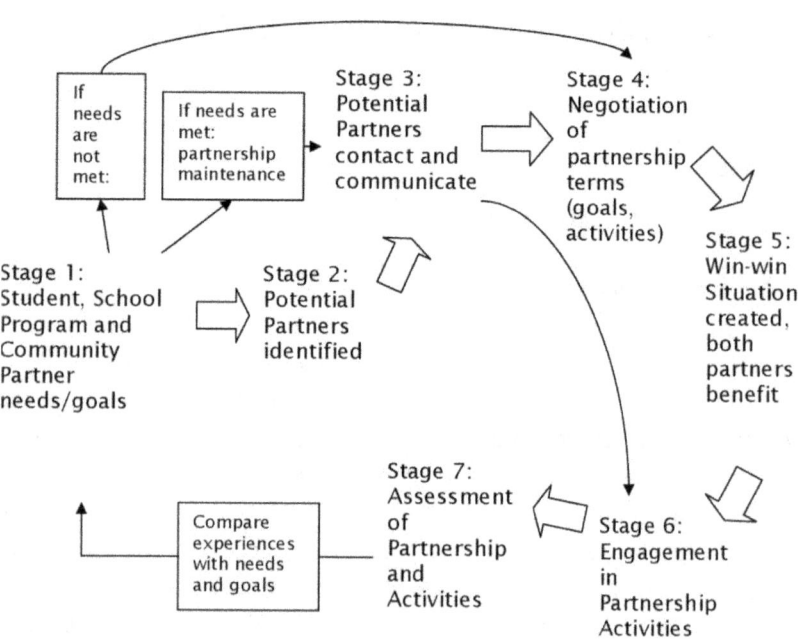

Figure 5.4 It's Who You Know "and" What You Know (Hands, 2005)

This process should not be rushed and should not be entered into without a clear understanding of self and intended outcomes. A willingness to compromise and collaborate is essential, but so is the awareness of when to walk away.

> **Top Tips for Finding the Right Partner**
>
> **DO**
> - Take your time.
> - Find a partner with the same goals and ambitions.
> - Have the attitude that this is an equal partnership.
> - Keep communicating.
> - Be open and honest.
>
> **DON'T**
> - Rush into things.
> - Expect perfection.
> - Overcomplicate the process.
> - Focus on risk at the expense of creativity.
> - Forget or neglect the wider eco-system.

WHAT DOES SUCCESS LOOK LIKE?

Success can come in many forms. The existence of a partner in and of itself is a success and should not be discounted. For many institutions, this constitutes a level of commitment and recognition of value. There is value in being recognised and partnered with, even if the outcomes are negligible. There may be less impetus on the part of the more senior partner to enter such an arrangement, but it largely costs them nothing. For the more junior partner, this connection represents validation and cache.

Successful partnerships are often more accurately measured in time, or space, but rarely both. Long-term partnerships demonstrate a sustained level of commitment in a world where arrangements and outputs often live and die by the involvement of individuals. Is a partnership that has been in place for more than a decade, but only resulted in marginal student exchange or output more or less valuable than a partnership that lasted less than a year but yielded healthier outputs?

An example of a long-term partnership, built on solid foundations, can be seen in the relationship between Université Grenoble Alpes and Swansea University as illustrated in Case Study 5.3.

Case Study 5.3: Université Grenoble Alpes and Swansea University and the Joint Doctoral Degree

Context

The Grenoble-Swansea partnership began in 2008 with a joint research initiative in nanoscience with the Joseph Fourier Universite, which amalgamated with a number of regional institutions to become the Université Grenoble Alpes. The partnership began small, with a few committed individuals and has grown to become one of both institutions' most important strategic partnerships. The beginning of the partnership was key. There was clear strategic alignment and a meeting of minds both in terms of what the institutions wanted to achieve in the research collaboration, but also more broadly in what they could achieve for both institutions by providing exciting opportunities for students to enhance their skills, global knowledge, and cultural agility.

Stages in the Journey

i) *The Beginning*

The Grenoble-Swansea partnership began as a research collaboration to develop a Franco-Welsh alliance in the areas of nanoscience, energy, and ageing which was supported by the French Embassy and Welsh Government. This was expanded in 2015 when the two institutions decided to develop an innovative model for international academic cooperation that would add value to close collaboration and academic differentiation. This new vision involved not only a wider spectrum of academic disciplines but also the senior management and administration of both universities in the development of a growing range of joint activities such as joint research and publications, student, and staff exchange and secondments, joint doctorates and masters, collaborative funding bids, a joint approach to trans-sector collaboration with industry both in the UK and France and the sharing of best practice and innovative policies.

ii) *Setting the Strategic Agenda*

The partnership is built on a common ground of shared institutional values and mission, and a set of actions have been designed to ensure that their core purpose and values are flowing through all aspects of their day-to-day activities including

- Strengthening their international activities and their status as major international universities.
- Growing international student numbers.
- Developing an ambitious policy of international influence.
- Securing their status as major research-intensive institutions who produce world-leading research and impact.
- Cultivating a distinctive culture and promoting an active programme of cultural events.
- Developing an enterprise culture and initiatives.
- Educating students to be global citizens by providing them with an inspiring international experience.
- Ensuring that their international policy has strong local, regional, and national impact.

The Grenoble-Swansea Strategic Partnership Plan clearly articulates the purpose of the partnership, defines its goals, sets targets, and apportions resource, and the implementation plan is monitored by a set of jointly run management committees.

iii) The Intervening Period

The partnership has developed to include a wide variety of initiatives including research, staff and student mobility, and joint curriculum programmes. Joint doctoral degrees can be seen as a challenge, but the collaboration between Swansea and Grenoble is a true 50-50 collaboration. Students spend 50% of their time at both institutions, funding is split 50/50. Supervision is joint, and successful candidates receive a double degree from the Université Grenoble Alpes and Swansea University.

The success of the joint doctoral programme is a good illustration of why the partnership works. Entry requirements are agreed jointly. Strictest regulatory requirements and skills training apply. If one institution requires a masters for entry onto PhDs, then that is the entry requirement that applies for the joint PhD. Likewise, if skills training is mandatory in one institution, then it is mandatory for the joint PhD. Students are given personalised learning agreements, a mobility schedule is agreed at the outset, and the student has access to student support services in both institutions.

Keys to Success

- Lay solid groundwork building the partnership relationship.
- Understand each other's requirements.
- Agree structure and requirements for programmes before students are recruited.
- Make sure your colleagues know about the joint programmes; internal communication is an important as external communication.
- Agree on key contacts in both institutions for queries.
- Keep channels of communication open.
- Be resilient and adaptable to change.

Lessons Learned

- **Communication:** The Partnership has gone from strength to strength helped by a dialogue at all levels of the two institutions to deliver tangible collaborations and measurable outcomes, top-down and bottom-up initiatives that have successfully engendered a high degree of engagement together with a wide ownership of, support for, and participation in the Partnership activities and regular programmes of focused visits to initiate and expand relationships.
- **Resources and targets:** Adequate operational and financial support to develop and sustain partnerships is essential, and there needs to be a commitment up front to provide this. The commitment needs to be written into the contract to ensure that it can survive changes in leadership.
- **Prioritisation:** Partnership activities have to be prioritised in an annual implementation plan and resources allocated effectively and efficiently through the operational plan procedure. The strategy is important, but the plan will make sure that things actually happen and targets are met.

CONCLUSION

Partnership choice is built on due diligence and market awareness; partnership development is built on time, resources, and cooperative bureaucracy; partnership sustainability is built on engagement communication and shared strategic direction – with an awareness of how success is measured. These stages all require different skill sets and demand different energy levels. All levels are important and must be understood and accepted from the initial planning process.

Choosing the right partner is half the battle but keeping the right partner is where the hard work begins. Clear lines of communication and shared goals/objectives help to underpin this but it stems from an awareness of self and a willingness to compromise and collaborate along the way.

In later chapters, we will return to the issue of partnerships but with a focus on the later stages of the process. This chapter has focused on the key elements of partnership selection and development and in subsequent chapters we will turn the page to the end of the story and think more critically about how we both manage partnerships in the long term, but also in how we end them – a process that requires an understanding of how we manage success; a framework for disentanglement and the ability to cut losses and walk away.

REFERENCES

Bryan, J., & Henry, L. (2012). Seven-stage partnership process model illustrating the equity-focused principles and process of building school-family-community partnerships. Adapted from A model for building school-family-community partnerships: Principles and process. Journal of Counseling & Development, 90, 408–420.

Hands, C. (2005). It's who you know "and" what you know: The process of creating partnerships between schools and communities. School Community Journal, 15(2), 63–84.

Ilieva, J., Lewis, V., & Frearson Emmanuel, E. (2023). Risk and Due Diligence in TNE Partnerships. Presentation given at UUKi TNE Annual Conference, London, UK. December 2023

The Role of Language and Cultural Responsiveness in Promoting Diversity, Equity, and Accessibility in Transnational Education

Stephanie Martin

Six

AN EDUCATOR'S JOURNEY INTO THE WORLD OF TNE

Raised by South African parents and educated in Australia, one might say I was the ideal candidate for a teaching career in the transnational education (TNE) system in the Middle East. I came from a diverse cultural background in terms of appearance and language – a tick for diversity. I was female – a tick for gender. But in hindsight, what was deemed most important to my new employers was the fact that I had gained qualifications in a Western education system and practiced teaching in the Australian education sector. I was not queried on my ability to speak Arabic, but instead, my proficiency in English was held in high esteem. As somewhat of a "bonus" package deal, I had also previously worked within the Queensland education system in Australia's east, which married perfectly with the institution's values.

Upon leaving Australia for the United Arab Emirates, I had a faint idea of the cultural considerations that I may need to make. But in retrospect, I realise that my understanding was superficial compared to what teaching in an international environment truly demanded of me. I considered that perhaps I would need to make slight alterations to my professional attire to suit the customs of my new host country – and this was confirmed during a brief employment induction. However, apart from adjusting to the extreme weather conditions typical of Middle Eastern summers and having a general understanding of Islamic obligations such as Ramadan, my way of adapting to the expectations of this new cultural environment was limited.

On arrival at my new place of employment, remarks were made about the fact that I was a teacher from Queensland, Australia, and I was perplexed at how this was met with such admiration and acceptance. I recall a new colleague and veteran expatriate noting to me quietly "You will do very well here" and another, chuckled "You know what you're

DOI: 10.4324/9781003649571-7

doing then". It felt strange to be so readily accepted simply because of two reasons: Where I hailed from and which emblem my passport displayed. I hadn't even commenced teaching yet.

When it came to the curriculum, I felt at ease – almost overprepared. The night before my first day of teaching, I sat in my adopted new home, glossing over all the past teaching resources I had brought with me from Australia: years upon years of worksheets, literary guides, activities, and even past university textbooks. I checked the number of students enrolled in my new classes and noted that each was significantly smaller than what I was used to in Australia. It sounded straightforward – easy. Almost too good to be true. And the truth is, it was.

My first week of teaching in the United Arab Emirates imparted invaluable lessons about the true essence of diversity, the sometimes superficial and often misconstrued notion of equity, and the stark contrast between theory and practice in TNE settings.

It emphasised what I believe many educators within the TNE sector will continually be challenged by if we remain remiss in the face of diversity and equity: That is, often there is a chasm of difference between our perceptions of the role of TNE in society and the realistic, lived experiences of TNE staff and students.

TNE IN THE GULF REGION AT A GLANCE

As global education evolves, the definition of TNE continues to become more elaborate and multifaceted. Earlier definitions of TNE are concerned with it merely involving higher education programs or education services, both virtual and in-person, where the location of the learners differs from the location in which the awarding educational institution is based (Knight, 2016). Other researchers describe it as "the mobility of educational programs and institutions across national borders, rather than the mobility of students" (Wilkins & Huisman, 2012, p. 628). TNE serves as a bridge between the contrasting global cultures of our society, particularly between East and West. Knight (2016) also suggests that TNE works to enhance the international repute of the offering institution by creating a sense of "presence" in the global market (Knight, 2016, p. 36). However, the significance of TNE runs deeper than matters of financial gain, or mobility and affordability for students abroad.

When I began my journey to the UAE, I was unaware of the numerous Western institutions that had emerged in the Gulf area over the last

15 years. The UAE has transformed itself into the main hub for transnational higher education, with Qatar and Bahrain also classed as the "centrepoints" of the region in terms of facilitating TNE programs in their own countries. Despite the large number of native Arabic speakers in the region, English has replaced Arabic as the language of instruction in the majority of UAE universities to cater for a growing demand for Western higher education and development of human capital to suit labour market requirements (Gray & Bashir, 2017).

The idea of "internationalisation at home" has become a popular choice for students residing in the UAE, as students are able to enter a new world of academia while maintaining the familiar surroundings of their home country (Bhandari & Blumenthal, 2013, p. 3). An increase in enrolment numbers reflects this, and it is predicted that by the end of 2024, at least one-third of the increase in international students will stem from the Gulf region (Kariwo et al., 2014). With a high expatriate population and an increase in migration and travelling, this also means a higher transient population of teaching staff who enter the UAE education market, opening the doors to new "cross-national, cross-cultural flows between global networks" (Alam et al., 2013). In considering these factors, we must also contemplate the extent to which educators are prepared for the diverse requirements of students in a transnational learning environment.

INCLU-VERSITY: DIVERSITY, INCLUSION OR BOTH?

Ask an educator to explain the difference between diversity and inclusion, and one may find that it takes more than a mere few seconds to answer. For decades, there has been confusion in professional education settings on how best to differentiate between both key terms in theory and practice (Gray & Bashir, 2017). When examining educator's perceptions of both diversity and inclusion, findings concluded that a significant number of educators experienced difficulty when differentiating between the two concepts (Hsiao & Lee, 2019). It is argued that such confusion exists as both terms are often used interchangeably, or as mere "buzz words" in curriculum policy, yet each represents a distinctly different focus that, if misunderstood, can contribute to substantial gaps in teaching and learning (Ainscow, Booth & Dyson, 2006).

Since diversity focuses on acknowledging and embracing differences and inclusion is concerned with providing equitable access for all learners, it is easy to observe how TNE may fulfil both criteria almost inevitably (Slee, 2011). Often, it is assumed that TNE environments instil diverse values by merely offering Western education programs to overseas countries and international students, and therefore by default, the diversity factor has already been fulfilled by the institution. In my early years as an educator in the Middle East, I too was guilty of this assumption. Ironically, while diversity initiatives like the implementation of TNE in developing countries may increase the "who" in terms of varying cultures in classrooms, one must consider that this does not automatically result in an inclusive and equitable environment for all students to thrive equally (Artiles, Kozleski & Waitoller, 2011).

Ultimately, the terms diversity and inclusivity attribute to equity, and each concept requires a deliberate effort from policymakers and educators to continue removing barriers within the curriculum and through culturally sustained pedagogical practices (Paris & Alim, 2017; Slee, 2011). When we teach for diversity, we acknowledge the varying differences in the classroom. When we teach for inclusion, we embrace the differing needs of each learning type. And when we teach for equity, we allow these differences in both cultural heritage and academic background to transform the ways in which we "think, teach, learn and act" to promote a higher understanding of the world around us (University of Delaware Center for Teaching & Learning, 2024, p. 1). Since its inception, TNE has presented opportunities for a diverse range of staff and students from varying cultural backgrounds to join forces – enter, internationalism. But this is only the beginning of the equation. What occurs afterwards in the teaching and learning stages ultimately distinguishes between TNE as a performative means of accessibility and TNE as the driver of intercultural understanding: its greater purpose (Gray & Bashir, 2017; Paris & Alim, 2017). And this, I learned in my very first week of teaching in a Middle Eastern TNE context.

BARRIERS TO EQUITY IN TNE

The term equity is most commonly found in educational policies and frameworks, but in my own expatriate teaching experience, the role of equity was somewhat misunderstood by many – perhaps even myself in the early stages. I arrived in the UAE armed with resources and the knowledge and qualifications previously attained in the Australian tertiary system. But little did I know that this would only transport me so far with the demographic of students in my new classroom. It was a paradoxically strange sensation: feeling somewhat prepared and secure in my own understandings of the curriculum being facilitated, and yet, having no faint idea of what to expect when delivering this content in a place that was far removed from the country that originally established the syllabus. Being placed in an environment where one had not fully grasped the cultural context of the surroundings was also, ironically, an alienating experience.

My first senior English class contained only nine students in comparison to the usual 23–30 students that I was accustomed to while teaching in Australia. Of those nine students, seven came from countries outside of the UAE and each one of them spoke at least two languages.

In other classes, where student numbers were closer to the low 20s, this multicultural quantity increased, and so too did the number of different languages spoken by students. Often, while I was explaining a concept, the students communicated with each other in Arabic, and initially, this was a new territory that I felt uncertain about. In Australia, it was not often that a teacher would not be able to understand the words being spoken by students in their classroom, unless of course that teacher was not a native English speaker. When I questioned colleagues about the best way to ensure that students were on task and discussing relevant classroom content, rather than the opposite, I was informed by members of the leadership team and colleagues to curtly remind students that this was in fact, an international school, and thus, Arabic was *not* to be spoken. In fact, the policy was that English was the only acceptable language of communication while at school. I was perplexed by this response. Was it logical that I, a newcomer to the Middle East, who did not speak the language of the region, would now demand that students who *did* in fact speak the language of the region abandon their mother tongue and pay homage to the language of the curriculum, and the language more suited to their teacher?

It had me puzzled and yet I took the advice of management and – with some hesitation – proceeded to tell students in that it was indeed an Australian school. Unsurprisingly, a young student looked at me and with innocent curiosity said, "But Miss, it's the UAE? We speak Arabic". Unsettled, and – upon reflection, I'm ashamed to admit – slightly defensively, I muttered that the curriculum was in English and therefore it was an English-only classroom. And there in that moment, on the surface it made sense: we were all going to speak a common language – the *lingua franca* – that both parties understood as a means of courtesy to the other. From a Western point of view, this is what seemed the most logical explanation – it was the polite thing to do in monolingual company. But an interesting thought crossed my mind as my students busied themselves in their work, and I was reminded of the educational environment that my parents were exposed to in South Africa. Having come from areas where South African tribal languages such as *Xhosa* and *Zulu* were prominent, my parents were well-versed in communicating in these dialects. However, they were also governed by the Eurocentric languages imposed by the apartheid ruling at the time: only *Afrikaans* and English were to be spoken, and curriculum programs were only delivered in these languages.

Of course, the nature of the apartheid era poses significant contextual differences which were far more severe than my first week of teaching in the UAE. But it begged the question: Would the Australian curriculum – or any Western curriculum program for that matter – be any less purposeful and effective if delivered in the language best understood by the student? And could students not learn about the likes of Shakespeare or how to write short stories and essays in their own mother tongue? The content, in essence, remains the same. The point of difference would be an increase in curriculum understanding and greater points of accessibility for students (Jenkins, 2014; Le-Ha, 2017).

LANGUAGE AS EQUITY IN THE TNE WORLD

When delving into the role of equity in TNE, past research focuses on the provision of accessibility, describing it as "ensuring that students from diverse backgrounds, particularly those from underrepresented or marginalised groups, have fair access to educational opportunities and resources provided by transnational programs" (UNESCO, 2023, p. 290). Developing countries, including those in the MENA region have been classed as belonging to these categories and TNE programs have therefore served as entry points for students who would not otherwise have access to Western curriculum programs (Bannier, 2016). Much research centres around the importance of equitable access to high-quality education experiences irrespective of geographical location, and others have expressed the need for the delivery of such education to be comparable to the awarding institution (Marginson & Sawir, 2011; Robertson, 2010). Hence, often research on equity in TNE has represented accessibility in the physical form of facilities and resources that align with the home country and its academic norms (Johnson, 2020). One key aspect of equity that is perhaps noted but not deeply acknowledged is the cultural capital that students bring to the learning environment.

Paris and Alim (2017) argue that for an extended period of time, the role of equity and access has subconsciously been centred around the following notion: "How can 'we' get 'these' developing and foreign countries to adopt Westernised cultural norms in the form of academia?" (p. 3). Similarly, Le-Ha (2017) offers a deeper, more critical lens to observe TNE through, arguing that we are at risk of espousing the ideal that education flows "from the West to the rest" (Le-Ha, 2017, p. 2). What I soon came to realise is that like my place of employment, many of the international campuses that exist globally stem from Anglophone countries, such as England, The USA, Australia, and Canada, and these countries alone offer the largest export of TNE programs (Bannier, 2016; Jenkins, 2014). As a result, English has become the common language of communication in TNE environments and also remained the sole language of instruction (Wilkins & Urbanovic, 2014). Whether or not I was capable of speaking Arabic in the classroom was of little importance to my perceived readiness for the role, as generally, TNE follows a model whereby it replicates the delivery of the home campus where methods of policy, assessment, teaching, and learning are concerned (Jenkins, 2011). Ultimately, what was deemed most essential was that I was fluent in the language of curriculum instruction: English.

In terms of accessibility in TNE, my initial perception was that the wider world favoured English as a universal language, and in this educational context, it served as the *lingua franca* between teacher and student and established a common ground on which to communicate.

In essence, it provided us both with an accessibility point into comprehending one another. However, what became one of the biggest lessons of my career was understanding that this "commonality" was, in hindsight, one-sided in terms of teaching and learning. In a sense, I expected them to do it all my way. My language of instruction, my native language expectations and overall, my language in terms of curriculum content. It occurred to me that such perceptions can subconsciously generate a sense of "linguistic supremacy", as Alim and Smitherman (2012) previously coined (p. 3). Where was the accessibility point for students who possessed lower levels of English skills?

I soon learned that TNE is more than the act of placing a Western education institution in a developing country or providing opportunities for students to study abroad in the West. TNE providers must also steer away from narrow perceptions of the home institution being somewhat of a "saviour" to the education system in developing countries (Jenkins, 2011). Alternatively, achieving equity in TNE environments requires a more in-depth exploration of culture and of our pedagogical practices when it comes to policy. Educational policy should promote true accessibility beyond the construction of facilities. It must offer support that meets the diverse needs of students from various linguistic and cultural backgrounds so that they too can fully participate in TNE programs and achieve success (Wilkins, 2016). It requires us to question the extent to which educators are providing an array of entry points into the curriculum to cater to the cultural capital of their students (Healey, 2015; Paris & Alim, 2017).

Much Ado About Language: Did You Know?

- Compared to many Asian, Arabic, and African languages – which rely heavily on non-verbal cues, shared cultural knowledge, body language and high-context communication – English is considered a low-context language. It is generally characterised by a stronger emphasis on explicit and literal verbal expression.
- Australia, the UK, and the USA are the leading exporters of TNE programs.
- In Europe alone, approximately 2,400 institutions deliver courses in English.

TOTO, WE'RE NOT IN THE WEST, ANYMORE

On reflection, the wiser, more seasoned, and culturally aware educator in me winces at the thought of my ignorance towards accessibility in that very first semester of teaching abroad. The first units to be studied were the likes of poetry and Shakespeare, two topics that had been my passion for decades. I was eager to begin and felt overly confident that my tried-and-tested resources – which had been previously used with students in Australia – would be just as successful with my new students. Thirty-something slides, a flurry of worksheets, and ICT resources sat ready on my desk, awaiting the likes of new, enthusiastic students who were eager to learn. As the token icebreaker activities drew to a close and sensing that the class was somewhat at ease, suddenly, I was back into curriculum mode.

With gusto, I presented the student with assessment outlines, due dates and the assessment policy stipulated by the Queensland Curriculum and Assessment Authority, distributed new assessment tasks, briefly deconstructing the criteria on which students were to be assessed, and dove headfirst into teaching all things poetry. I had selected a well-known poem by a renowned Australian poet which detailed the painful history of Indigenous Australia's stolen generation. When I finished reading the last line of the text, I raised my eyes, ready to witness the same reaction I always did from students who had heard this prose for the first time: shock, awe, and overwhelming empathy. Instead, I was taken aback by the glazed, blank stares of nothingness that ogled back at me, as if I had just spoken to them in a different language. What I failed to realise at the time was that ironically, I had.

When I quizzed students on the key messages and takeaways from the text, and what the experience of those marginalised indigenous groups might be likened to, the blank stares and awkward silences continued. A student queried what the "stolen generation" was and in that moment, I realised that the assumptions I had carried with me into the room had created a learning barrier where students could not relate to or identify with the curriculum content presented to them. Additionally, there was a second issue. Not all students spoke fluent English, nor were all of their reading levels on par, and yet here I was presenting a two-page piece of prose with complex language and themes as if it was their norm. In an effort to avoid this with my next classes, I searched the prescribed reading list from the syllabus in the hope of finding more suitable poetry for other classes. 84% of the poets were Anglophone, European or Australian, or Indigenous Australian writers (QCAA, 2009). There was no Middle Eastern or even African influence in any of these prescribed texts. To add to this, I soon learned that there would be no adjustments or accommodations made by the assessment panel in the home country, Australia, to accommodate 91% of the students in the host institution who were ESL learners. Advice from the governing body mandated that curriculum content, assessment, and verification procedures were to remain unaltered. It was here that I began to question the "international" integrity of TNE institutions and whether the concern for maintaining quality assurance was given greater status than the importance of diversity, inclusivity, and equity for students.

CANCEL LANGUAGE, CANCEL CULTURE

With approximately 138 countries opting for compulsory English education courses worldwide, the many benefits of learning to communicate in English, particularly for academic purposes, cannot be ignored. English ranks as one of the top five languages in the world in terms of popularity as a spoken language, accounting for an estimated one-eighth of the world's population (University of Winnipeg, 2024). But what many educational policy makers and expatriate educators may fail to recognise is the vast difference between high cultural context and low cultural context languages. This was a concept I understood from my family's South African bilingual background, but one that I had not connected to Middle Eastern education culture. As a language, English is exceptionally literal. Despite the excess of functional grammar rules and, lest we forget, the exceptions to the rule, much of what we say in English is explicit (Bannier, 2016; Halliday, 2007). In contrast, many Asian, Middle Eastern, and African languages are quite the opposite and are therefore classed as high context cultural languages (Bannier, 2016).

Languages such as Arabic can be idiomatic and phrasing often relies heavily on an understanding of Islamic culture, or requires comprehension of how best to use tone, eye contact, and gesture – that is, it requires a wider understanding of the culture itself (Feghali, 1997). My first exposure to this was through the Arabic phrase, "*Inshallah*", which translates to "If Allah wills" or "If God wills it" (Merriam-Webster, 2024). Upon first understanding, my assumption was that the term, which comes directly from the Qur'ān, was used in religious discourses only. However, I was surprised when, after a rather stern conversation with a student who had not submitted his assessment, his response to my scolding was this very phrase. "I'm expecting your assessment to be emailed by 9am tomorrow", I had warned, signalling the end of the conversation. But the student turned to me and with an almost coy smiled, uttered, "*Inshallah*, Miss". My perplexed facial expression may have been more transparent that I had realised, because he looked at me reassuringly and said, "It means if God wills it, Miss, it will happen".

On the surface, I knew the direct translation of the phrase. For a newcomer to this culture, what puzzled me was how casually the student had stated the phrase in a casual, everyday context. While English speakers may occasionally say "God willing", I had very seldom heard this being uttered by a teenager. I soon became aware that there is a definitive context where the phrase can be used to communicate various things. I noticed an interesting set of contextual patterns, particularly when male students had been instructed to fulfil a task that they were hesitant to complete, or during disciplinary interventions. "Make sure you have this completed by tomorrow", "Will your work be ready by then?" and "I don't want to see a repeat of this behaviour again" were often met with the same response: "Inshallah, Miss". Suddenly a phrase which instils much religious reverence had also been used in the context of "hopefully", "let's see" or "maybe". And here, it became evident to me that social and cultural contexts are vital when learning to partake in dialogue with bilingual individuals – this is ultimately how meaning is created (Bannier, 2016; Jenkins, 2011). It comes down to what Halliday (2007) has described as the harmony between language and culture and the challenges faced by students who engage in TNE study:

> When we learn the language, we also appropriate the social context within which the meaning is created. By learning French or English, for example, we also acquire French or English cultures. We try to integrate their social contexts so that we can understand what is said and why. This discussion explains partly how the competence of ... graduates sometimes becomes "inefficient competence" due to semantically impoverished classroom situations they experience when they come back to their countries of origin.
>
> (Halliday, 2007, p. 4)

But the question remains: why does this matter when it comes to our policy, curriculum design, and pedagogical methods?

With the UAE hosting the largest number of TNE institutions in the Middle East Gulf region and exporting nearly 17,000 students to study abroad programs, student mobility is on the rise (UNESCO, 2023). This means that our ESL students are most likely studying a program that is delivered in a different language from their mother tongue, and more than likely, the language of instruction is English. Furthermore, sociocultural stress facts such as language barriers and a limited familiarity with new academic rules and cultural systems continue to be a burden for international students embarking on the TNE journey (Roemer, 2016). While adopting this monolinguistic approach continues to open more transnational partnerships to overseas countries, we must also remember that educational imperialism continues to be a global concern – a neocolonial disguise, as Le Ha (2017) has coined (Bannier, 2016; Barnawi, 2018; Robertson, 2010).

QUALITY ASSURANCE OR RECOLONISATION?

Maintaining quality assurance across academic standards and guaranteeing equivalence between both home and host countries has proved to be a crucial aspect of TNE and one of its most significant challenges. Healey (2015) emphasises the need for compliance and regulatory processes across partnerships and Lim (2010) highlights that curriculum programs should support the needs of the host country, while still maintaining high standards in academia. However, aside from the cruciality of sustaining excellence and streamlining processes, what must be considered when developing such procedures is how governing institutions can incorporate the local cultural, social, and education contexts into their quality assurance policies (Leask, 2004). Thus, cultural sensitivity must also be considered and a mutual understanding of what "culture" and "internationalism" look like is essential for stakeholders.

In light of this, it has been argued that TNE organisations "claim to be international by default, however, where written and spoken English are concerned, most institutions uphold standards suited to native speakers, and there is a sense of 'business and usual', where bilingual students must simply meet these expectations" (Jenkins, 2011, p. 34). The same may be said for academic staff who are non-native English speakers, where the pressure to "function as close as possible to native-like standards in terms of professional practice, assessment and…everyday language use" may be present (Jenkins, 2011, p. 35). Such student barriers are common in the UAE, where students cannot enter TNE higher education programs without having obtained a satisfactory score in secondary school standard English or where standardised tests are used as a means of entry, such as IELTS, GAMSAT, and TOEFL. EMSAT, a UAE initiative for students studying locally has adopted a similar approach; however, the test accommodates both English and Arabic speakers (Ministry of Education, 2024). Australia has recently increased the stakes for all international students, with the government introducing a new legislation which increased standardised entry test scores by .5% (Minister for Education and Youth, 2024). While there are quality assurance provisions in place to cater for ESL candidates during testing conditions, such as the allowance of a bilingual dictionary for a portion the test, and while testing panels have established policies for diversity, inclusivity and equity, a heavy focus on quality assurance and "sameness" often outweighs the notion of true accessibility for international students (ACER, 2022).

A noteworthy example of this is the fact that while 138 countries worldwide include English as a mandatory part of the curriculum, approximately 40 countries either do not offer English as a subject or offer it as an optional language course (Hartshorne, Tenenbaum & Pinker, 2018). Hence, one must question if TNE truly caters to the minority of minority nations who do not offer English education still need to meet the language requirements of TNE programs to be accepted entry. In my own expat teaching experience, many students had previously schooled in local institutions during primary years, where only Arabic was spoken. These students experienced significant difficulties being submerged immediately into a highly academic, English-dominant learning environment where 75% of teachers were Western and not trained as ESL instructors. Put frankly, the level of student achievement in English when compared with Australian standards was far lower. Therefore, it seems that many of the discourses, ideologies and values within the education programs being taught in Western institutions cater largely for native English speakers, making the very assumption that I did of my students in my initial stages of teaching abroad (Turner, 2011). While quality assurance procedures and unified academic standards are vital aspects to uphold the repute and prestige of education institutions, there is perhaps a gap that is yet to be filled in terms of true accessibility for all minorities.

When observing the distribution of TNE globally, Turner (2011) highlights that anything other than "the English norm" within the world of academia has, in the past, been portrayed as requiring remedying (Turner, 2011, p. 21). There is an unspoken notion that while TNE institutions may be international by default in terms of a diverse student composition, the values instilled within language policy – and to some extent, cultural practices – may largely revolve around the national approach of the Western home country (Alsharari, 2017; Jenkins, 2011).

I became accustomed to this idea of Western-dominant approaches as an expat teacher when an Australian institution in the Middle East opted for a song titled *This is Australia* as the daily school bell. I considered this to be an oddity at the time, as despite the fact that the curriculum was Australian, we were very much not in Australia, and 94% of student clientele were also not Australian. While this could be seen as a demonstration of proud patriotism to the home country, perhaps it is also a classic example of an overwhelming eagerness to establish the dominance of the home institution rather than striving for balance between both cultures, allowing them to co-exist and flourish equally. Where quality assurance procedures were concerned, I learned that for some, success was measured through the perception of sameness and uniformity (Alam et al., 2013).

In matters of equity and quality assurance, the question is what shall we do with the student who is brilliantly gifted in Physics and who dreams of one day becoming an international engineer, but whose home country has not offered scholarly English courses? It comes as no surprise that within the UAE, a language-identity crisis is beginning to unfold. Since the language of medium for the majority of HE courses is English, a large number of Emirati and Arab expatriate students have previously struggled to meet university entrance requirements via standardised testing (Alsharari, 2017). Over seven years, a pattern occurred in my own senior English classrooms whereby students enrolled in university-recognised authority courses, only to find that the curriculum itself did not make sufficient adjustments or allowances for ESL learners. The consequences of this inclusion failure gave students two options: remain in the English course and fail or enrol in a low-level English course which resulted in limitations to TNE university pathways.

In a TNE environment, a student's ability to read, write, and speak proficiently in English plays a monumental part in academic performance, particularly where British, American, Australian, New Zealand, and Canadian curriculum programs are concerned. Often, parents queried staff on why their child was failing English, and the response remained inherently the same: "This is a rigorous curriculum program where a sound level of English proficiency and critical understanding are required. Unfortunately, your child does not meet the requirements of the course and it would be best to enrol in the English course that meets their level of capability". What my internal voice would have preferred to say was, "Unfortunately, the curriculum program that we have adopted and implemented in this Middle Eastern institution does not recognise that we are in fact, in the Middle East, where children speak English as a second or third language. Due to our somewhat excessive commitment to quality assurance, we are unable to bend the rules and make reasonable adjustments for your child to ensure that as a non-native speaker, they can access the curriculum. Our only solution is a swift transfer to an English course that will not challenge them and that may hinder their ability to apply to top tier universities abroad".

While some may view this critique of policy as unwarranted, the fact is that when observing the path forward for TNE, perhaps we must first question our fixation on sameness, uniformity, and conformity. Rather than do away with what does not inherently "fit" our mould, perhaps it is time to welcome an intersection between cultures that runs deeper than the surface level approach of simply grouping international students in the same room and calling it diversity – a box ticking exercise. Instead of adopting an approach which merely disseminates education practices "from the West to the rest", we can begin to examine culture, curriculum, and knowledge in an equal space, where both East and West can learn from and educate each other (Le-Ha, 2017, p. 2).

SHAKESPEARE IN THE DESERT: REDISCOVERING THE TRUE PURPOSE OF TRANSNATIONAL EDUCATION

As globalisation continues to grow and as we continue to navigate the waters of international education, it seems that we must constantly remind ourselves of its core purpose. If, as Waters and Leung (2013) suggest, the true goal of TNE is to develop and enhance the social and cultural capital of both the student and the institution itself, then TNE must continue to look beyond multiculturalism as diversity-by-default and opt for an asset-based approach to pedagogy, rather than simply a "tolerance" of difference (Ladson-Billings, 2014; Paris & Alim, 2017). By adopting cultural pluralism into our institutional values and empowering TNE educators with this knowledge, we allow the ideologies, traditions, and stories of new subcultures to be embraced, appreciated, and understood, as opposed to only promoting the dominant culture of the home country (Knapp & Wilkerson, 2023). While the reliability, validity, and credibility of programs and teaching practices remain paramount, there is an urgency for us to cease the idea of full assimilation and avoid asking cultural groups to become duplicates of the primary culture. In the past, TNE models have been framed around an unspoken concept of "sameness", where integration has underpinned success in terms of "assimilation to Eurocentric norms" (Darling-Hammond & Liberman, 2012; Paris & Alim, 2017, p. 4). On the contrary, viewing our curriculum through the lens of decolonisation theory encourages individuals to bring their own stories, experiences, languages, and cultural values into the learning environment and society itself (Jenkins, 2011; Paris & Alim, 2017; Stein & Andreotti, 2016). It is a task that often appears easier said than done, but once comprehended and embraced, it is an achievable and worthy goal for TNE overall.

As an avid Shakespeare fan and classical literature enthusiast, one of my greatest passions as an educator was exploring the Elizabethan world – its complex themes, eloquent language, and universality – and instilling this appreciation of the classics in students. After perusing the prescribed reading list from the curriculum, which at the time predominantly consisted of Keats, Austen, Shakespeare, Kipling and other Western playwrights, poets and novelists, I sat wondering how any of the required texts would serve purpose or be of any relevance to students who had no ties to this world of literature. Not to mention that many students were not 100% proficient at communicating in English. It all felt very far removed. But over the course of seven years teaching internationally, I discovered that one cannot simply replicate the same style of teaching as executed back in the home country of origin and expect the outcome to be the same. In fact, the teachers who came from abroad and attempted this tended to experience less classroom satisfaction, a higher level of disengagement from students towards the subject and in turn, these were the educators who tended to long for things to be as they were "back home". It resulted in staff dissatisfaction, a disconnect from the culture of the host country (and in turn, their students), and contributed to a higher level of staff turnover, whereby teachers wished to return to the familiarity of their home country to teach.

The notion of cultural pluralism, which aims to bring forth the values and ideals of subcultures was a concept that formed the very basis of my pedagogy, particularly in literature studies (Knapp & Wilkerson, 2023). When approaching the teaching of literature through this lens texts must be selected in a way which allows for reflection of the attitudes and values of various cultures, and which also serves to represent different subcultures in its nature (Knapp & Wilkerson, 2023; Ladson-Billings, 2014). As Knapp and Wilkerson (2023) emphasise, the literature does not merely "… tolerate the values and ideals of subcultures but would embrace and celebrate them" (p. 1). Initially, I questioned how this could be possible when the offering of texts was largely Western. However, as I stumbled across Shakespeare's The Merchant of Venice, a play I had studied in tertiary years, I resolved to the fact that if the curriculum could not be flexible in its nature, I would be. It required me to be adaptable, but to also revisit the purpose of learning. Amongst the endless red tape and the need for quality assurance and assessment procedures in TNE, I had forgotten a simple concept: the art of teaching, and the sheer pleasure found in *learning*.

I found myself pondering the very question, *why* are we offering this education to students in the Middle East in the first place? The answer could not be simply because "we" do it better and are therefore disseminating this curriculum globally – a narrow and misconstrued view of TNE (Jenkins, 2011). And secondly, why was learning Shakespeare an important part of an ESL student's education journey? The latter was a query often raised by students in Australia: "Miss, why do we need to learn about Shakespeare? He's old, and he's dead!" one student had previously quipped. My fallback response always centred around the fact that as English speakers, we ought to know how the English language evolved over time and afford some appreciation to the playwright who contributed some 1700 words to our vocabulary. Additionally, as any fan of "The Bard" would agree, it is the universal themes within classical literature that make these texts timeless. But such reasoning felt less relevant to students who were already bilingual, some trilingual, and who only required competent skills in modern academic English to enter university. The key, I discovered, was as Ladson-Billings (2014) describes, to use culturally relevant pedagogy practices as the place where "the beat drops" for students (p. 76). To this day, I thank Act Three, Scene One of Shakespeare's *The Merchant of Venice*, and Shylock's profound monologue for opening the door to equity, diversity and accessibility at a small international institution all the way in the sands of the UAE.

Given the complexities of conflict that exist in the Middle East, there were cultural and religious intricacies that as an educator, I needed to be aware of before introducing this text to primarily Arab students who had never studied Shakespeare before. Of course, the infamous feud between Christians and Jews as it exists in the play may not have been of much significance to a Western scholarly cohort, but here in the UAE, establishing historical context was crucial. Viewing my lesson planning through the decolonising theory prompted further consideration of three questions:

1. To what extent does my unit reflect diverse entry points of accessibility and align with the prior experiences of my students?
2. Is the unit content relevant for all student backgrounds in my classroom?

3. Is the learning content contextualised so that all learners can connect new ideas with prior experiences, perspectives, and learning?

(University of York, 2023)

Another aspect that was considered in my preparations was what topics and issues were of grave importance to this demographic of students. How might I teach the themes of mercy and injustice to Arab students through the eyes of a British poet and playwright? Ultimately, it was this intersectionality of culture and history that revealed the greatest lesson of TNE overall. That is, that accepting and embracing – not ignoring – the cultural capital in the room is the key to a rich, diversified, and worldly learning experience.

What happened next was nothing short of magic. After weeks spent researching the cultural context of the play, then reading, acting, and viewing parts of the film adaptation, it was time for the critical thinking to arrive. Using the famous monologue from Jewish "antagonist", Shylock, in which the character queries his Christian foe, "Hath not a Jew eyes?" and the renowned line, "If you prick us, do we not bleed?", students were asked to rewrite the monologue passage. However, rather than use the two religious groups from the play, I instructed them to consider a marginalised group in society who they felt needed a voice and a platform in which to be heard by humanity. Twenty minutes later, I experienced what Ladson-Billings (2014) describes as "the beat drop" in culturally sustaining pedagogy practices (p. 76).

What followed was a series of heartfelt monologues being read out by students in the classroom, each highlighting a different minority group in society, and each student pouring a little of themselves onto the page, subliminally revealing issues that were of personal significance to them and sharing this with peers. Some focused on gender, others on people of colour, religious groups, sexual orientation, and even groups on lower socio-economic scales. A number of students revealed that their family lineage stemmed from oppression, and that they had scribed the monologue with their ancestors in mind. And in this very moment – and unashamedly, with a prickle of tears in my eyes – I relearned the purpose of TNE and its place on a global scale. Yes, the curriculum we deliver is gold. But it will remain as unchanged, untouched gold – something to be viewed by spectators, not active learners – if we continue to strive for sameness. Instead, we must ask ourselves how we can enhance the TNE learning experience and improve it further. What creates a more transformative learning experience and adds meaning to the content we teach is the incorporation of student capital in its various forms and the embracing of diverse funds of knowledge that students bring into the classroom (Paris & Alim, 2017).

RETURNING TO THE ESSENCE OF TNE: GLOBAL PERSPECTIVES THROUGH LEARNING

In considering the ever-evolving role of TNE, there are aspects one should consider as vital components in the international education sector. Firstly, diversity, equity, and accessibility extend far beyond checkboxes and token gestures of inclusion and multiculturalism (Le-Ha, 2017). Each concept is more than merely theory. As educators, we must actively continue reshaping the curriculum to suit who is in the room, and not vice versa (Bannier, 2016; Jenkins, 2011). All students should be able to engage with and benefit from the educational experiences that TNE programs offer; however, at present, barriers to this ideal still exist in the form of standardised entry testing, rigid curriculum content, and English-only instruction (Ryan, 2013). While it is agreed that individuals must be provided with an equal opportunity to engage in the benefits of TNE HE programs, regardless of gender, ethnicity, religion or language, researchers argue that this sector remains generally elitist in nature, with inconsistencies in the number of enrolled students stemming from wealthier societal backgrounds (Brooks & Waters, 2011; Marginson, 2016).

Perhaps the time has come for a shift in our perception of TNE. Instead of solely emphasising the preservation and status of Western programs, perhaps it is time that we remind ourselves of the bridge between cultures that internationalism offers. A bridge, meaning that we resist the one-way, "re-colonial" approach of "West to the rest" and instead, we encourage a synthesis of richer cultural experiences that also embraces the "East to the West", and beyond. As Ladson-Billings (2014) suggests, "the future is multilingual and multiethnic, regardless of attempts to suppress that reality", and thus, acceptance of this is essential (Ladson-Billings, 2014, p. 6). While there is no "quick fix" for the gaps that currently exist in TNE practices, as a profession, we are drawing closer towards addressing a greater need for versatility and a sense of balance between policy and practice.

As Hallett and O'Hara (2024) propose, this "balancing act" requires dexterity and establishing an equilibrium between academic standards and relevance and flexibility for international students (Hallett & O'Hara, 2024, p. 1). Paired with this, there is a critical need to focus on preparing educators for the TNE environment. This involves staff re-evaluating how curriculum programs are presented to international students and questioning, "Why do we do it this way"? If the answer is simply, "because that's how we've always done it", therein lies the critical lesson to be learned. TNE allows learning to transcend borders and classroom walls, but for diversity and inclusion to truly flourish, the concepts of accessibility and equity must go beyond physical spaces. Policies must continually evolve to address the deeper needs of international students and create an environment which celebrates their many funds of knowledge.

Do's and Don'ts for an Expat Educator:

DO

- Get to know the cultural backgrounds of your clientele: your students.
- Familiarise yourself with the country's culture and customs.
- Learn a few local greetings from experienced staff or trusted locals.
- Prepare to be surprised and throw "what you thought you knew" out the window.
- Find the beauty in difference.

DON'T

- Constantly make comparisons to your home country: You're on this journey for a reason – embrace it.
- Be hard on yourself during the early adjustment phase.
- Be afraid to meet new people from different cultures.
- Assume that everyone speaks your home language.

REFERENCES

Ainscow, M., Booth, T., & Dyson, A. (2006). Improving Schools, Developing Inclusion. London: Routledge.

Alam, F., Alam, Q., Chowdhury, H., & Steiner, T. (2013). Transnational education: Benefits, threats and challenges. Procedia Engineering, 56, 870–874. https://doi.org/10.1016/j.proeng.2013.03.209

Alim, H., & Smitherman, G. (2012). Articulate while Black: Barack Obama, language and race in the U.S. New York, NY: Oxford University Press.

Alsharari, N. (2017). Internationalization of the higher education system: An interpretive analysis. International Journal of Educational Management, 32(3), 359–381.

Artiles, A. J., Kozleski, E. B., & Waitoller, F. R. (Eds.). (2011). Inclusive Education: Examining Equity on Five Continents. Cambridge, MA: Harvard Education Press.

Australian Council for Educational Research. (2022). GAMSAT information booklet 2022 [PDF]. Retrieved from https://gamsat.acer.org/files/GAMSAT_Info_booklet_2022.pdf

Bannier, B. (2016). Global trends in transnational education. International Journal of Information and Education Technology, 6, 80–84. https://doi.org/10.7763/IJIET.2016.V6.663

Barnawi, O. (2018, July 24). International Students Increasingly Attracted to Vietnam. University World News. https://www.universityworldnews.com/post.php?story=20180724132007428

Bhandari, R., & Blumenthal, P. (Eds.). (2013). International Students and Global Mobility in Higher Education: National Trends and New Directions. New York, NY: Palgrave Macmillan.

Brooks, R., & Waters, J. (2011). Student Mobilities, Migration and the Internationalization of Higher Education. London: Palgrave Macmillan.

Darling-Hammond, L., & Lieberman, A. (2012). Teacher education around the world: What can we learn from international practice? Teacher Education Around the World Changing Policies and Practices. https:doi.org/10.1080/02619768.2017.1315399

Feghali, E. (1997). Arab cultural communication patterns. International Journal of Intercultural Relations, 21, 345–378. https://doi.org/10.1016/S0147-1767(97)00005-9

Gray, K., & Bashir, H. (Eds.). (2017). Western Higher Education in Asia and the Middle East: Politics, Economics, and Pedagogy. Maryland: Lexington Books

Hallett, R., & O'Hara, M. (2024). Transnational education: Challenges and opportunities. Advance HE. Retrieved from https://www.advance-he.ac.uk/news-and-views/transnational-education-challenges-and-opportunities

Halliday, M. A. K. (2007). Language and education (Volume 9 of the Collected Works of M.A.K. Halliday). Continuum.

Hartshorne, J. K., Tenenbaum, J. B., & Pinker, S. (2018). A critical period for second language acquisition: Evidence from 2/3 million English speakers. Cognition, 177, 263–277. https://doi.org/10.1016/j.cognition.2018.04.007

Healey, N. M. (2015). Managing international branch campuses: What do we know? Higher Education Quarterly, 69(4), 386–409. https://doi.org/10.1111/hequ.12082

Hsiao, Y. J., & Lee, K. (2019). Confusion between diversity and inclusion: Examining teacher perspectives. Teaching and Teacher Education, 83, 101–111. https://doi.org/10.1016/j.tate.2019.03.010

Jenkins, J. (2011). Accommodating (to) ELF in the international university. Journal of Pragmatics, 43(4), 926–936. https://doi.org/10.1016/j.pragma.2010.05.011

Jenkins, J. (2014). English as a Lingua Franca in the International University: The Politics of Academic English Language Policy. Milton Park; Abingdon; Oxon: Routledge

Kariwo, M., Gounko, T., & Nungu, M. (Eds.). (2014). A synthesis of the issues, challenges, and dilemmas. In Comparative Analysis of Higher Education Systems (pp. 215–218). Rotterdam: SensePublishers.

Knapp, A., & Wilkerson, G. (2023). Cultural pluralism in literature: Definition & examples. Retrieved from https://study.com/academy/lesson/cultural-pluralism-in-literature-definition-examples.html

Knight, J. (2016). Transnational education remapped: Implications of the 2011 UNESCO/Council of Europe guidelines. Higher Education, 72(1), 1–14. https://doi.org/10.1787/9789264038493-3-en

Ladson-Billings, G. (2014). Culturally relevant pedagogy 2.0: The remix. Harvard Educational Review, 84(1), 74–84

Le-Ha, P. (2017). Transnational Education Crossing 'the West' and 'Asia': Adjusted desire, Transformative Mediocrity, and Neo-Colonial Disguise. London; New York: Routledge.

Lim, F. (2010). Do too many rights make a wrong? A qualitative study of the experiences of a sample of Malaysian and Singapore private higher education providers in transnational quality assurance. Quality in Higher Education, 16(3), 211–222.

Marginson, S. (2016). The worldwide trend to high participation higher education: Dynamics of social stratification in inclusive systems. Higher Education, 72(4), 413–434. https://doi.org/10.1007/s10734-016-0016-x

Marginson, S., & Sawir, E. (2011). Ideas for Intercultural Education. London: Palgrave Macmillan. https://doi.org/10.1057/9780230339736

Merriam-Webster. (2024). Inshallah. In Merriam-Webster.com dictionary. Retrieved June 1, 2024, from https://www.merriam-webster.com/dictionary/inshallah

Ministry of Education. (2024). Ministerial Resolution No. (19). https://www.mohesr.gov.ae/En/Legislation/Documents/Ministerial%20Resolution%20No.%20(19)%20of%202024%20Concerning%20Admission%20Standards%20for%20Higher%20Education%20Institutions%27%20Programs.pdf

Minister for Education and Youth. (2024). Education Services for Overseas Students Amendment (Quality and Integrity) Bill 2024. Retrieved from https://ministers.education.gov.au/clare/education-services-overseas-students-amendment-quality-and-integrity-bill-2024

Paris, D., & Alim, H. S. (Eds.). (2017). Culturally Sustaining Pedagogies: Teaching and Learning for Justice in a Changing World. New York: Teachers College Press.

Phan, L. H. (2017). Transnational Education Crossing 'The West' and 'Asia': Adjusted Desire, Transformative Mediocrity, and Neo-Colonial Disguise. London: Routledge. https://doi.org/10.4324/9781315759098

Proceedings of the Australian Universities Quality Forum 2004: Quality in a Time of Change (2004) pp. 144-149 Accessed online 22nd September 2025: https://find.library.unisa.edu.au/discovery/fulldisplay/alma991591287560183161USOUTHAUS_INST:ROR

Queensland Curriculum and Assessment Authority (QCAA). (2009). English senior subjects. https://www.qcaa.qld.edu.au/senior/senior-subjects/english

Roemer, A. E. (2016). Veiled incivilities: International students and campus/classroom climate at predominantly white universities (Publication No. 10156541) [Doctoral dissertation, University of Denver]. ProQuest Dissertations & Theses Global. http://aus.idm.oclc.org/login?url=https://www-proquest-com.aus.idm.oclc.org/dissertations-theses/veiled-incivilities-international-students-campus/docview/1818564054/se-2?accountid=16946

Ryan, J. (2013). Cross-Cultural Teaching and Learning for Home and International Students: Internationalisation of Pedagogy and Curriculum in Higher Education. London: Routledge.

Slee, R. (2011). The Irregular School: Exclusion, Schooling and Inclusive Education. London: Routledge.

Stein, S., & Andreotti, V. D. O. (2016). Decolonization and higher education. In M. Peters (Ed.), Encyclopedia of Educational Philosophy and Theory. Singapore: Springer Singapore, Science+Business Media. https://doi.org/10.1007/978-981-287-532-7_479-1

Turner, J. (2011). Language in the Academy: Cultural Reflexivity and Intercultural Dynamics. Bristol: Multilingual Matters.

UNESCO. (2023, October 4). Equity, inclusion and the transformation of higher education. https://www.unesco.org/en/articles/equity-inclusion-and-transformation-higher-education

University of Delaware Center for Teaching & Assessment of Learning. (2024). Diversity and inclusive teaching. University of Delaware. https://ctal.udel.edu/resources-2/inclusive-teaching/

University of Winnipeg. (2024). Countries in which English is a mandatory or optional subject. Global English Education. Retrieved from https://www.uwinnipeg.ca/global-english-education/countries-in-which-english-is-mandatory-or-optional-subject.html

University of York. (2023). Reflective questions: Decolonising and diversifying the curriculum. Retrieved from https://www.york.ac.uk/staff/teaching/inclusive-learning/ourcurrentwork/decolonisinganddiversifyingthecurriculum/reflectivequestions-decolonisinganddiversifyingthecurriculum/

Waters, J., & Leung, M. (2013). Immobile transnationalisms? Young people and their in situ experiences of 'international' education in Hong Kong. Urban Studies, 50(3), 606–620. https://doi.org/10.1177/0042098012468902

Wilkins, S. (2016). Transnational higher education in the 21st century. Journal of Studies in International Education, 20(1), 3–7. https://doi.org/10.1177/1028315315625148

Wilkins, S., & Huisman, J. (2012). The international branch campus as transnational strategy in higher education. Higher Education, 64(5), 627–645. https://doi.org/10.1007/s10734-012-9516-5

Wilkins, S., & Urbanovic, J. (2014). English as the Lingua Franca in transnational higher education: Motives and prospects of institutions that teach in languages other than English. Journal of Studies in International Education, 18, 405–425. https://doi.org/10.1177/1028315313517267

Conversation Not Confrontation – Women in Leadership in TNE
Judith Lamie

Seven

INTRODUCTION

We all tread our unique paths to leadership in higher education. Nowhere can this be more challenging and rewarding than in international higher education. In this chapter a range of female international higher education professionals from around the world reflect on the topic of women in leadership in transnational education. They share their thoughts and reflections on a number of aspects, from systemic barriers and training opportunities, to mentoring and celebrating success, as well as sharing stories from their own personal journeys.

Our esteemed international colleagues include:

Sirin Myles:	Co-Founder and Director, The IC Global Partnership
Dr Vicky Lewis:	International Education Consultant
Joyce Achampong:	Executive Director, Pivot Education Consulting Group
Stephanie Martin:	Co-Founder Edvance Consultants
Melissa Abache:	Senior Regional Manager, International Recruitment and Marketing, University of Cambridge
Dr Lobar Babakhodjaeva:	Associate Professor, Westminster International University, Tashkent, Uzbekistan
Professor Angela Yung Chi Hou:	Professor, College of Education, National Chengchi University, President Chinese Taipei Comparative Education

The panel were posed a series of questions including:

i. Could we do more to celebrate the achievements of women globally?
ii. How have things changed for women leaders in our field?

DOI: 10.4324/9781003649571-8

iii. What can educational institutions do to address the continued inequality in leadership roles in IHE?
iv. Can you talk about the role of mentors in your career development?
v. What are the challenges faced by female leaders when working abroad (particularly in male-dominated cultures) and how have you dealt with them?
vi. What advice would you give your younger self?

Meet the Panel

Judith: Thank you so much for agreeing to share your thoughts on women in leadership in transnational education. Before we delve into the topic, can you tell us a little about yourself?

Vicky: I'm Vicky Lewis from the UK. I grew up on the south coast of England and worked in France, Germany, Wales, and Scotland before ending up close to my childhood haunts again in the coastal town of Bournemouth. Since 2013, I've been working as an independent consultant supporting higher education institutions in the development of their international strategies.

Stephanie: I'm Stephanie Martin, South African by blood, and "adopted Australian", as I often call myself by passport! I have worked in the education sector for 15 years, beginning my career in Australia. For the last seven years, I have resided in Dubai, UAE, working as a leader and teacher in secondary international schools and as an assistant lecturer in the higher education sector. I'm the co-founder of Edvance Consultants, a female-led organisation helping schools, universities, and early years centres to create impactful change through innovative research-based practices.

Sirin: I'm Sirin Myles, Co-Founder and Director of The IC Global Partnership. Originally from Türkiye, I worked as Director of Education Counselling and Marketing at the British Council. Since 2000, I have lived in the UK, working in the internationalisation of Higher Education at UK universities. For the last four years, I have been jointly leading The IC Global Partnership, an organisation I co-founded with the late Charlene Allen. Our mission is to support professionals in internationalisation and global engagement and build strong international education communities.

Through our Academy, Executive and Consultancy branches, we provide a one-stop international resource and knowledge hub for our IC Global Community.

Joyce: I'm Joyce Achampong and I'm Executive Director, Pivot Global Education Consulting Group and Associate Director Impact, Institution of Mechanical Engineers. I also sit on the advisory board of the Perivoli Africa Research Centre (University of Bristol). I started my professional career in international development in Canada and then worked in health education and policy for a few years. I found my way into international higher education working at the UK arm for an American headquartered organisation that supported University Advancement (alumni relations, comms, marketing, and fundraising).

Melissa: My name is Melissa Abache, I'm Venezuelan (and since late 2023 also Turkish!), and I recently joined the University of Cambridge in the UK in the Student Admissions and Access Department as a Senior Regional Manager in the International Student Recruitment and Marketing team. In this role, I am responsible for engagement with stakeholders in the Southeast Asia region, and additionally I manage two Regional Managers responsible for North America, Latin America, sub-Saharan Africa, and Australia and lead strategy for postgraduate recruitment and marketing activities. Prior to this, I worked for five years in the NGO, private, and public sectors, before moving to Istanbul in 2011 where I initially undertook freelance consulting projects, whilst I learned the language, before arriving at Koc University, where I spent a happy ten years.

Lobar: I'm Lobar. I have undergraduate degree in Business Management with Finance, a Masters in International Tourism and a Master's in Business Computing. My PhD and DSc is in Education with focus on technology-enhanced learning. I am currently Associate Professor at Westminster International University in Tashkent (WIUT), Uzbekistan. In 2011 I became Head of Research and Consultancy, after that I was Deputy Dean on teaching environment. For five years, I was a Dean of Faculty managing around 3,500 students and 200 academic staff. In 2020 I decided to focus on research and defended

	my Doctorate degree, and since then I teach, do consultancy work, and research.
Angela:	My name is Angela Yung Chi Hou. I am a professor in the College of Education at the National Chengchi University in Taiwan. I am also the President of the Chinese Taipei Comparative Education Society. I teach courses on higher education policy, quality assurance, institutional governance, and international education. I began work as a teacher in a secondary school and then decided to pursue a PhD, and over time, realized how much I was interested in higher educational policy.

Celebrating Women in Leadership

Judith:	I thought it would be interesting for us to begin by reflecting on how we celebrate women in leadership. There is a clear and obvious example of this in International Women's Day (IWD) which was first celebrated in 1911. The United Nations officially recognized IWD in 1977 and a number of countries designate the day a public holiday. **Could we do more to celebrate the achievements of women globally, have you experienced these celebrations, and do you think we need a special day to celebrate this?**
Vicky:	When International Women's Day is mentioned, my thoughts immediately go out to women (and girls) whose right to education has been suppressed, as is the case under the Taliban regime in Afghanistan; or who live in societies where other everyday freedoms are curtailed. Although it's a day for celebrating women's achievements, it's also important to shine a light on – and take action to challenge – the extreme inequalities that persist in some parts of the world.
Joyce:	We should be looking at this year round, not just on one day. As seen recently from the film Hidden Figures, we have always been there, our stories just haven't been told since we aren't the ones traditionally telling the stories.
Stephanie:	Absolutely! IWD still appears tokenistic. The pink cupcakes, ribbons, and slightly overused "empowerment" quotes are not a fix for what occurs in professional settings during the

remaining 364 days of the year. Women should not feel compelled to create their own table as an immediate response to being denied a seat at the existing one. Research also highlights that women often overexert themselves out of fear of not being "enough", constantly questioning whether they are qualified enough, intelligent enough, or have done enough, largely due to the lack of recognition they've received over the years. In hindsight, this may have been a driving force behind my own motivation in the past: a desire to prove my worthiness.

Sirin: Celebrating women's achievements and setting role models will create awareness and confidence in the minds of other females to apply for senior and influential roles. Any opportunity for celebration and raising awareness is important. At The IC Global, we celebrate International Women's Day every year through IC Cafes, bringing female and male colleagues to share their challenges, experiences, and solutions in order to foster a culture of inclusivity, mutual respect, and empowerment.

Melissa: I think the volume and nature of celebrations around IWD is enough at present, especially in countries where gender equality has advanced significantly in the past 100 years. This does not mean those celebrations and awareness raising efforts should be diminished in countries where the advances have been not as significant or are in a reversal path in areas like reproductive rights (the United States comes to mind) or access to education (Afghanistan comes to mind).

I think in the global north and parts of the global south, young girls and teenagers do not need further evidence that they can aspire to learn or work in whichever field they want. They do not need more role models in the media they consume; they can see it all around them. In short, no one needs convincing that women can achieve as much as they want.

Lobar: I agree with Stephanie. In my country it is a public holiday, but as I get older, I no longer believe that it must be the holiday as we celebrate it. I have a lot of questions in my head regarding this holiday such as: why there is no Man's day? Why am I getting this message with "the beautiful half of the world" – aren't we more than that? Is this what those women in 1911 fought for?

Recently, I was one of organizers of the Women in STEM event. We created an event where young professional working in engineering, medicine, physics, and math presented their research findings in an engaging and interesting way. I believe this was a celebration of their achievement, and such events must be promoted and organized more.

> ### What Did Our Panel Want to Be When They Grew Up?
>
> **Vicky:** Everyone presumed I'd be a teacher, so I was determined not to go down that path. I was keen to do something that involved traveling and writing.
>
> **Stephanie:** A famous actress!
>
> **Sirin:** Inspired by Jules Verne's 'Around the World in 80 Days' something to do with travel, or acting!
>
> **Joyce:** A statistician – I loved numbers and problem-solving.
>
> **Melissa:** The city as an object of study was my passion and I started my professional life as an urban planner.
>
> **Lobar:** When I was little, I would put my toys in the room and teach them.
>
> **Angela:** A teacher in a secondary school.

Changing Times

Judith: You all have an extensive amount of experience in international higher education spanning a number of decades, **how have things changed for women leaders in our field during the course of your career?**

Vicky: At my first University Management Team meeting at Bournemouth University in 2000, there were more men called David (4) around the boardroom table than there were women (3). I was also the youngest by quite a margin. However, one of the three women was the Vice-Chancellor (pretty unusual at the time, since only 11% of UK Vice-Chancellors were female in 2000), which certainly helped to make it less daunting. And I had some very good (male) line managers over the years who encouraged me to chisel away at the glass ceiling.

Over the course of my career, there's been a gradual increase in female HE leaders here in the UK, and a move away from some of the more egregious sexist behaviours I used to experience (e.g. in a meeting of peers, automatically expecting a woman to pour the tea and/or take the minutes). However, the culture at the top of some institutions can sometimes still come across as a bit "macho".

Recently, there seems to have been an influx of new female Vice-Chancellors in the UK who are modelling a more emotionally intelligent and compassionate form of leadership with very open communication. And there are some vocal male allies. So, I would like to think we're entering a new, more egalitarian phase of HE leadership.

Stephanie: Having schooled in a private all-girls school in Australia that proudly honoured female leadership, I entered my tertiary years believing that anything was possible for women. I'd been exposed to a school principal who had completed her doctorate and who sought to empower young women of the future. Needless to say, it was inspiring. But in the course of my career, I have noted that there still remains a chasm of difference in the path that women walk in comparison to our male counterparts. We're definitely seeing more women in the education industry making executive decisions, leading departments, and certainly in the higher education sector, there has been a greater move to promote female leaders.

There is greater conversation also taking place around providing equal opportunities regardless of gender. But in my work with leaders in various organisational settings, I still witness the larger and perhaps more overwhelming number of women who experience higher levels of imposter syndrome. This leads to less women in the profession vocalising their ideas, promoting their own strengths and professional assets, and often questioning whether they are worthy of further professional growth. We've certainly come a long way, but we still have a long way to go.

Sirin: During my time as a Regional Manager in a UK university, there was female representation at the executive table, whilst in a subsequent role as International Director at a different institution, there had been none and indeed, during my tenure there, the females who applied for those roles, were unsuccessful.

The IC Global's pioneering research[1] showed that the gender balance for International Directors at UK higher education institutions is more equal, with 53.2% assumed male and 46.8% assumed female, compared with Pro Vice-Chancellor Research (PVC-R) and Pro Vice-Chancellor International (PVC-I), which had over 70% assumed male. The majority of International Directors have a non-academic background (74.5%), the opposite of PVC-Is who were mostly from an academic background (77.3%). 90.7% of International Directors are from a non-STEM discipline background, whereas the figure is lower for PVC-Is (62.5%) and even lower for PVC-Rs (34%).

In recent years, I have observed and am observing a conscious effort to increase female representation at the executive table together with enhanced diversity and inclusion.

Joyce: There are more women in positions of leadership outside the traditional university. They sit as leaders of associations and learned societies, more so than as Vice-Chancellors (VC) and Presidents in the UK. There has been a visible increase in women at the DVC or VC level in the UK and a growing number of women VCs around the world which is great to see, and I hope this is more than a trend, but continuation to recognize excellence from different backgrounds. Board rooms seem to be seeing more balance with these same women on them, but not as much as they should at this stage.

Melissa: In the ten years since I joined the higher education sector in Türkiye, I can see how increasing numbers of women (and particularly young women below 45 years old) became part of senior leadership teams in several foundation (private) and public universities in Türkiye. Whenever I attended sector events to advance internationalisation topics in Türkiye there would always be a stark contrast between the make-up of the university managers invited to attend (usually gender balanced or tipping towards a predominance of women) and the make-up of the government officials (predominantly male) we were having dialogues with.

Two other interesting things I witnessed in my role were firstly, women leaders in higher education and particularly in international offices in Türkiye not being held back from travelling to countries or zones considered high-risk for business or academic travel due to political instability, terrorism or other issues. Secondly, in the past five years I noticed a small but significant growth in the number of educational agencies and independent educational consultancies (IEC) that were started by or led by women in Türkiye and some of the countries our team would regularly engage with for student recruitment (Azerbaijan, Pakistan, UAE, Russia, India to name a few).

Finally, I have also observed with delight the growth of women researchers, especially from the Global South, in the field of international education. These researchers are important to practitioners like me, as they demonstrate how a career in international education can continually evolve and may provide opportunities for applied research and policy making in universities, international NGOs, multilateral, and government organisations.

Lobar: There has been a steady increase in women's representation in Uzbekistan's public administration over the past seven years, rising from 27% to 35%. Currently, women constitute 32% of deputies in the Legislative Chamber of the Oliy Majlis and 25% of the members of the Senate, with women represented in every district. According to a Spot report, the labour market situation for women in Uzbekistan was analysed by HeadHunter. Based on the analysis, the following five sectors had the largest share in hiring women in 2023: Medicine, pharmaceuticals, and pharmacies (76%); Educational institutions (69%); Accounting (65%); Human Resource Management (62%); and Arts and culture (58%).

The lowest levels of employment offerings for women were noted in mining, heavy machinery, and the automotive sectors – at respective rates of 21%, 19%, and 17%. Additionally, the areas and professions attracting the most interest from women were highlighted. According to the 2023 results, the majority of women's resumes were recorded in administrative positions (9.5% of the total), education (8.4%), and accounting (8%).

In higher education back in 2002, it was only one Rector in the republic, whereas now there are a number of them. They are still underrepresented. At WIUT, we have now only male in executive positions. Senior management positions have some women but it is still underrepresented. There have been changes, but we cannot talk about equal distribution in leading positions as of now.

Angela: Things have changed over time, and there is more representation now for women. I was invited by the university leader to serve in different administrative positions, including Vice President of International Education.

Judith: There have been changes, and many of these have been for the better, but it would appear that there is still some way to go, not least, reflecting on Stephanie's comments around imposter syndrome, in how women view themselves as leaders.

Addressing Inequality

Judith: There has clearly been progress across many areas, as Lobar illustrates with regard to Uzbekistan, but there remains a considerable distance to go particularly in some sectors. Those of us who work in academic institutions are in a positive position to help address this imbalance, but are we doing enough, and what can we do to help further. There has been a rapid increase in higher educational attainment for women globally, but there remains a significant challenge for women when it comes to managing to break into leadership roles in IHE. **What can educational institutions do to try to address the inequality and imbalance?**

Vicky: I suspect slightly different approaches work in different cultural contexts. Here in the UK, gender-specific, sector-wide professional development initiatives like Advance HE's Aurora programme (for women up to senior lecturer or professional services equivalent level) can be very valuable, as can coaching and mentoring. The same principles apply when it comes to broadening the leadership pipeline for other underrepresented groups.

It's also helpful to see different kinds of leadership modelled, and for female leaders (at all levels of leadership) to be supported in being both visible and audible (i.e. people –

and not just other women – going out of their way to amplify female voices). However, there are still systemic barriers, which need to be dismantled so that the onus is not on potential female leaders to adapt their behaviours to "fit in" to structures built up over decades (even centuries) with male leadership in mind.

Stephanie: It starts with making male leaders aware of this. Often, this is either not done or not done well, and when I have witnessed this striving for awareness being executed poorly, executive leadership teams have come away feeling as though it is yet another feminist movement protest, which is not the case. It takes honest reviewing of systems and structures in place and being open to asking the female employees how they feel that the policies in place support and empower them. If there is an imbalance, we must ask ourselves why? And if the significant gap is due to varying levels of competence rather than oversight or bias, then IHE institutions must also question how they are empowering the women in their organisation to be able to grow, expand, and transition into leadership roles. Again, this comes down to the support in place for women and also opening the conversation to address the gap, rather than shying away from it or perhaps feeling threatened by the outcome.

Sirin: The IC Global's research shows that at PVC level, there is heavy representation of males; however, at Director levels, there are more females. We also observed that teaching, internationalisation PVC roles are more represented by female PVCIs, yet research PVC roles are mostly held by male colleagues.

Research shows that female colleagues would only apply for higher-level roles when they feel more than 70% ready for the role and they have completed similar-level tasks previously. However, male colleagues feel ready to apply for such roles with much less experience. Institutions and their leaders should actively encourage female colleagues to apply for such roles. Coaching and mentoring could also play a significant role in raising awareness of female colleagues' skills and abilities and building their confidence. Coaching and mentoring can also help to build clarity for female role holders to purposefully get ready/feel ready for applying and transitioning to higher-level roles.

Joyce:	Reflect on who is hiring and what additional skills are needed for a role, see more than the traditional trajectory, and value different experiences and what they could bring.
Angela:	Women's participation in academic community is being protected by national regulation. In all high-ranking committees, one-third of the representatives should be female.
Melissa:	I think that looking at countries where this is not an issue would be a good start. When I think of countries like Türkiye, Colombia, Spain, China (to name a few) I remember that most of the senior or director colleagues I met so far at international conferences, online meetings, and recruitment travel are women. This also reflects the fact that those countries have entered the HE internationalisation process relatively later than the more established destinations or usual suspects like the UK, US, Australia, Canada, and thus, could be more open to give opportunities for career growth to young women who come with very high levels of relevant qualifications. I also observed that several women colleagues in leadership positions had benefited from their universities' policies of providing free or highly subsidized management training or opportunities for obtaining a management formal qualification (e.g. MBA, PMP). Lessons could also be learnt from countries like the UK where the existence of policies that mandate that universities should have maternity leave cover temporary contracts, secondment contracts, flexible maternity and paternity leave arrangements, and even the provision on campus of nursery places are a significant benefit to encourage more women to continue their careers in IHE if they decide to have children and then advance towards leadership positions in international office to Director or even PVC level or equivalent. Finally, we can all look towards the salary transparency practices of universities in Nordic countries and in the UK as ways of advancing more women to join the sector and have a better sense of their value in the university workforce. Universities have always been bastions of new ideas and practices that help advance women's rights and equality. They can continue to play this role going forward and use their outreach channels to showcase real examples to other

	organisations of how these issues can be overcome (e.g. fixing the leaky gender pipeline of science, providing comprehensive and flexible support and infrastructure for women returning to work after childbirth or extensive care duties, making salaries transparent).
Lobar:	I think IHE must promote their success stories involving women, invest more into public relations and marketing showing to the society that it is possible and represent real cases of woman in power and their achievements.

Mentoring

Judith: Picking up on Vicky's point about coaching and mentoring, **have mentors figured in your career development?**

Stephanie: Interestingly, gaps in competence can often be viewed as a weakness rather than an opportunity, and talent management is a concept that many organisations fail to execute well. Quite often, there are excellent individuals within the organisation who are waiting to grow and transform their expertise, but they lack mentorship. Mentoring was never formally in place in any of my prior workplaces, but on reflection, it is something I would have greatly benefited from, like so many others. Despite this, as someone who always seeks to improve and enjoys rising to new challenges, I found myself always questioning how I could "do better".

The problem I encountered was that not everyone was equipped to be a mentor, even though they were in positions of leadership. The quality of advice I received depended greatly on whom I was asking. "Mentoring" by those who were more managers than leaders unfortunately adopted more of a "we want you to jump, but only this high" approach, where true growth was only measured in the interest of the organisation. But when conversing with those who understood the very essence of leadership, I found that I was empowered to do more and seek more. My achievements and accomplishments, particularly in academia, were acknowledged and embraced. Their guidance and encouragement were instrumental in my development and success.

Sirin: My mentors were often strong females who were fair and solution driven. During one of my institutional roles, my mentor, who was allocated to me by one of my institutions, was not suitably matched to my needs so the experience lacked impact, that mentoring could have achieved. Mentoring can be incredibly impactful and would allow the mentee to gain time and truly speed up in achieving what they want/aim for via the mentor's lived experiences.

Joyce: I have had very few formal mentors who have come from the same background and trajectory I have. I am good at relating to others, so engage with them and learn from them that way.

Angela: My supervisors indeed guided me how to develop research capacity through the process of academic writing.

Melissa: I have never formally joined a mentorship scheme or programme but have certainly been a beneficiary of all the advantages of having a mentor from my first professional role as a social researcher in Venezuela until today. My mentors have been the ones who have guided me to training, scholarships and project opportunities I was not aware of, have been there to try to answer tricky questions when it came to dealing with difficult conversations that are inevitable when you start managing people and encouraged me to think of problems as opportunities.

Other key learnings I was able to gain thanks to my mentors are: 1) it is okay and even a good thing to have a "wiggly" career in IHE and to pivot when needed, 2) that it is okay to admit one does not know everything about every topic in our field/sector and that asking questions from your team, colleagues in other institutions and academics is crucial to develop insights and a strategic perspective on our work, 3) that trying to advance big bold new ideas in complex and large institutions like universities takes time, is about politics (internal and external) and often can work out better if it starts as a pilot or as a ground-up initiative. There are many other things I have learnt from all my mentors (men and women!) but that would be a whole book chapter.

Lobar: I was lucky to have very interesting and wise people on my way. One of them Evelyne Rugg, she was Academic Registrar and later Director of Education Policy and Strategic Partnerships at University of Westminster (UK). She was very calm, respectful, straight to the point, able to see potential in other people, passionate about her work and very hard working. She taught me that decisions must be made with consideration and all facts taken into consideration, triangulation of information always must be made and all sides must be heard.

I also had male mentors, one of them was Alan France. He was my line manager when I was a Dean. He never doubted me because of my gender, he trusted my decisions and supported them. He is a great believer in communicating with people.

And my main and most important mentor is my father. He has four daughters. From our childhood, he never even mentioned that we can do less because we are girls, we were never told that our main priority is to build a family – unfortunately this is how the majority of families in my country treat girls in the family. He always insisted and invested a lot in our education. He was the one who pushed me towards research. And he would always say that I must be self-sufficient and independent.

Judith: It can be a variable experience when it comes to mentors. Sometimes we have them, sometimes we don't. Some people may have the best of intensions, but their advice can seem limiting. Others, who we may not think of as mentors as such, provide us with important and influential sounding boards. As Melissa mentions, it's okay not to always know the answers (how else can we learn), it's normal to ask questions, and having a "wiggly" career path (which should be adopted as the new terminology from now on from journeys through IHE) is equally fine.

Another area that can have a bearing on women in leadership is the role and influence of cultural norms, and it is to that topic that our panel now turn.

Cultural Norms

Judith: **What are the challenges faced by female leaders when working abroad (particularly in male-dominated cultures) – and how have you dealt with them?**

Vicky: A key challenge, when in a mixed group, is the situation where the people you're meeting automatically defer to the males in your group, or address their remarks to the men, even if your own role is at the same, or a more senior, level. It forces you to think and behave in a hierarchy-conscious way, which (I find) goes against the grain. When I was younger, I suspect I didn't deal with this particularly well. Nowadays, I travel less and the nature of my role means that I rarely find myself in this situation. However, I think I'd be more confident now to enlist the active support of men in my group to redirect the conversation. I might even try to open up dialogue about how we all make assumptions and it's worth allowing these to be challenged.

Stephanie: My own experience reflects that of many women in the Gulf education sector who work in TNE settings: at leadership level, there is a higher volume of male dominance in these roles. A challenge that many women who are also mothers encounter is the return to professional work duties. When answering to a largely male-dominant leadership team, there is little understanding and meaningful support in place for female employees that allows them to adjust and balance their new life. In terms of leadership strategies, research has shown time and time again that there is a significant difference (whether we want to accept this or not!) in male versus female leadership styles. Women are often found needing to adopt more authoritarian approaches in early stages of their career to be taken seriously as a leader, for being too empathetic or emotionally intelligent may be viewed as somewhat less competitive in a male-dominated environment.

There is no straight remedy or answer to this, I believe it is a work in progress. However, now when I work with leaders, having been informed by my own experience and the experience of others as well as research, these are the questions I ask when it comes to policy frameworks and employee wellbeing. First and foremost, it comes down to making male leaders aware of the challenges faced by women in the profession, because – try as they might – more often than not, this is overlooked and leaders remain blissfully unaware.

Sirin: In male dominated cultures, I have personally observed visiting teams with male role holders typically addressing male role holders or team members. Just last month, a female leader in the sector shared the same experience with me. I have also heard through team members in the past, that female international visitors to the country are treated as "honorary" men.

Early in my career, having come from a culture where female colleagues would typically take care-giver roles, including serving refreshments during meetings, I started doing the same when I started my role in the UK. I then realised this action or assumption could lead to female colleagues not being treated as equals during conversations, when influencing or making decisions. At the same time, I remember reading a book about female role holders consciously not offering drinks to assert their equality in meetings. This highlights an experience where a female leader of an academic school was asked to serve drinks. She responded, "Is that because I am female?" The male Dean apologised and offered to serve the drinks instead, raising awareness of the need to avoid stereotypes or assumed roles to all those in the room.

As a female from a male-dominated and hierarchical culture, I often waited to hear the opinions of colleagues in higher-level roles, either male or female. However, as a female, I observed men jumping in with their thoughts and suggestions, and by the time female colleagues offered their opinions or ideas, the same or similar ideas were already being discussed and owned by male colleagues. Therefore, female colleagues lost their chance to lead with their thoughts and were seen as "followers".

Extroverted and introverted preferences also influence colleagues and introverted female colleagues struggle most in this case. Nancy Kline, in her book "Time to Think", shares a useful strategy that could be used in meetings to ask each colleague to give everyone equal time to think and speak in meetings without any interruption.

Joyce: Getting a seat and the table and the recognition of the efforts to get there, lots of having to prove you are more than qualified to be in the room, which can come off arrogant to onlookers, but is understood by most women as a necessity!

Melissa: I was very lucky to work for ten years in a university where gender balance and advancing women was a priority at every level, and this was reflected in the number of women professors, students, and senior administrators. It (Koc) was the first university in Türkiye to devote resources to a Gender Equality Office and even before it was compulsory to have a Gender Equality Plan due to EU research funding regulations, it had been steadily advancing a culture and small programs and initiatives to advance gender equality in research and professional development and advancement for its staff. Having said that, there were challenges that remain which have to do with national policies concerning maternity and paternity leave, salary transparency laws, and others.

I only had a very small number of occasions when my gender was a factor in terms of how I was treated by hosts whilst visiting a partner university or organisation, and this was more about their intention to make sure I would be safe in a new city. The challenges I ever felt and observed were the culture of senior male academics being considered the wisest voice in the room when deciding on what to do, how to do it, or whether to do something, due to a cultural deference for age and seniority.

I did experience and observed with other women international education leaders that we tend to be more aware and concerned with risk management in terms of travel safety than male colleagues. This means that reminding people of why procedures are needed before, during, and after travel becomes our job instead of what should be standard practice. I also remember somewhat amusingly that there were some partner university delegations who came to our campus, and the women staff members (no matter how senior they were in terms of their roles) were always given or assumed the role or task of gift bearer, note taker, photograph taker, protocol watcher during our meetings. This always struck me as curious as to why we as women continue to feel this need to take on the role of caretakers of groups, even when we are all travelling abroad for business.

Angela: In my society, your performance is measured on merit-based, including your leadership, research output, and teaching quality.

Lobar: I believe the challenges are not greatly impacted by geographical position. During my conversations with colleagues from other countries, we share the same views and same obstacles in getting into leading positions. Probably culture is the factor which influences it more. Europe is more female represented, and Asia is less. Challenges are misconceptions about women roles and abilities to manage a bigger group of people, being able to balance work and life and etc. Some of my colleagues note that women are underpaid being in the same positions as men, preferences for management positions are always on the male side, and most importantly, woman themselves in most of the cases do not believe in their own success as managers and leaders.

Judith: It's always interesting having a difference of opinion. We know there are no right answers, but it is welcome to note those institutions that actively seek to promote gender equality, such as Koc University, although there still may be challenging instances, which may seem harmless enough – can you hand out the gifts, take photographs, make tea – but do reinforce what may be an underlying cultural bias that we do well to call out.

Words of Advice to Our Younger Selves

Judith: Do we do enough to believe in ourselves? Can we see ourselves succeeding as leaders? I recall a chat with a male colleague ahead of becoming a Head of Department for the first time. I wasn't sure that I was "old enough" (and I remember actually saying that) and I'd never been a Head before so didn't have the experience (although I had been a programme leader), which concerned me (there are echoes of Stephanie's earlier point here). He, whilst not overtly advising me, said that he thought I had demonstrated that I had the skills and that there always has to be the first time when it comes to taking the plunge into leadership. **What advice would you give your younger self and/or someone embarking on an IHE/TNE leadership role today?**

Vicky: I would encourage my younger self to recognise the value of both female mentorship and investment in my own professional development. I saw the benefit of building up my academic qualifications, but I overlooked the kind of confidence-building development that I needed. As someone who ended up in a leadership role at a relatively young age, I thought I had to be self-sufficient and work everything out myself. It didn't occur to me to proactively seek out help and support (and such support was less visible in those days anyway). So, to any woman embarking on a leadership role today, I'd urge them to ask for help, build a strong support network and keep investing in their own professional development.

Stephanie: Never dim your light out of fear of being "too much". Embrace it proudly and use it to inspire others to shine their light a little brighter, too.

Angela: Be yourself and work towards the life goal you set.

Sirin: My advice to someone embarking on an IHE/TNE leadership role is to say "yes" to all internal project opportunities. Ask to do more, expand your role and involve yourself in internal or external projects to gain a wider knowledge and understanding of other areas. Build strong relationships with wider stakeholders. Research, learn and seek coaching and mentoring support.

Joyce: Create space to engage meaningfully with people, create connections that you can learn from and who can learn from you. Walk into a room like you belong and eventually you will!

Melissa: I have learned so many lessons along the way. IHE is a sector full of people who love to travel and interact with other cultures (yes, it is still very true!) but also of people who are largely motivated by a desire to create positive change in student's lives (because many have been former international students themselves). I would say to my younger self, embrace this drive to create teams that bring new ideas for supporting international students, that improve how we communicate with those students and their advisors and very importantly, that can be strategic thinkers and connect the dots of how their work impacts the institution's culture (not just its finances). I would also

	advise myself to make sure I understand the whole institution's politics and take time to meet for coffee, lunch, whatever it takes, with your President/PVC/Rector and senior colleagues across departments so you understand their needs, goals and challenges and they can also understand what you mean when you start talking about internationalisation in meetings.
Lobar:	I would say, believe in yourself, build your confidence and trust people. A leadership role does not depend on gender, leadership is about building a team, trusting that team and developing yourself and others.
Judith:	Wise words from Lobar to draw our panel discussion to a close.

Top Tips from the Panel

- Build a strong support network
- Work on your confidence
- Challenge inequalities
- Trust people and build a self-assured team
- Inspire others
- Involve yourself in internal and external projects
- Research, learn, and seek mentoring support
- Bring students and teams together – they inspire us
- Walk in the room like you belong and (eventually) you will

THE FINAL WORD

It seems only right that our final reflection should be from Charlene

> I am proud to be part of a sector that speaks a global language, creates a global community and develops global opportunities that are life changing not only for students but staff too.
>
> (Charlene Allen, LinkedIn post April 2024)

Charlene may no longer be with us, but her inspirational words are.

NOTE

1 Find out more about The Route to Pro Vice-Chancellor International: https://www.theicglobal.com/insights/the-route-to-pro-vice-chancellor-international/

Eight

Lost in Translation – Culture, Community, and Communication on Our International Travels

Judith Lamie and Christopher Hill

INTRODUCTION

What do we think of when we hear the world culture? Is it something that happens, "out there" or can we find it closer to home? Culture can be seen in different ways: from the personal perspective, thinking about other places and the cultural norms that exist there, the food, the festivals, the behaviours and the language; and from the professional view and institutional culture, in the classroom and across the institution, a term that can both facilitate and prevent.

How do we articulate the notion of culture within an organisation, or even within ourselves? For those of us in international higher education, this is a daily reality – both in conversation and reflection. This chapter attempts to pull back the curtain and examine – or at the very least, highlight – the day-to-day experiences, and our reactions to these, that shape so much of our individual and collective responses. The value of this type of examination and self-reflection is the increased awareness of things we had simply taken for granted. Things that are in place because they have always been in place. Things that just simply are, even if we don't agree with, or understand them. Through the presentation of two in-depth case studies, we will look at how we situate ourselves in places we find ourselves; how we navigate these new realities; and how we take this learning and understanding and move forward.

WHERE YOU GO, THERE YOU ARE

First we will begin with a story; Sharon's story. Are you sitting comfortably? Then we will begin …

> **Case Study 8.1: Sharon Davies-Smith's Story: "Are We There Yet?"**
>
> **Context**
>
> Sharon Davies-Smith, College Director/Principal and Chief Operating Officer – The College, Swansea University. Sharon's journey to

international higher education began in education, moved to the corporate world, and then found its way back. Sharon was a hall tutor, teacher, commercial buyer for Sainsbury's and Next, and then returned to education to her current role at Swansea University.

This is Sharon's reflection of her first, long-anticipated, visit to Japan.

Stages in the Journey

i) The Preparation

Decision to go – this was a BIG decision; I have always been fascinated by Japan and for many years have wanted to go. I planned (somewhat subconsciously) to go "when I retired", but last year my very fit and healthy 70-year-old aunt was diagnosed with bone cancer out of the blue and within six months had sadly died. This was a tremendous shock and upset and made me realise that you should maybe not put off things for "the future" as that is not guaranteed to any of us. Seize the day!

So, I decided I would go in 2024, whilst I could. Whilst my parents were still well and able and wanting to come with me and my daughter and whilst my aforementioned daughter was still in primary school and could miss school.

Having made the decision to take the trip in 2024, I then spent AGES planning and researching it! Working out where I wanted us to go, how long to spend in each place, and how to undertake the trip; totally independently (as we normally would for all previous holidays), semi-autonomously (e.g. with TrailFinders) or with a guided tour? Eventually, after much discussion, debate, comparison, talking to others who had visited Japan, and internal angst I settled on a guided/accompanied tour.

Having booked the trip, I then set about scheduling out what would be covered with the tour and what else we would need to fit in (and how) on our free days. I scoured forums and social media, especially Instagram accounts, for ideas and tips. And of course, I reached out to colleagues who had lived in and visited Japan themselves for more tips. I asked specific questions on a Visit Japan forum and quickly received very informative and helpful answers. I'm always struck by how generous people are with their knowledge and information. This all really helped me to feel fully prepared ahead of leaving.

ii) The Arrival

Our arrival into Tokyo Haneda airport was on time and relatively straightforward. I had read about longish queues at immigration and so was prepared for these on arrival. Although tedious, at least I was forewarned! I didn't love standing in an endless snaked back and forth queue of passengers in a very warm and stuffy space... a Covid legacy is heightened awareness of germs in general and I really didn't want any of us to come down with any type of illness during the trip. It was well organised with plenty of staff directing things, and moved forward – although not at great pace – and so we eventually proceeded through to baggage reclaim. Although we hadn't been to Japan before we are relatively well-travelled through Europe and the United States and everything was very similar. With its level of "same-ness" Haneda, Tokyo, could have been any number of airports across the world!

It was surprising to hear over the tannoy that after retrieving our bags that we then needed to fill in more customs declaration forms online on a computer terminal! We were poring over this when an exceedingly helpful official came over and assisted us. Although he didn't speak any English and we didn't speak any Japanese he was extremely helpful through pointing out the buttons to press and through his constant commentary – none of which we understood other than his lovely smile, and genuine friendliness and desire to assist! We passed through customs into the arrival hall with great excitement – we were finally in Japan!! It all seemed surreal that we were finally there after all the planning and anticipation. To be honest, this surreal feeling persists even after our return home!

We were very pleased to see our tour guide and to find the rest of the group – this was a very "soft landing" into a new country with completely unfamiliar language. It was a relief to be able to just be guided out of the airport and onto a coach and to our first hotel. It felt luxurious actually to be so looked after. On reflection, knowing that this was going to happen had also made the journey there easier and much more enjoyable – I hadn't had to worry about arriving and finding our way onwards by whatever means from there. It was a very lovely and easy welcome to this new country to be picked up and transported to our hotel.

iii) Observations During the Journey

We started our trip in Tokyo – I was very surprised how "familiar" this felt – I guess just like the best bits of any other major city. I was pleased to discover more traditional aspects of Japan, such as lower rise, timber buildings, and the "old" temples and shrines. But in general it was very easy to assimilate into Tokyo, perhaps having lived in and stayed in London many times, also New York. for example.

In addition to this I noted that there were some aspects of the Japanese culture that are similar to that of (again, the best bits of) the UK –polite, queuing, no pushing and shoving, pretty quiet and calm; quite different from the cultural norms of other countries where perhaps the local "norms" may feel really uncomfortable to begin with.

For us, both the physical environment and the societal norms seemed very familiar and reassuring. In a way this was fantastic but was also slightly disappointing – Japan didn't feel as "foreign" as I had expected (even wanted?) it to!

We did quickly notice – and appreciate – the impeccable tidiness of Japan – in all areas that we went to in Tokyo, Hakkone, Hiroshima, Kyoto, Nara, and all the stops in between. I don't think I saw a single piece of litter or graffiti. No-one was talking on their mobile phones, let alone listening to music or video without headphones. Public transport was blissfully calm, quiet, and clean. It is amazing to me how beautiful a place can be in these aspects when all of society behaves in the same way.

Of course, at first the language – especially signage and on packaging and labels – was tricky, almost disconcerting, as I could not even recognise any of the characters. I don't necessarily speak Polish, but I can have a guess at some words because I recognise the characters and the combination, but with Japanese, this was absolutely no go! However, after a while, and with the considerable help of Google translate (and Google lens – what a great invention!) then you quite quickly become more at ease and used to not being able to read or understand the Japanese writing.

When in a completely new country (i.e. not the UK or somewhere you have been numerous times, Europe for us, for example) you realise how brand-dependent you are. In a convenience store in the UK, Spain, Malta, or Italy, I recognise and trust brands on sight, but you have to learn all of this from scratch in a completely new domain. Even down to learning that the red background on a vending machine (very obviously, once you know) indicates hot coffee as opposed to the blue background for an iced coffee! You only make that mistake once….!!

We had different Japanese guides with us – each of whom had different, but in some cases very strong, accents. You definitely had to "tune in" and listen carefully. I think working a lot with international students has helped this part of my brain – I found it much easier to understand these guides than a lot of the other tour participants, some of whom were quite rude about the accents. I was uncomfortable with that arrogance – the guides' English was 10,000x better than any of our Japanese!! I especially liked being able to ask these tour guides more day-to-day questions about life in Japan – I wanted to understand about schools and home ownership, and societal trends. Of course, I wanted to know about the tourist information, but I also wanted to delve a bit deeper, and I felt very fortunate to have the opportunity to talk to "real life" Japanese citizens too.

Another element that I realised helped us to feel quite comfortable and "at home" was that the driving in Japan is on the left, the same as in the UK. It didn't register for a few days, but I realised when getting into a taxi on day 3. I think this aspect – of getting on and off coaches, into taxis, and even getting about town as a pedestrian – really prevents the discombobulation that you sometimes can feel abroad, especially in big cities. When a country drives on the same side as yours. I suppose everything is "where it should be" in your mind! You have to consider things less, and it is less jarring.

The journey around Japan was fascinating, and I am so pleased that we saw so many places. I felt we had a real insight into Japan and not just one destination, which is often what you do when you go on holiday. Seeing Mount Fuji so clearly across two days was a real highlight – this is such an iconic landmark and symbol of Japan, and there is no guarantee that the weather will cooperate. I was fully prepared to NOT see it. We felt very lucky and blessed – as Annie, my daughter, noted "You can't make that happen even if you are rich with loads of money" and these days you can't say that about many things!

I hadn't done a "touring" holiday in this way before, and I loved it. It was, however, quite gruelling – definitely not a "fly & flop"! Not ever really properly unpacking, but instead living out of suitcases was odd and not very settling. Constantly packing bags and having them outside the hotel door for 7am for onward transit was disruptive. We covered 15,000–20,000 steps every day and encountered snow, rain and sun so hot that some fellow travellers got sunburned, all in the space of 12 days! I'm also not sure we really had the opportunity to just "breathe" into a place and allow ourselves to sit back, observe, and absorb, as it was so scheduled and busy trip. I really feel as though I would like to go back and do it all again just to have more time to take it in and really embed it into my memories.

iv) The End

I was so sad to leave Japan – especially knowing that I may not go back. It is so far away and it was such an expensive trip that there is no given that I will return. That's a very different feeling from when you leave somewhere closer to home like Croatia or Menorca – you know it is relatively easy to return if and when you decide to; you can just hop on a plane, even if you may never actually do that. The major obstacles to my returning are both the price and the flight – 14.5 hours on a plane is off-putting, and the jet lag on return was gruesome!

However, I'm sure that memory will fade and I have already been heard to say "Next time we go" to my daughter!

Lessons Learned

- Preparation is essential to maximise the enjoyment and minimise the discomfort of being in a new place. Apart from anything else, it makes you more efficient in terms of time! Plan ahead with technology too, download Google maps for the areas you are going to be in so you can use it without data.
- Global technology helps hugely – Uber is so useful because you don't have to try to explain where you are or where you want to go – you just plug it into the app and "bingo"! Language barrier is no longer a problem. Google translate and Google lens are amazing, but for some things you need Wi-Fi and/or data, so plan ahead to make sure you have connectivity!
- Take time to "enjoy the moment". Just sit and absorb the place; the people; the new perspectives. I already feel I need to go back and do it all again and take it in more.
- Someone else organising everything and being "in charge" can be surprisingly liberating. I miss this as much as I miss Japan itself!

Preparation

There is tremendous value in preparing but there should also be the awareness that we can't prepare for everything. Often, the expectation that we are fully prepared will mean, when something inevitably goes wrong, we are less equipped to deal with it as it feels more like a failure than a natural part of the process. Part of the joy of travel is experiencing the unknown and coming away a little better for it. We learn a lot about ourselves in these moments and win or lose in the actual moment, our ability to adapt and survive is seen as a win – often at a distance and with the benefit of time, but a win nonetheless.

There are varying motivations for travelling to study or work abroad. At times, it is a necessity to improve upon current circumstances, or because the provision or resource is not available at home; the opportunity is part of an internal job structure; or wanderlust. For each of these, and there are of course a host more, there comes a point when we have to marshal our sense of fear, concern, worry, and in addition excitement, and simply jump.

We can prepare. We can read. We can talk to people in the know. We can watch endless YouTube videos or consult travel guidebooks depending on your generation and appetite. We can balance it against what we know and compare this to what we expect. But at some point, we have to let go and go.

Communication

Communication across cultures can be challenging and often very humbling. This in itself has great value for those of us who work in international higher education as it makes us more empathetic to international students and colleagues visiting and studying in our home environments. The frustration of not being able to make oneself understood is palpable, and the feelings of inadequacy are very real. This is a normal part of everyday life for international students and staff travelling and working abroad but is nonetheless difficult to navigate because of its frequency for others.

There are ways around this, of course. As Sharon points out above, there are even tech solutions we can use to support engagement and understanding.

> **The Benefits of Cross-Cultural Engagement**
> 1. Increased understanding of others.
> 2. Enhanced understanding of yourself.
> 3. New viewpoints and ways of approaching problems.
> 4. Opening the mind to new possibilities.
> 5. Boost to creativity.
> 6. Improved verbal and non-verbal communication skills.
> 7. Expanding your professional and personal networks.
> 8. Practise the art of reflection.
> 9. Interesting stories to tell.
> 10. You get to write books about your experiences!

Community

Arrival and adjustment to new surroundings are difficult and often quite scary. There will be opportunities, however, to adjust and adapt – even if the period of stay is a short one. There is of course the option of cocooning oneself in the hotel room and shutting out the noise and uncertainty. There is value in this. There is also the opportunity to talk to people; to watch people go about their daily lives; to learn; and to absorb. There is no expectation that you will fall in love with the place in which you find yourself, or that you will take on any of the things, customs, activities or foods that you experience, but you never know. It might just get under your skin.

Travel and international exposure do not come with a specific time stamp. The length of stay does not necessarily translate to a deeper and more sustained understanding – although this is of course possible. A short work trip abroad can open our eyes to new experiences and ways of doing things that will impact our approach to work when we return home.

> **Case Study 8.2: Andrew Disbury's Story: "I Put a Spell on You"**
> **Context**
> My first degree was a BA (Hons) Chinese and French at the University of Leeds, comprising year 2 as an exchange student at Fudan University, Shanghai, China on a bilateral exchange scheme that had

only recently been signed between to two countries. There was also a term of year 3 at the Université de Caen Normandie in France.

Neither of these study abroad experiences cost any additional money, and at the time, the full four-year bachelor's degree was free at point-of-use and supported by a maintenance grant.

Without all these technical instruments, I would never have been the first in my family to go to university, much less study abroad.

My French level on entering university was post-A Level, while I began Chinese ab initio. I had studied French, German, and Latin at school. At university, I also studied one year of Italian. Subsequently, I studied Japanese and am currently studying Spanish. It is only recently that I realised what an unusual Englishman this makes me. For the purposes of these comments, I will focus on studying in China, inevitably the rarer, more different, and more transformative of the two study abroad experiences.

Stages in the Journey

i) The Preparation

Year 1 of the degree was focused on language acquisition in Chinese to enable the second year in China. Study abroad preparation classes were offered, but for the first-year undergraduate adjusting to big city life at university and away from home for the first time, the importance of these classes was not properly understood. There was little about topics we now think of, such as risk appraisal, cultural and psychological preparation for post-Cultural Revolution China, and how 19-year-olds could develop coping strategies for the isolation they would face. Many of these personal experiences that we endured led directly to a professional commitment to student safety and well-being in my subsequent working life.

One cultural and political aspect of studying in China in the early 80s we had no way to understand was the all-encompassing role that The State assumed for everyone, and by extension for its foreign student guests. We were particularly amused when every period of "free time" was organised for us by the Foreign Students' Office. Also, so soon after the Cultural Revolution when so many had lost their lives in a civil war, any contact with anything foreign was potentially life-threatening for the staff and our fellow students. We did not understand how much pressure our teachers were under with the spotlight of this new bilateral exchange agreement firmly on them. Who knew what they had suffered (or even done to each other) not five years before? And now they were expected to behave like teaching foreigners Chinese was entirely normal again.

The French department began our university life by telling us no matter our A-level grades, we had all learned nothing at school and they would therefore be treating us as remedial students. Needless to say, Chinese was more exciting than French from the get-go. Studying in France was completely different from the all-embracing vice-like grip of studying in China.

ii) The Arrival

After an arduous journey from London to Shanghai via Hong Kong, we arrived at night into what we knew to be a large city that was in almost total darkness. Standing in the "baggage claim" area, basically a huge pile of everyone's luggage that we had to sort ourselves and pass over our heads to our student group amid the hustle and bustle of hundreds of local and Hong Kong passengers. We travelled at what felt like a snail's pace through the darkened streets of the city refreshed by bottles of the brightest orange fizzy drink that practically glowed in the dark. Allocated to our twin rooms in the foreign students' building, it was only later exploring the campus that we realised how "up market" our concrete dorm building was compared to the 8-to-a-room Chinese student's conditions. We had hot water twice a day, and heating in the winter. They had hot water once a week and no heating at all. We had our own cafeteria that attempted nods to Western food with milk, yogurt, bread, as well as a variety of freshly-cooked Chinese dishes each mealtime. The Chinese student dining hall looked like somewhere that fed animals.

Never having left the so-called "first world" before, this all came as a tremendous shock. As did the luxury hotels reserved for foreigners' use, and the "Friendship Store" where we could spend foreign currency to buy not only imported goods but domestic goods not available in local stores like unrationed bicycles, the family car of the era. We used grain coupons, cloth coupons, and a special permit that allowed foreigners to spend the Renminbi that our allowance was issued in. It was quite literally another world.

iii) The First Six Months

If anyone had given me a ticket to come home, I would have left and never returned. And how my life would have been different as a result. As someone who had not grown up an ethnic minority, I was totally unprepared for becoming "coloured". Fortunately, the staring, name-calling, and random touching (in the summer wearing t-shirts and shorts it was quite common for blond boys' legs and arms to be stroked by complete strangers in wonder that our "yellow" hair grew everywhere) was almost uniformly positive once we could understand it. Compared to African students' experiences in China at that time, we were looked up to and almost revered for being "foreign" (i.e. "white Western"). But everything about daily life was a huge shock, including the squat toilets which it took me about 20 years to master.

Also shocking was the organised nature of a socialist society. We were also too young to understand that following the Cultural Revolution universities had only just re-opened, and that welcoming international students again was completely new. We had no idea the risks and pressures for our teachers and roommates of just us being present on campus. We also had no concept that we had been provided with the lap of luxury compared to Chinese classmates' dormitories and we could not fathom why they would treat foreign students better than their own.

iv) The Intervening Period

Around Easter, as spring was making things feel more optimistic, I decided I could not discount billions of people in one part of the world by reducing them simplistically to being "The Chinese", an amorphous mass of unfathomable inscrutability. So one day I went out on the street resolved to allow a conversation to happen with the first person who said to me "Hello, you are American?" And it changed my life as the doors opened up to this other world. A few years later, I met up again with that first friend. His English and my Chinese had both improved in the intervening years, and we laughed at how fluent we had thought we were in that first year, and how little we must have understood of each other.

I realised through making this friend and then many others, that my real driver for foreign language learning was not to read and write in the target language, but rather to speak and listen to real, live people. This communication, and through it the acculturation and emotional intelligence that was acquired alongside it, became something that drove me personally, but also later on made me successful in many business negotiations up to the top levels of governmental bilateral relations in education. I have observed many times in business meetings in China the shoulders of my interlocuters visibly relax as they realise "he gets us". My main value to UK colleagues has been the ability to decode the situation, to eavesdrop on what people are saying to each other (not just what the interpreter is telling us in English), and provide advice and suggestions on what the problems really are and how to achieve the compulsory win-win solution to them. This emanated directly from my early desire to communicate.

One very vivid memory was trying to understand what we later learned was the Falklands War from Chinese TV news broadcasts: we had never heard of the Falklands, much less the Malvinas Islands, as the news referred to them, but we understood images of Margaret Thatcher, Union flags, ships, and missiles. We had been brought up to believe the next war would be nuclear and totally nihilistic. Therefore, as we deciphered the news bulletins, we began to prepare mentally for no longer having a home to go back to and becoming impoverished refugees in China.

v) The End

By the time it came to leave I was under China's spell. The only thing I wanted to do, including during my term studying in France, was to return to China upon graduation. I devoted myself to one goal: obtaining a post-graduation scholarship from the British Council to return to China and continue a journey that has now lasted 44 years. I went back to Fudan University in 1984 and then taught English in the pretty town of Suzhou. In 2005 when working in Beijing I returned to Suzhou for a very happy 20th reunion with my class of postgraduate students who by then were living and working all over the world. In spite of me only being a couple of years older than them, they persist in calling me "Teacher" to this day.

On April Fool's Day 2004, I attended a reception at the New Zealand Ambassador's Residence in Beijing. There I met the Chinese man who three years later became my husband. And thus my education and my profession became my family.

A consequence of the isolation we felt in our first time in China was a very intense "Huis Clos" (Sartre) sentiment among our Leeds University classmates: by the end of the year abroad we could no longer stand each other, and on returning to Leeds avoided each other as much as possible for the following year, reengaging with the life we thought we might lose. But by the final year, we realised we truly needed each other, as only our other classmates could understand what we had undergone. Over 40 years, this sense of community has endured, and more than half of our class, whether still connected with China or not, is still in touch and still linked in a very deep way by the bond of studying abroad.

Key Themes

- **Communication:** preparing to study abroad; understanding that you cannot yet know what you don't know; learning strategies for induction and integration; settling in with a flying start; dealing with the low ebbs; and developing multi-cultural emotional intelligence as a key tool in one's skill set.
- **Community:** within the confines of the structures of study abroad, creating your own experience through others, both fellow foreign classmates as well as those from the destination country; learning to give each other close support and personal space to cope individually with the constant pressures of being a foreign student; when returning to domestic studies, applying the learning to support foreign students on campus, and continue global engagement while technically at home.
- **Boundaries** and bottom lines: knowing your personal red lines beyond which you cannot adapt (and maybe pushing them a little to see which ones are really solid); and developing personal coping strategies for when they're reached.

Lessons Learned

- How open is an open mind? My personal answer is that my closed young provincial and religious mind of youth turned out to be pretty adaptable, and to this day, I continue to grow and learn in the face of new opportunities to communicate and build community.

- I have learned over the years that I can always do more than I think I will be able to, and in spite of my constant imposter syndrome, a product of the English class system undoubtedly, I am usually better at things than I think I am.
- Do once, use many times – understanding your transferable skills and how to apply them in new situations and contexts is not something that was embedded in degree programmes in my era – we graduated knowing languages but not how to apply them – but the contemporary opportunities to acquire knowledge while being conscious of its application really benefit the learner of today.
- Acculturation and flexibility aren't personality weaknesses; they are your secret weapon – I used to think that how my English accent changes depending on where I live or who I am speaking to meant my personality was somehow "weak". Now I understand it is all part of my emotional intelligence and communicative competence as a linguist. And I can no longer fathom people whose accent remains stubbornly stable no matter where they live or who they speak to. And the bane of my life are academic colleagues who complain about foreign students' English when they themselves are purely monolingual.

Did I aspire to become a university leader when I was growing up? Absolutely not, it was beyond anything I thought someone like me could ever do. However, I did want to be a teacher, and still my 13 years as a lecturer are among some of the happiest of my career.

Did my study abroad experiences inform my professional practice? Absolutely yes, as I had been that study abroad student and had lived the highs and lows of the "year abroad cycle" personally, to great extremes. Therefore, when recruiting international students over the years and arranging for domestic students to study, work, or volunteer abroad, I have taken the task before them very seriously. I have been able to attend pre-departure briefings around the world and say to parents, grandparents, and other influencers that I understand their emotions as their young person prepares to leave for the UK, as my parents had felt the same way, albeit without having to make the tremendous financial investment overseas families are making now. And that when their young person arrived in the UK, the first person they would meet on campus at the university would be me.

PROFESSIONAL CULTURE

Just as there is an opportunity to learn through engagement with regard to personal cultural norms, so too is there when we consider pedagogical culture. Too often, the rhetoric can be that professional cultures are in opposition in TNE, especially when we consider institutions where the original programme comes from the West and the delivery takes place in the East. This is simplistic of course as there is a wide variety within a single institution, let alone a country or an entire region, but typically the culture of learning in the former can be viewed as student-centred, whereas the latter is very much teacher-led.

The key in all of this is adaptability and compromise. If we are teaching overseas ourselves, then we will have to adapt significantly to what is the dominant pedagogical environment; we are in effect visitors in their space. But we do have opportunities to listen and to learn and to also politely make suggestions as to changes that could be implemented if appropriate. When you work in the education sphere you must never feel as though you cannot at least make some educated and thoughtful proposals.

Academic accreditation and quality assurance are naturally benchmarks of international education, and these govern the practice and regulations under which our activity takes place and yet, the role of interpersonal engagement and cultural awareness – from both a management and a teaching perspective – are often overlooked or fall victim to assumptions.

> There is a dearth of detailed individual accounts about pedagogical strategies used by foreign academic instructors to overcome linguistic and learning culture differences for active learning engagement in China's transnational universities where diversity in staff and student composition is accompanied by diversity in pedagogies employed.
>
> (Che, 2023)

There is a very real need to reflect on our experiences and our responses. When faced with uncertainty, we need to strike a balance between quality assurance and what "we believe to be right" and the knowledge that we are not always going to be approaching the problem in the right way for the context. Learning experiences take place within a local (to the institution) and regional context. There is life outside of the seminar room or the lecture hall. Context and culture are not everything, but they are certainly something that we need to be actively mindful of professionally and personally, for our institutions, our students, and ourselves.

> **Top Tips**
>
> **DO**
>
> - Be curious.
> - Try to engage with others.
> - Prepare but be open to uncertainty.
>
> **DON'T**
>
> - Don't take loss of influence personally.
> - Assume you are always in the right.
> - Be afraid to ask questions.

CONCLUSION

The more you travel and engage with people in higher education, the more you recognise yourself and your challenges in the stories you hear and the experiences you share. There are of course unique issues and contexts that differ considerably across borders but there are shared values and realities that unite us.

We face challenges regarding funding; we experience frustration with bureaucracy; we don't often know the names of the people who work in the same corridor. We struggle with getting numbers through the doors; we struggle with numbers in our classrooms. We work in a shared setting in vastly different contexts. This is a great place to start and one that provides an opportunity for engagement across languages, cultures, and distances.

> Most striking, in the initial conversations, is a shared understanding of the need to respect place, and people, as we transpose and adapt models of education across global contexts. This need for local flexibility and relevance is counterbalanced by the requirement to set shared – or equivalent – academic standards and learning outcomes to frame the student learning experience rigorously.
>
> (Hallett and O'Hara, 2024)

We have likely all experienced examples of kindness and support on our travels. We have seen challenges that put our own firmly into perspective. We have seen opportunities to learn and to grow. We have gained from our travels.

We all have a job to do, and we are all operating under a system of constraints. We are not always right, even if we are always trying to do the right thing.

> **Did You Know?**
>
> A good traveler has no fixed plans and is not intent on arriving.
>
> (Lao Tzu, 780–490 B.C.)

REFERENCES

Che M.A. (2023). Benefits and Challenges of Transnational Education: Reflections from a Sino-British Joint Venture University, in *International Journal of Chinese Education*, Volume 12, Issue 1, January 2023

Hallett, R. and O'Hara, M. (2024). *Transnational education: challenges and opportunities*. AdvanceHE Blog found at https://www.advance-he.ac.uk/news-and-views/transnational-education-challenges-and-opportunities

Managing Transnational Education Partnerships – An Evolving Journey
Nigel Healey and Rob Hickey

Nine

INTRODUCTION

Over the last 25 years, however, a combination of declining public subsidies and burgeoning global demand for higher education have encouraged public universities in the Global North – most notably in the main English-speaking or Anglophone destination countries – to recruit a growing number of international students to their campuses; and when the limits to international student mobility were reached, to provide their educational services on a commercial basis to students in their own countries, either indirectly via a partner organisation or directly via an international branch campus.

For the exporting universities, managing these transnational ventures stretched their organisational capabilities. Few ambitious academic leaders were willing to risk their career prospects by taking on management roles in remote locations far from "head office". Professional services in public universities were ill-suited to coping with cross-border operations, lacking the expertise and capacity to deal with transfer pricing, international taxation, and unfamiliar employment legislation – weaknesses exacerbated by the difficulties of doing business in a foreign language and an alien culture.

While these challenges have been well-documented in the literature, transnational education has been quietly and steadily maturing. As transnational partnerships and international branch campuses have become more deeply established, the management and organisational structures have evolved to make them more sustainable and better "fitted" to local conditions. This chapter draws on a number of case studies and interviews with a range of actors to explore the way that the management of transnational partnerships is adapting to the "new normal" of spatially distributed educational provision.

DOI: 10.4324/9781003649571-10

THE MARKETISATION OF HIGHER EDUCATION

While higher education has always been inherently internationalised with researchers, students, and ideas moving constantly between universities and across borders since the medieval era, it is only relatively recently that internationalisation has become associated with marketisation (de Witt & Merkx, 2012). Historically, higher education has been seen by most societies as a "public good", reflecting the wider social benefits of an educated population in terms of greater economic productivity, increased civic engagement, and reduced criminality and poor health (Slaughter & Leslie, 1997). For these reasons, higher education has typically been provided free at the point of use by public universities, or heavily subsidised by the taxpayer in countries where universities are more autonomous like the UK and Australia. The exception has perhaps been the United States, where tuition fees have long been the primary funding route for higher education. Even here, however, there has historically always been a cost differentiation between subsidised public state universities and private institutions.

This *status quo* came under strain as tertiary enrolment ratios have risen. As Figure 9.1 illustrates, the percentage of the eligible age cohort globally that enrols in tertiary education has grown from 10.5% in 1974 to 41.8% by 2022. In other words, over two in every five school leavers will

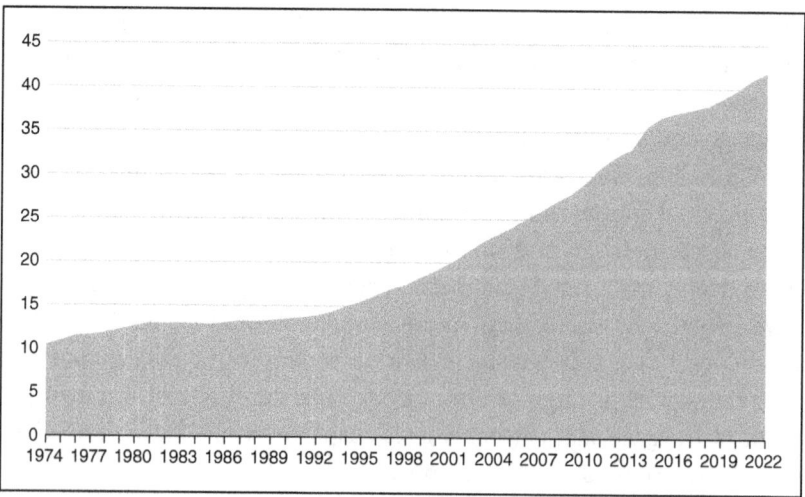

Figure 9.1 World Gross Tertiary Enrolment Ratio (%)
Source: World Development Indicators DataBank (2024).

Table 9.1 Gross Tertiary Enrolment Ratios for Selected Anglophone Countries

	1974	1990	2022
Australia	21.8%	34.6%	106.3%
Canada	46.9%*	89.9%	77.8%**
Ireland	12.0%	28.3%	78.8%**
New Zealand	25.8%	38.8%	79.4%**
United Kingdom	16.5%	26.8%	82.7%
United States	48.7%	69.7%	79.4%

Source: World Development Indicators DataBank (2024)

Notes: *1976; **2021

enter tertiary education across the world. Over this same 50-year period, the number of students in tertiary education has grown from 39.1m to 254.3m (Source: UNESCO Institute for Statistics, 2024).

For the richest nations, tertiary enrolment ratios are much higher than the global mean. Table 9.1 shows the increase in gross enrolment ratios for the six Anglophone countries for selected years. As the proportion and number of school leavers entering universities and colleges rose during the 1970s, the burden on the taxpayer of supporting students grew. By the 1980s, the cost of subsidising public universities began to strain public expenditure and, in succession, the UK (1980), Australia (1986), New Zealand (1989), and Canada (1996) allowed their universities to charge international students tuition fees which could be set at a commercial unregulated rate, to encourage institutions to diversify and grow their revenues.

These Anglophone countries have now become major recruiters of international, full fee-paying students. The recruitment of international students is often termed "export education", as it is a way of exporting "invisible" education services, in the same way that attracting international tourists to the country is a service export.

Table 9.2 shows the picture in 2019, the latest year for which there is data unaffected by the COVID-19 pandemic. Collectively, these six destination countries account for the enrolment of 38% of all internationally mobile students. Referring back to Table 9.1, the influx of international students from the 1980s means that for the Anglophone countries, their recorded tertiary participation rates are now artificially inflated by international enrolments – to the extent that Australia's ratio is over 100% – which is offset globally by deflated participation ratios in sending countries such as India and China.

Table 9.2 International Enrolments

	International enrolments as % of total enrolments			% market share of global market
	2010	2014	2019	2019
Australia	21%	18%	28%	8%
Canada	n/a	10%	16%	5%
Ireland	n/a	7%	11%	0%
New Zealand	14%	19%	21%	1%
United Kingdom	16%	18%	19%	8%
United States	3%	4%	5%	16%

Source: OECD (2023)

FROM EXPORT EDUCATION TO TRANSNATIONAL EDUCATION

Despite the rapid growth of export education, the vast majority of students enrolling in higher education are unable or unwilling to study overseas. Table 9.3 shows that global enrolments in tertiary education have grown from 51.2m in 1980 to 254.3m by 2022. However, while the number of internationally mobile tertiary students studying outside their own country also appears, at face value, to have grown rapidly from 1.1m to 5.6m over the same period, the percentage of internationally mobile students has remained low at around 2% of all enrolments.

Table 9.3 Global Enrolments

	1980	1985	1990	1995	2000	2005	2010	2015	2022
Internationally mobile tertiary students (m)	1.1	1.1	1.3	1.7	2.1	3.0	4.1	4.8	6.4
Global tertiary enrolments (m)	51.2	60.3	68.7	81.7	99.9	139.0	181.7	217.7	254.3
Internationally mobile as % total	2.1%	1.8%	1.9%	2.1%	2.1%	2.2%	2.3%	2.2%	2.5%

Source: World Development Indicators Databank (2024)

There is a raft of reasons for students being resistant to travelling abroad for study, despite the willingness of universities in countries like the UK and Australia to admit them. These include linguistic, cultural, and financial barriers (Wilkins, 2012). Nevertheless, the apparent 2–2.5% ceiling is striking, given the globalisation of business and the prevalence of English as a second language. Over the same 40-year period, and according to the same source, the share of imported goods and services as a percentage of global gross domestic product has grown from 20% to 30%.

Given the financial importance of international student recruitment to universities faced with declining public subsidies, there has been growing interest in the scope for delivering education to students that are unwilling or unable to move to the exporting university to receive their education. This interest has been cyclical (Healey, 2020). In certain periods, it has spiked when international student recruitment from an important source country was adversely impacted by an economic shock. For example, Malaysia was an important source market for Australian and UK universities in the 1990s. When demand for overseas study collapsed after the 1997 "Asian Financial Crisis", many universities that depended on export education pivoted to delivering their programmes in Malaysia through third parties.

At other times, offshore delivery has assumed greater prominence when there were other downward pressures on export education. In the UK, after 2010, when political resistance to immigration led to a more restrictive international student visa regime, the UK Government encouraged universities to expand their offshore enrolments as a way of offsetting revenue lost from international student recruitment. More recently, interest in expanding offshore operations has reintensified as Australian and UK universities begin to reach the limits of their ability to recruit international students to their campuses, with a greater number of public and private institutions entering the market, more restrictive immigration rules, and shortages of student housing.

The term "transnational education" (TNE), sometimes called cross-border education, is used to describe "any teaching or learning activity in which the students are in a *different* country to that in which the institutional providing the education is based" (Global Alliance for Transnational Education, 1997); that is, a university in country A teaches students in country B directly, without the students having to travel to country A to receive the education (e.g. Knight, 2003, 2007).

At a time when people are more digitally connected than ever before, the consumption of services across borders is ubiquitous. Many people spend a high proportion of their waking hours in the virtual world, listening to streamed music, watching videos on their smartphones, and engaging with social media from across the planet. For many people, the quest for information on anything from the sports results to how to fix their washing machine starts with a Google search and often involves watching an explanatory YouTube video.

While online provision appears to be the obvious solution to delivering educational services to students in other countries, the market for higher education has proved remarkably conservative. UK universities such as the University of London, the Open University and the University of Liverpool have all established a significant online presence globally and collectively the UK's 288 universities and colleges had 140,900 students studying wholly overseas in online programmes in 2022/23, up a modest 17% on 2018/19 (HESA, 2024).

This compares with 2.9m students studying on campuses in the UK and 434,000 students studying wholly overseas in face-to-face programmes, suggesting that online education has not yet achieved market acceptance for students paying full-cost for higher educational qualifications (HESA, 2024). Some governments, notably China, do not recognise online degrees, a view shared by many employers. Many students want the social experience of learning that comes from studying full time in a campus setting. While this may change dramatically in the future as higher education is reshaped by artificial intelligence (AI) and virtual and augmented reality (VR and AR), at present, TNE remains dominated by in-person delivery modes.

The literature classifies different ways that universities can provide in-person teaching to students in another country, typically distinguishing between franchising, where a third party delivers the curriculum on behalf of the university, and an international branch campus (IBC) where the university establishes a satellite campus offshore (Healey, 2015; Knight, 2016). The UK's Higher Education Statistics Agency (HESA) collects data using the classifications set out in Table 9.4. Collaborative provision is where the students are studying with a third party, but are registered as students of a UK university, while an overseas organisation means that the students are registered with the third party but qualify for a UK university degree on completion.

Table 9.4 Students Studying Wholly Offshore at UK Universities

	2018/19	2019/20	2020/21	2021/22	2022/23
Overseas campus	28,985	30,960	35,075	37,785	40,060
Distance, flexible or distributed learning	119,985	126,900	139,535	138,015	140,900
Other incl. collaborative provision	163,770	173,815	195,990	224,035	248,095
Overseas organisation	347,375	95,195	111,995	130,995	146,045
Other arrangement	5,510	4,460	5,305	0	0
Total students	665,625	431,330	487,900	530,825	575,100

Source: HESA (2024)

In practice, however, the arrangements for TNE delivery are complex, multi-faceted, and dynamic. This can be best illustrated by considering the two extremes of the TNE spectrum of control (Table 9.5). At one extreme is the "pure" IBC, where the university builds and operates a wholly-owned satellite campus overseas, employing the administrative and academic staff (perhaps by seconding them from the home campus), recruiting and admitting students, following its standard curriculum, assessment and examination and, in all respects, ensuring that the IBC is a clone of the home campus. At the other extreme is a "pure" franchise, where the university licences a third-party college to offer its degrees on an accredited basis, but has no involvement in student admissions, teaching, and assessment.

Table 9.5 The TNE Spectrum of Control

"Pure" IBC	UK University Controls:	"Pure" franchise
√	Institutional branding and marketing	Î
√	Student recruitment and admission	Î
√	Curriculum	Î
√	Learning resources	Î
√	Assessment and examination	Î
√	Administrative staff	Î
√	Academic staff	Î
√	Institutional management	Î

Source: Authors

In reality, it is almost impossible to find an example of either extreme in practice. In the case of IBCs, many host governments require the IBCs to be joint ventures with local partners. The IBCs are normally established as private companies and hire their own staff. Local quality assurance agencies require adjustments to the curriculum to meet local standards. The University of Nottingham Malaysia, often portrayed as the Malaysian campus of the University of Nottingham, is actually a private company in which the university has a minority stake, with staff that are all locally hired, and a curriculum that is controlled by the Malaysian Qualifications Agency.

In the case of franchises, most universities insist that the home curriculum is followed and retain control over assessment and examination to ensure standards are maintained, often processing student results through examination boards on the home campus. They frequently second staff from the home campus to the franchise partner for periods, sometime years, to maintain quality control. The University of Bolton Academic Centre – Ras Al Khaimah, for example, is actually a franchise operation run by Western International College, a private company, but it is a purpose-built academic campus with strong University of Bolton branding.

Not only are both IBCs and franchises almost always somewhere along the spectrum between the "pure" extremes, but depending on the extent to which control over their various functions and activities is retained or delegated, it is quite possible to envisage IBCs that are more like a franchise and *vice versa*. It is the complexity and changing balance of control over the TNE operation that makes its management so challenging.

> **Did You Know?**
>
> - According to Universities UK[1], transnational education is delivered in 225 countries and territories around the world.
> - A British Council survey[2] of HEIs suggests that dual and double degrees are now the dominant model of TNE, followed by online learning and franchise or validation arrangements.
> - The number of International Branch Campuses around the world continues to grow rapidly, from 82 in 2006 to 333 in 2023[3].

THE CHALLENGES OF MANAGING TRANSNATIONAL EDUCATION PARTNERSHIPS

The following subsections explore a range of challenges experienced by the managers of TNE partnerships. These are drawn from a large number of interviews carried out by the authors over a ten-year period, as well as a review of the growing literature on the issue. The final section offers a series of suggestions as to ways in which these challenges can be overcome, or at least mitigated, based on best practice.

Managing One's Own Career as a Senior Academic

One of the most striking challenges is that of appointing and supporting an effective academic manager and champion for the TNE partnership. For universities that want to retain strong direct control of a TNE partnership, the usual approach is to second a loyal and trusted senior member of staff to represent their interests. Even when the university is prepared to take a more arms-length approach, they are likely to choose one of the senior staff to act as the liaison person with the in-country management of the TNE partnership.

A common problem is that these roles are not seen as attractive for career academics. As with any administrative role, they are time-consuming and negatively impact the incumbent's research productivity. Unlike serving as, say, a head of department or dean, these roles are not seen as contributing to the core mission of the university or building the social capital that will support their future career development (Healey, 2016). They could be perceived as not providing a logical stepping stone to an advanced career either internally or elsewhere in the sector. Indeed, often they are perceived as career-threatening: at worst, they are high-risk jobs that could poison a career if the TNE venture fails or falls from favour; at best, they are a job that risks pushing the managers "out of sight, out of mind" and sidelines them in a dead-end role without a meaningful chance of further progression.

As a consequence, the academic managers of TNE partnerships, whether based in-country or operating remotely from the home campus, are often staff near the end of their careers, who have the luxury of taking the positions without jeopardising either their research productivity or promotion opportunities. They are also likely to be mature in their personal lives, with a lower chance of family issues becoming a barrier to successful relocation and acclimatisation to a new country. This has certain benefits. They are likely to know their own universities intimately, have strong personal connections in the key professional services departments such as finance and human resources, and take a long-term view without being overly risk-averse. On the other hand, however, it means that they are less likely to be heavily invested in the TNE partnership, to the extent of wanting to understand local cultures and learn the language of the host country. The contrast could not be greater than with, say, the diplomatic corps, where future ambassadors will be groomed and prepared over decades to take on important assignments in other countries.

Managing Academic Staff

Successfully operating a TNE partnership involves the active engagement of academic staff. In the case of an IBC, this may mean managing a mixture of seconded staff from the home campus and staff that are locally hired and employed by the IBC. In a less mature IBC, there may be the added complexity of managing a high proportion of "casual" temporary staff, who may also be employed by other universities. For more arms-length partnerships, the manager may have to engage staff from the home campus that act as "link tutors", flying out to undertake training of locally hired staff and taking part in quality assurance processes.

Managing these academic staff presents new and distinctive challenges. In general, it is relatively easy to engage staff from the home campus in a TNE partnership initially, but very hard to retain their enthusiasm. Younger staff are often attracted by the prospect of regular travel, but this attraction wanes over time as the novelty wears off and the threat to their career progression and their impaired research performance becomes increasingly apparent. Some universities that have hired academic staff to help manage offshore operations, including explicit conditions in their employment contracts requiring them to travel for extended periods to the TNE partner, find that despite having permanent contracts, young staff members tire of the constant juggling of their personal and professional lives and look for more stable employment.

Where the managers are in-country, recruiting and hiring academic staff locally, the problems can be more insidious. Invariably, the locally-hired staff do not enjoy the same salaries and terms and conditions as seconded staff or staff at the home campus. Initially, they may be pleased with the opportunities offered by working at an institution associated with a major university from the Global North, but typically resentment builds up over time as they begin to perceive themselves as second-class citizens rewarded less for the same effort. In interviews with locally-hired staff, they often complained of the low salaries, limited opportunities for career development, or precarious contracts. Their sense of alienation is intensified by the contrast with their counterparts working as permanent staff at the home campus. There was also disquiet that they were employed on terms and conditions that would be unlawful in the university's own country.

The challenges of managing staff are not restricted to those that are locally hired. Seconded staff range from those on long-term assignments, with pensions and salaries based on those in the home campus plus housing, travel, and school allowances, to those that are shorter-term flying faculty. Like academic management roles in the TNE partnerships, long-term secondments are only attractive to certain groups, often senior staff near the end of their careers. This means that they may be less motivated and willing to adjust to local conditions than younger staff.

On the other hand, many managers report that difficulties with flying faculty (Smith, 2014). Typically, this involves the growing reluctance of younger staff to make repeated visits overseas, as the novelty wears off, pressure to publish in the interests of promotion grows and resistance to their absences from families intensifies. Some universities have resorted to hiring faculty members whose contracts require them to travel frequently to support the TNE operations. While this is partially successful and, by filtering out applicants uninterested in a peripatetic career at the outset, it may mean that they are more committed to TNE, but often the same pressures eventually build to the point where they resign these positions in favour of home-based careers.

Managing Local Students

Most universities with TNE partnerships have decades of experience of teaching international students on campus, and typically employ a significant proportion of foreign teaching and research staff. Their home campuses are diverse and cosmopolitan. However, internationalisation of the student body takes place within a specific cultural context: the foreign students have chosen to travel overseas for study and are a minority population at a campus embedded in the home country.

TNE students, in sharp contrast, are living and studying in their own country, spending part of their days studying in a foreign "academic bubble", but otherwise remain in their cultural and linguistic comfort zone. This bifurcated daily life makes it harder for them to adjust to the alien learning and assessment style to which they are exposed by the TNE partnership. Managers' report that it is much harder to induct and teach students using the problem-based pedagogies and learning styles that they relied on when working at the home campus (Waterval et al., 2014). Their acquisition of English language skills is also often inhibited when compared to international students studying abroad who are completely immersed day and night in the language of instruction.

The fact that most TNE partnerships deliver the curriculum using locally-hired academic staff may exacerbate this issue. Many home universities try to foster critical thinking and encourage students to challenge their teachers. In societies with high power-distance relations, students are culturally unwilling to question their lecturers, and local academic staff may resent interventions from students, reinforcing cultural norms to the detriment of the learning outcomes the TNE partnership is seeking to achieve.

As many TNE partnerships do not have residential facilities, they are forced to recruit commuter students who continue to live with their families. Similarly, TNE partnerships, including physical IBCs, have historically not necessarily provided the same level of social facilities and extracurricular activities for students as traditional university campuses. One consequence of these issues is that the TNE students may not develop the same independence, resilience and social capital as students studying away from home, with teachers reporting that they are much less mature and worldly than the international students they are used to teaching (Heffernan et al., 2010; Tran et al., 2021).

Managing Quality in Transnational Education Partnerships

Most TNE managers believe that one of their central challenges is maintaining the quality of the education — both in terms of the education experience and the academic qualification (Cheung, 2006). The value of the TNE award lies in the proposition that it is equivalent in standing to the same qualification gained at the home campus. If this confidence is eroded in the eyes of students, their parents, or employers, the value proportion of the partnership collapses.

Critics of TNE frequently point to the fact that, compared with the home campus, the TNE operation is a poor imitation (e.g. Altbach & Knight, 2007; Altbach, 2010). Its buildings and facilities are more basic — the ancient libraries, impressive sports complexes, and comprehensive student residences are all absent. Its academic staff are less well-qualified and on more precarious employment contracts, weakening their commitment to the institution. Its research culture is stunted, and its commuter students take an instrumental approach to their learning.

While these criticisms have merits, TNE partnerships typically focus on ensuring that their academic quality assurance systems are rigorous, to try and maintain the parity of the learning outcomes. Using staff from the home campus to moderate assessments and second-mark assignments and examination papers, as well as using the external examiner system to oversee the quality of awards, can all counter the charge of differential standards.

Indeed, in some TNE partnerships where the curriculum and the quality assurance systems are common to both home campus and TNE students, the academic performance of TNE students can sometimes be demonstrably superior, despite the relatively more limited infrastructure and learning resources of the TNE venture (e.g. Heffernan et al., 2010; Wilkins & Juusola, 2018). This may be because the TNE provider can recruit better-qualified entrants onto its programmes than its home-based counterpart. This is particularly likely when the home university is relatively lowly ranked in its domestic market, but the TNE operation is based in a country with considerable unmet demand for higher education.

It may also be because many TNE students live at home with their families, and their parents take a close interest in the progress of their studies. One manager interviewed, who was serving as a seconded head of department in Sri Lanka, reported that some parents requested weekly meetings to receive updates on their child's academic performance and attendance, intervening when their child missed a class (Healey, 2016). In jurisdictions where data protection legislation would make such sharing of confidential information unthinkable, this monitoring of students by parents is alien, but presumably contributes to higher academic performance, all other things equal.

Notwithstanding strenuous efforts to preserve academic standards through quality assurance systems, some managers concede that other cultural factors can undermine their efficacy. This ranges from the reluctance of some junior staff to fail students of higher social status to a strong sense of entitlement on the part of students – "my parents have paid for this qualification" – and concerns about academic integrity, and even the bribery of staff by wealthy students to gain academic favour.

Managing the Balance Between Content and Pedagogy That is Locally Relevant and Institutionally Consistent

There are two contrasting viewpoints in the so-called "Integration–Local Responsiveness" trade-off debate (Shams & Huisman, 2012; Healey, 2018). One perspective argues that TNE partnerships of various shapes and sizes should seek to mimic the programmes, teaching styles, and content of the awarding institution (Shams, 2016). This would demonstrate the equivalence demanded by many overseas governments and would align with the expectations of students, and with the marketing and branding used. Another viewpoint that TNE managers need to consider, however, are the motivations for modifying the academic programmes offered, the pedagogy employed, and the content used to cater for the local context, job market and economic requirements, as well as cultural norms around how students have learned before arriving (Dunn & Wallace, 2006; Heffernan et al., 2010). The most elegant example of the contrast in these two approaches is perhaps the branch campuses led by the Universities of Nottingham and Liverpool in China. Since its creation, Nottingham Ningbo has adopted the "convergence/globalisation" model, which means an unequal marriage with a comparably less well-established Chinese partner. Nottingham controls the curriculum offered, based on a traditional British degree that mirrors those provided in the UK and dominates governance, awarding one UK degree to students. By contrast, Xi-an Jiaotong Liverpool University is built on a "localisation" model, led jointly by equal partners of similarly strong academic standing. The partnership has developed and they co-control a shared curriculum which reflects local employment needs and projected future requirements. Management and governance is balanced, with a Board structure that is constructed to favour local stakeholders, and a degree is awarded to students by both universities (Feng, 2013).

The choices around institutional harmonisation and local relevance present a challenge for TNE managers, as they seek to avoid the hazards of a polarisation between global integration and local responsiveness. In many cases, the most pragmatic solution has been a hybrid model where the curriculum is localised whilst trying to offer equivalent courses and quality as at the home campus.

Building a Research Culture

In most cases, research has much less prominence in TNE partnerships than at the home campus (Knight, 2007; Lane, 2011). This is primarily because the primary objective is commercial – recruiting and teaching students in a competitive environment which relies wholly on tuition fees. While some of the staff may be seconded on a short- or medium-term basis from the home campus, feeling the need to maintain their research productivity to keep their promotion hopes alive, most of the academic staff are typically hired locally on fixed-term contracts and often do not have doctoral degrees.

In such circumstances, encouraging local staff to engage in research necessarily entails cross-subsidising their pump-priming research grants and conference attendance from tuition fees paid by students to cover their education, and asking staff with high weekly teaching loads to undertake research in their own time. TNE managers' report that local staff, often those with doctoral degrees, are attracted to work in TNE partnerships in the hope that, in time, they will be able to transition to a regular academic contract at the home campus (Chapman et al., 2014). For this reason, they may be willing to invest their own time in writing research papers. Certainly, some universities have supported this tendency by seconding some senior academics to the TNE partnership to mentor local staff, but there is invariably a sense of tokensim, given the absence of access to meaningful research grants and long-term promotion prospects for local staff.

Managing Relations with the Home Campus

One manager interviewed summed up a common complaint: "the biggest challenge from day one has been the UK campus" (Healey, 2016). Many managers express frustration with the inevitable power imbalance between the senior management at the home campus and the managers of the IBC and a general sense that the TNE operation is, at best, a distraction from core activities back at the home campus, and at worst, an unwanted thorn in their side (Lane, 2011).

Strains in the relationship between the managers of TNE partnerships and colleagues at the home university range from ignorance and indifference at one extreme to outright hostility at the other. This manifests itself in various practical ways: failure to schedule online meetings involving home-based and TNE staff at times which work for the latter group, which is located in a different time zone; routinely using online learning and conferencing tools that are unavailable or illegal in the country where the TNE partnerships are based; a refusal to change meeting schedules to accommodate the needs of a TNE venture in another jurisdiction; and changes in curriculum and assessment made by home-based course directors and module leaders when consulting the TNE-based staff who have to deliver parallel courses overseas.

A more structural issue is the fact that academic regulations and official policies and procedures have been designed, and often evolved over decades, for the needs of the home campus. These may simply be misaligned with the aims of the TNE venture. There are countless examples. Diversity, equity, and inclusion (DEI) policies, for example, which guide relations between students and staff, are grounded in liberal, progressive cultures. In major TNE markets such as the United Arab Emirates and Malaysia, in contrast, laws limit sexual expression and forbid same-sex marriages. TNE managers in these jurisdictions have reported their fear that local legislation undermines their institutions' perceived commitment to DEI and constrains their ability to host seconded gay and lesbian staff.

Structural misalignment is regularly compounded by the innate conservatism of large bureaucratic organisations like public research universities. Not only have the human resources and finance departments of the home universities been shaped by decades of receiving and accounting for public money, with limited experience of managing cross-border transfers of staff and dealing with foreign tax authorities, but their staff may be resistant to changing the way they operate to accommodate the needs of a relatively small TNE operation compared to the turnover of the home campus. Every TNE manager can cite examples of inflexible bureaucracy at the home campus, refusing to adapt processes or seek innovative solutions to new TNE problems.

Part of this structural misalignment may be intractable. This is because the policies and procedures of the home university – including HR, finance, information systems, and libraries – are shaped both by the institution's history and mission, and the legislative provisions of the home country. In many cases, they are simply inappropriate to a TNE venture, which is a private, for-profit institution operating in a foreign jurisdiction with a different language, culture, and legal system.

Managing Relations with Host Governments

While higher education is steered and subsidised by governments in all countries to a greater or lesser extent, in the Anglophone countries, universities are autonomous institutions and governments often interact with them through the mediation of arms-length funding bodies. The managers of TNE partnerships frequently report that in the host countries, their relationships with the Ministry of Education were much more direct, with one British manager of a Malaysian TNE partnership explaining that "universities here are not self-governing. This is something in British higher education that we just take for granted. Here, we are directly accountable to the Ministry of Education" (Healey, 2016).

In this operating environment, TNE ventures are vulnerable to changes in government policy towards foreign universities. The Chinese Ministry of Education, for example, has shifted its stance on Sino-foreign educational partnerships quite radically over time. In 2014, in response to concerns over the variable quality of many TNE partnerships, the Ministry abruptly issued a directive closing large numbers of programmes. More recently, the Ministry has changed its stance on 2+2 degrees, using its authority to register partnerships to force foreign universities to transition from 2+2 to 4+0 arrangements and so-called "joint education institutes" (4+0 in-country partnerships which are licensed to charge higher tuition fees and recruit students with a higher Gaokao score).

TNE managers must also deal with host regulators, which ministries set up to oversee the academic quality of the programmes offered by TNE partnerships. These regulators may impose a range of considerations on the staffing and resources required by the TNE partnership to maintain its accreditation. A well-known example is the Malaysian Qualifications Agency which sets minimum qualifications for academic staff (they must hold a qualification at least one level higher on the national qualifications framework than the level at which they teach) and minimum contact hours. The Chinese regulator also requires a range of mandatory courses as part of an accredited degree, which the TNE partnership must offer over and above the curriculum provided by the foreign university. The Knowledge and Human Development Agency (KHDA) in the United Arab Emirates, in contrast, forbids TNE partnerships to offer curriculum that is not completely aligned with the content of the degrees delivered by the home campus. It also mandates that the physical space provided to staff and students within the UAE meets strict minimum standards.

Managing Relations with the Joint Venture Partner

TNE partnerships often involve the home university working with a joint venture (JV) partner. In traditional franchise operations, the JV partner is often a private college without its own degree-awarding powers or, in some cases, the autonomy to award qualifications but not the reputation in the local market to charge a commercially-viable tuition fee. In most IBCs, the JV partner is either a local educational institution, or more often an infrastructure partner that finances and builds the campus and employs the local staff.

The challenges of managing the relations with the JV partner range from a principal-agent tension to a power imbalance. This varies considerably with franchise partnerships. In the best-case scenarios, the private college is using the franchise as a means to build its own brand and lean on the relationship with the home university to strengthen its capabilities. Institutions like Taylor's University and Sunway University started out as largely passive JV partners, delivering the franchised degrees of Australian and UK universities. However, they harnessed these partnerships to develop their organisational capabilities, becoming first private university colleges, and then fully recognised private universities in the Malaysian higher education system.

In some cases, however, the private colleges were created to extract the maximum value from the TNE partnership, without a long-term vision. Tensions steadily grew between the college and the home university, with the former seeking to maximise enrolments regardless of the academic standards of the intake, while pressurising the home university to turn a blind eye to plagiarism and poor academic standards. This was often compounded by the private college making wildly inaccurate marketing claims about the status of the home university and the quality of the programmes. Scandals uncovered by the BBC Panorama investigation into the TNE franchise partners of the University of Wales revealed, alongside weak governance by the home university, widespread allegations of corrupt practices by the private colleges franchising the University of Wales's degrees. These revelations were so damaging that they led to the winding up of the University of Wales by the Welsh Government.

While there are sometimes similar principal-agent issues with the JV partners of IBCs, more generally, the complaint from the TNE managers is the power imbalance. As one manager of an IBC complained, the relationship with the management team of the joint venture partner "is complicated because we are minority shareholders in the joint venture. So it's not a partnership of equals". Another noted that "from a governance point of view I think the issue is with the balance of power… this building isn't owned by [the university]…We always struggle with it". Working with private sector JV partners is particularly challenging for the managers of IBCs, who have mostly had little previous management experience within academia, let alone in a commercial environment.

Managing Pressure from Competitors

TNE partnerships operate as private, for-profit institutions. Typically, they rely on tuition fees alone, with no public subsidies from the host government (Qatar is a notable exception, which provides financial support to IBCs through the Qatar Foundation) and recruit students in a fiercely and increasingly competitive environment. Most TNE higher education markets are stratified. Most TNE operations, with the exceptions being the branch campuses of elite western universities like NYU or INSEAD in Abu Dhabi, do not compete directly with the higher status public research universities, but rather with local private colleges and other TNE partnerships. Research has shown that there is little or no competition for students between the TNE venture and either the home campus or other universities in the home country – for students who can afford to travel overseas for study, enrolling at a local TNE provider is a very poor second-best (Tsiligiris & Ilieva, 2022).

Waters and Leung (2014), for example, found that in Hong Kong, there is a clear hierarchy, with students preferring, in turn, to first study at one of the public Hong King universities, then travelling overseas, then either a private local university or college, or a TNE provider. In other words, TNE ventures typically inhabit a space in the competitive hierarchy which is highly competitive and commercial.

Whilst domestic and migrant population and student numbers in regions like the Middle East and Southeast Asia have grown so quickly that demand absorption has driven the establishment and success of many TNE partnerships, one way that some have thrived in the face of this intense competition is to offer programmes and delivery models which tap into new, previously unserved markets. For example, in Singapore, some UK universities offer intensive, part-time degrees which can be completed by working students in only three years, by running classes four or five nights a week. This allows them to access a market for higher education that is off the radar of local competitors. The University of London uses distance learning, either with local provider support or purely online, and niche degrees to carve out a market and reach new students. These include law degrees delivered to incarcerated prisoners and specialist programmes aimed at women in traditional Muslim countries who cannot access more mainstream higher education.

HOW HAVE THESE MANAGEMENT CHALLENGES EVOLVED OVER THE LAST 25 YEARS?

In comparison to the age of many university systems around the world, and indeed hundreds of individual institutions that can be traced by centuries, TNE remains an extremely young phenomenon. The past 25 years have seen huge changes as this approach to providing higher education has matured: new delivery models, new geographical markets, more institutions, and more students. HESA data on universities' TNE enrolments (see Table 9.4) shows that almost all UK institutions are now involved in some form of offshore distance learning, franchising, collaborative provision, or IBCs. The number of IBCs being monitored by C-BERT, a US-based research group, has steadily grown, and as Figure 9.2 illustrates, the range of home countries of IBCs is diversifying, with India and China emerging as key players from the Global South.

As TNE has developed and matured, the challenges for managers working in this sector have evolved. In general, a mixture of experience economies, the sharing of best practice, and the increasing centrality of TNE to the strategy and operations of many exporting universities mean that TNE management has become more professional and mainstream. However, at the same time, the diversification of markets has meant that

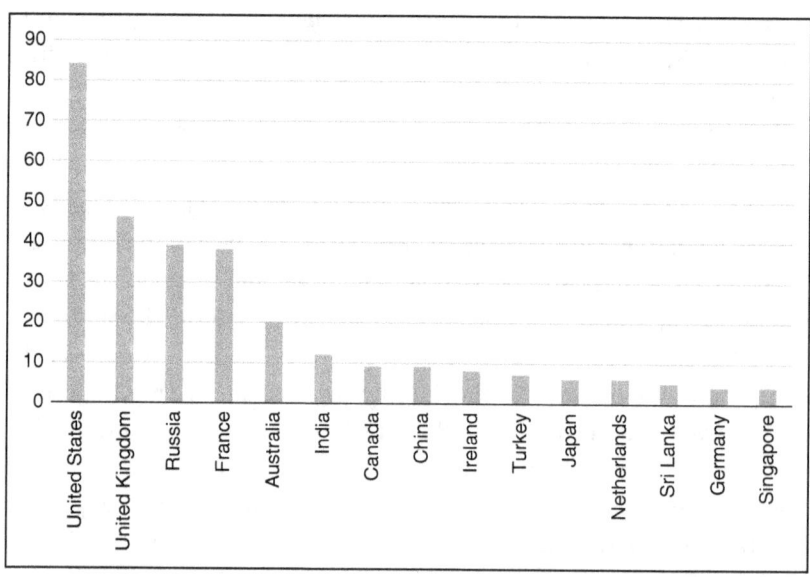

Figure 9.2 Top 15 Home Countries of International Branch Campuses 2023
Source: C-BERT (2023).

new TNE ventures are constantly being established in unfamiliar environments where new cultural, linguistic, and legislative barriers have to be encountered and overcome. The next sub-sections explore how each of the main managerial challenges has developed over the last 25 years.

Managing One's Own Career as a Senior Academic

TNE is assuming an ever-increasing importance within HE. In the UK, for example, it generated £1.07 billion (6.7% of total education-related exports) in 2010, rising to £2.40 billion (8.6%) by 2021 (Department of Education, 2024). Together with the rising importance of export education, this has led to the professionalisation of international higher education – what twenty years ago was a set of interesting projects in universities looking to branch out and explore new markets is now core business within many institutions. A seat is now typically reserved around the Executive Board table for a Deputy or Pro Vice Chancellor (DVC, PVC) with "international" or "global" in their job titles, who would often command a sizeable team of staff at the home campus or overseas. A review of university websites suggests that, in 2024, a strong majority of UK universities employed a DVC or PVC International, or equivalent. This professionalisation is also reflected at sector level. In the UK, Universities UK now operates an arm's length UUK International organisation, focused on lobbying for the interests of institutions on the global stage, commissioning research and data collection, and forging cross-border links.

For the TNE manager, this means that career opportunities are perhaps beginning to change. The professionalisation of international higher education opens up progression routes within the home institution, but also inflates the profile, grading, and likely remuneration available to those leading TNE partnerships.

Managing Academic Staff

The growth of the scale and importance of TNE could also provide some mitigations for the challenges facing TNE managers around managing their academic staff. Many of the most popular markets for TNE, such as the UAE, Qatar, Malaysia, and Singapore, are increasingly being seen as aspirational places to live and work, and IBCs in particular are becoming a preferred career choice for internationally mobile staff, especially through the emergence of independent research cultures.

In many so-called *education hubs*, entirely new employment ecosystems have emerged, with an eclectic mix of international academics attracted to start and continue their careers (Knight, 2011). Dubai perhaps provides the best example, with over 20 IBCs from nine sending countries and dozens of other TNE operations based at partner colleges and institutes (C-BERT, 2023). This means that TNE is beginning to become a viable choice for academics of all backgrounds, career stages, and personal situations. Clusters of TNE, alongside established domestic systems, provide more stability than was the case with standalone outposts, but also create research and career development opportunities of their own.

Managing Local Students
Over the last 25 years, there has been exponential growth in the number of internationally mobile students, with the number enrolled outside their home country more than trebling from 2.1m in 2000 to 6.5m by 2023 (UNESCO Institute for Statistics, 2024). For host countries such as the UK and Australia, this has meant two things: first, teaching international students on the home campus is now core business with many universities having almost as many international as domestic students. For example, latest UK data (relating to 2023) shows that 47.4% of the students enrolled at the University of Cambridge were international, with the percentages for the University of Oxford (45.6%), Imperial College London (49.6%) and University College London (49.9%) close to 50% (HESA, 2024).

Secondly, as source markets have evolved and responded to changes in international student visa regimes, the national mix of international students has changed, first with the dominance of the Chinese market for UK universities, followed by the temporary surge in West African enrolments and latterly the inexorable rise of South Asia as the largest source region. For academic staff, teaching international students from a range of national, linguistic, and cultural backgrounds has become the norm, so that teaching at an IBC is increasingly similar to teaching at the home campus. Both content and pedagogy need to be sensitive to the needs of a mixed cohort of students.

Managing Academic Quality in Transnational Education Partnerships
As TNE has become more important and widespread, academic quality has come under increasing scrutiny from both host and home regulators. For example, concerns over the perceived poor quality of many TNE

partnerships encouraged the Singapore government to establish the Council on Private Education (CPE) in 2009. In a relatively short period of time, it closed down two-thirds of the 2000+ providers that were deemed to be of insufficient standing (Garrett, 2015). In China, the Ministry of Education has also been swift to deregister foreign TNE providers that fail to achieve targets in terms of enrolments and progression, sometimes changing requirements with little notice. The Malaysian Qualifications Agency regulates both the curriculum and the delivery of programmes by foreign providers, including setting minimum standards in terms of the qualifications of teaching staff and the number of contact hours per programme.

At the same time, home regulators like the UK's former Quality Assurance Agency have carried out academic audits of the TNE partnerships of UK universities. There is clearly a risk to the standing of the national higher education sector if the brand is damaged by the actions of a few rogue providers. The increased scrutiny by host and home regulators, coupled with experience economies of years of assuring the quality of TNE activities and facilitated by dramatically improved online communications tools like MS Teams and Zoom have together transformed the management of academic quality since 2000.

Managing the Balance Between Content and Pedagogy that is Locally Relevant and Institutionally Consistent

If academic quality assurance for TNE partnerships has improved over the last 25 years, the tension between local relevance and institutional consistency has, arguably, become more intense. In part, this is because host regulators often place demands on the curricula of TNE programmes, in terms of content and contact hours. Most notably, the Chinese Ministry of Education requires a number of mandated courses to be included in an accredited programme. However, as TNE partnerships have matured, the traditional "mother-child" relationship between the home institution and the TNE operation has become strained by the increasing assertiveness of the latter, seeking greater autonomy and responsiveness to local student demand. There are examples where, bound by the host regulator's stipulation in some markets that TNE operations must offer the same curriculum as the home campus, a programme developed for the host market has been introduced at home.

Building a Research Culture

For most of the last 25 years, TNE partnerships have been teaching-focused. Almost exclusively financed by student tuition income, they have tended to rely on temporary staff, employed on teaching-only contracts with high contact hours. Over time, however, there has been growing recognition that building a basic research culture is critical to long-term sustainability, both in terms of staff recruitment and retention and building a reputation in the local market (Lane, 2011; Garrett, 2018).

TNE partnerships have also evolved from the former reliance on franchising degrees to private colleges towards double and joint degrees with peer universities. The latter tend to emphasise research-informed teaching, especially at postgraduate level where capstone research projects are often important graduating requirements.

Finally, in some host markets, notably China, Sino-foreign universities (IBCs) are eligible for research funding, encouraging staff to focus on research that aligns with the priorities of the host government. The University of Nottingham Ningbo, for example, has established a China Beacons Institute, with locally-funded research programmes in areas including intelligent manufacturing, green chemicals, energy and life science, and health care.

Despite the advances made in integrating a research base to TNE partnerships, multiple challenges remain including the disproportionate reliance on non-doctorally qualified teaching staff, access to host research funding councils and the potential misalignment between the disciplines demands by fee-paying local students – overwhelmingly business management and computer science – and the research needs of the host society (McBurnie & Ziguras, 2007).

Managing Relations with the Home Campus

As discussed above, the relations between the home campus and TNE partnerships will evolve, as they become more financially valuable and with greater advocacy via a senior member of the university leadership team. As a minimum, this should ensure that the Vice Chancellor, or a senior nominee, is always present at the TNE graduation ceremony, but often it will be the case that TNE in general, and specific partnerships in particular receive regular senior attention. From one perspective, this could be seen as a challenge for the TNE manager, with possibly increased scrutiny and pressure, but from another, it could mean increased support and investment to succeed.

The practical challenges for TNE managers of operating remotely, and in most cases in a different time zone, from the sending institution's main campus are also changing, from a technological and cultural capacity. The emergence of video conferencing as the default method of engagement in many institutions now mean that meetings with remote partners or campuses are no longer seen as novel or strange. At universities where intra-campus communications are often Zoom or MS Teams-based, or where home working is commonplace, this also means that those working overseas no longer feel as "different" as they once did. The extent to which this supports the cultural acceptance of TNE is not supported with any empirical evidence, but logic would suggest that it should trend in that direction.

Managing Relations with Host Governments

The management of relations with host governments has become more complex and nuanced over the last 25 years. On the one hand, host governments have become more confident and assertive in terms of dealing with foreign universities. In some cases, the aim of enhancing the quality and diversity of the national higher education systems by welcoming foreign TNE providers has come to the fore, but with host governments increasingly demanding specific disciplines and partnership arrangements. In other cases, host governments may seek to attract foreign universities to help them create export hubs to attract regional internationally mobile students, or seek leading Western universities to set up IBCs to promote soft power agendas.

As host governments have become more sophisticated and discerning in their choice of a foreign university, it forces exporting universities to ensure that they can align, and constantly realign, to the needs of the host country if their TNE partnerships are to remain viable.

At the same time, the political landscape for TNE is becoming more complicated and multidimensional. Once dominated by universities from the Global North, universities from the Global South are now actively involved in establishing IBCs, often as part of their government's geopolitical ambitions. China and India, for example, have both become important exporters of IBCs but as part of initiatives like the Chinese "Belt and Road" which involves bilateral/multilateral government relations. There is a danger for universities from the Global North that their once dominant position in TNE is eroded by non-commercial, politicised competition from the emerging global superpowers in the South.

Managing Relations with the Joint Venture Partner

One of the biggest changes has been the power dynamics between home universities and JV partners. In the late 1990s, most TNE involved universities collaborating with private, for-profit colleges to offer franchised and validated degrees. The potential "principal-agent" problems were clear, with universities seeking to minimise their financial exposure by contracting delivery to a third party, while the JV partners sought to maximise their financial returns by "selling" the university's degrees, sometimes with little regard for the quality of either applicants or the integration of assessments and examinations.

There has been a marked shift in the nature of TNE partnerships, with a decline in franchising and validation, expansion in IBCs and distance-learning, but most notably a greater focus on TNE through joint and double degrees with peer universities in third countries. Increasingly, IBCs are established as partnerships with universities in the host country — the foreign-Sino IBCs of the University of Nottingham/Zhejiang Wanli University and the University of Liverpool/Xi'an Jiao Tong University are the best-known examples.

Managing Pressure from Competitors

Two decades ago, many TNE operations were amongst the very few operating in their territory, with the home university system largely catering for a different segment of the student market and local competition limited. This is no longer the case in many of the more popular host markets for TNE in the Middle East and Southeast Asia. Competition is fierce in many, with home system universities growing through state investment, many offering franchised or validated courses with "western" partners, a rise in private, independent for-profit providers, and continued and significant investment in bricks and mortar IBCs.

For TNE managers, this means a renewed emphasis on providing relevant, distinctive and attractive programmes, taught in a way that meets the needs and expectations of students. Depending on the nature of the provision, pricing will also be important, as will the retention of good-quality academic staff. With maturity, however, have come more resources and better knowledge of local markets in the host countries of TNE partners and IBCs. TNE managers now have better data on the students they are seeking to cater for and have been able to modify their operations to fit.

CONCLUSION

For many of the Anglophone public research universities, venturing into TNE partnerships has been a major challenge to their organisational capabilities. Arcane decision-making systems based on principles of collegiality, bureaucratic structures shaped by decades of public subsidies and political direction, and a culture rooted in the principle that higher education is a public good, all combined to militate against successful overseas ventures. Some high profile TNE enterprises were scuppered by faculty resistance in senates (e.g. University of Warwick); others failed because the business cases were overly optimistic and lacked rigour; others stagnated, ignored or positively disavowed by faculty at the home campus, becoming casualties of the inevitable change in senior university leadership which saw the departure of a key TNE champion (e.g. UNSW's abrupt decision to abandon its Singapore campus in 2007 following the arrival of a new Vice Chancellor is an extreme case in point).

However, over the last 25 years, there have been deeper underlying forces at work which have gradually propelled TNE into the mainstream. First, universities in countries like Australia and the UK have become increasingly "public" in name only, with a minority of their funding now coming from taxpayer funds. This marketisation of the sector has meant universities having to operate more like commercial entities, professionalising their support services and sharpening their decision-making. Second, this marketisation has forced universities to dramatically expand international enrolments, to cross-subsidise domestic students where numbers are often capped and tuition fees are still publicly controlled. As source markets have evolved over time, the mix of international students on home campuses has shifted steadily from Southeast Asia, to China, West Africa, and India, compelling faculty members to adapt their pedagogies and forcing administrators to come to grips with new markets.

Third, the relentless growth in global demand for higher education, the tightening constraints on further increase in international enrolments and the opening up of host markets to foreign universities has driven the expansion of TNE, to the extent that it is now a core part of the business model for many Anglophone universities. The increased importance of international recruitment and TNE has also seen the emergence of a new cadre of university managers. In the past, international offices were largely administrative functions that concerned themselves with coordinating student exchange and dealing with international student marketing and recruitment. In the last decade, C-suite level positions like pro vice chancellor and deputy vice chancellor/vice president (global) have become commonplace, with organisational structures that include managers for transnational partnerships.

Whether TNE remains embedded in the organisational architecture of universities is an open question. The forces driving the demand for TNE – rising living standards and educational aspirations in developing countries which lack the domestic capacity to absorb demand – may prove transitory as investment in local institutions drives up national tertiary participation rates. There is evidence that some TNE partnerships may gradually transform into national universities (e.g. Sunway and Taylor's Universities in Malaysia), suggesting that in some markets TNE is not a stable endpoint. Nevertheless, over the last 25 years, TNE has evolved from being a fringe activity, managed by enthusiastic amateurs in the face of bureaucratic inertia on the part of the home universities, to being a core business for most Anglophone universities.

Top Tips for managers establishing an International Branch Campus (adapted from Hickey & Davies, 2022):

1. Align with the institutional strategy.
2. Understand the political and regulatory landscape, and secure host government support.
3. Evidence your decision-making, considering all TNE options.
4. Prioritise managing your internal and external stakeholders.
5. Secure local representation within the governance regime.
6. Balance teaching, research, and the student experience.
7. Deliver programmes that are influenced by both the home campus and local context.
8. Aspire to provide programmes at a range of levels and disciplines.
9. Think long term around financial returns.
10. Source at least some staff locally.

NOTES

1 Universities UK, 2024. *Measuring transnational education: changes to the TNE data landscape.* Published online, available from: https://www.universitiesuk.ac.uk/universities-uk-international/insights-and-publications/uuki-blog/measuring-transnational-education

2 British Council, 2022. *The Value of Transnational Education Partnerships.* Published online, available from: https://www.britishcouncil.org/sites/default/files/value_tne_fullreport.pdf
3 Cross-Border Education Research Team, 2023. *C-BERT International Campus Listing March 2023.* [Data originally collected by Kevin Kinser and Jason E. Lane]. Available from: http://cbert.org/intl-campus/. Oxford, OH: C-BERT.

REFERENCES

Altbach, P., 2010. Why branch campuses may be unsustainable. *International Higher Education,* 58, pp. 2–3.

Altbach, P., and Knight, J., 2007. The internationalization of higher education: Motivations and realities. *Journal of Studies in International Education,* 11, pp. 290–304.

British Council, 2022. *The Value of Transnational Educational Partnerships.* https://www.britishcouncil.org/sites/default/files/value_tne_fullreport.pdf

Chapman, D., Austin, A., Farah, S., Wilson, E., and Ridge, N., 2014. Academic staff in the UAE: Unsettled journey. *Higher Education Policy,* 27, pp. 131–151.

Cheung, P., 2006. Filleting the transnational education steak. *Quality in Higher Education,* 12(3), pp. 283–285.

Cross-Border Education Research Team, 2023. *C-BERT International Campus Listing March 2023.* [Data originally collected by Kevin Kinser and Jason E. Lane]. Available from: http://cbert.org/intl-campus/. Oxford, OH: C-BERT.

Department for Education, 2024. *UK revenue from education related exports and transnational education activity.* Published online, 21 March 2024, available from: https://explore-education-statistics.service.gov.uk/find-statistics/uk-revenue-from-education-related-exports-and-transnational-education-activity

Dunn, L., and Wallace, M., 2006. Australian academics and transnational teaching: An exploratory study of their preparedness and experiences. *Higher Education Research and Development,* 25(4), pp. 357–369.

de Wit, H., and Merkx, G., 2012. The history of internationalization of higher education. In D.K. Deardorff, H. de Wit, and J.D. Heyl (eds.), *The SAGE handbook of international higher education,* Thousand Oaks, CA: Sage, pp. 43–57.

Feng, Y., 2013. University of Nottingham Ningbo China and Xi'an Jiaotong-Liverpool University: Globalization of higher education in China. *Higher Education,* 65(4), pp. 471–485.

Garrett, R., 2015. The rise and fall of transnational higher education in Singapore. *International Higher Education,* 39, pp. 9–10.

Garrett, R., 2018. International branch campuses: success factors. *International Higher Education,* 93, pp. 14–16.

Global Alliance for Transnational Education, 1997. *Certification Manual.* Cited in: Adams, T. (1998). The operation of transnational degree and diploma programs: The Australian case. *Journal of Studies in International Education,* 2(1), pp. 3–22.

Healey, N.M., 2015. Managing international branch campuses: What do we know? *Higher education quarterly,* 69(4), pp. 386–409.

Healey, N.M., 2016. The challenges of leading an international branch campus: The 'lived experience' of in-country senior managers. *Journal of Studies in International Education,* 20(1), pp. 61–78.

Healey, N.M., 2018. The optimal global integration–local responsiveness tradeoff for an international branch campus. *Research in Higher Education*, 59, pp. 623–649.

Healey, N.M., 2020. The end of transnational education? The view from the UK. *Perspectives: Policy and Practice in Higher Education*, 24(3), pp. 102–112.

Heffernan, T., Morrison, M., Basu, P., and Sweeney, A., 2010. Cultural differences, learning styles and transnational education. *Journal of Higher Education Policy and Management*, 32(1), pp. 27–39.

Hickey, R., and Davies, D., 2022. The common factors underlying successful international branch campuses: Towards a conceptual decision-making framework. *Globalisation, Societies and Education*, 22(2), pp. 364–378.

Higher Education Statistics Agency, 2024. *Open data and official statistics*. Online, available from: https://www.hesa.ac.uk/data-and-analysis.

Knight, J., 2003. Updated definition of internationalization. *International Higher Education*, 33, pp. 2–3.

Knight, J., 2007. *Cross-border tertiary education: An introduction*. Paris: OECD Publishing, pp. 21–46.

Knight, J., 2011. Education hubs: A fad, a brand, an innovation? *Journal of Studies in International Education*, 15(3), pp. 221–240.

Knight, J., 2016. Transnational education remodelled: Toward a common TNE framework and definitions. *Journal of Studies in International Education*, 20(1), pp. 34–47.

Lane, J.E., 2011. Global expansion of international branch campuses: Managerial and leadership challenges. *New directions for higher education*, 155, pp. 5–17.

McBurnie, G., and Ziguras, C., 2007. *Transnational education: Issues and trends in offshore higher education*. Florence: Routledge.

OECD (Organisation for Economic Co-operation and Development), 2023. *Education at a Glance 2023*. Online, published 12 September 2023. Available from: https://www.oecd.org/en/publications/education-at-a-glance-2023_e13bef63-en.html

Shams, S., 2016. Sustainability issues in transnational education service: A conceptual framework and empirical insights. *Journal of Global Marketing*, 29(3), pp. 139–155.

Shams, F., and Huisman, J., 2012. The role of institutional dual embeddedness in the strategic local adaptation of international branch campuses: Evidence from Malaysia and Singapore. *Studies in Higher Education*, 41(6), pp. 955–970.

Slaughter, S., and Leslie, L.L., 1997. *Academic capitalism: Politics, policies, and the entrepreneurial university*. Baltimore: The Johns Hopkins University Press.

Smith, K., 2014. Exploring flying faculty teaching experiences: Motivations, challenges and opportunities. *Studies in Higher Education*, 39(1), pp. 117–134.

Tran, L., Lea, T., Phan, H., and Pham, A., 2021. "Induction and off you go": Professional development for teachers in transnational education. *Oxford Review of Education*, 47(4), pp. 529–547.

Tsiligiris, V., and Ilieva, J., 2022. Global engagement in the post-pandemic world: Challenges and responses. Perspective from the UK. *Higher Education Quarterly*, 76(2), pp. 343–366.

UNESCO Institute for Statistics, 2024. *International Students*. Online, published 24 January 2024. Available from: https://www.migrationdataportal.org/themes/international-students

Universities UK, 2024. *Measuring Transnational Education: Changes to the TNE Data Landscape*. Online, available from: https://www.universitiesuk.ac.uk/universities-uk-international/insights-and-publications/uuki-blog/measuring-transnational-education

Waters, J., and Leung, M., 2014. 'These are not the best students': Continuing education, transnationalisation and Hong Kong's young adult 'educational non-elite', *Children's Geographies*, 12(1), pp. 56–69.

Waterval, D., Frambach, J., Driessen, E., and Scherpbier, A., 2014. Copy but not paste: A literature review of crossborder curriculum partnerships. *Journal of Studies in International Education*, DOI: 10.1177/1028315314533608.

Wilkins, S., 2012. Student choice in higher education: Motivations for choosing to study at an international branch campus. *Journal of Studies in International Education*, 16(5), pp. 413–434.

Wilkins, S., and Juusola, K., 2018. The benefits & drawbacks of transnational higher education: Myths and realities. *Australian Universities' Review*, 60(2), pp. 68–76.

World Development Indicators Databank, 2024. *World Development Indicators*. Online, available from: https://databank.worldbank.org/reports.aspx?source=2&series=SE.TER.ENRR&country=

Developing TNE Partnerships – The End – Planning or an Amicable Separation

Judith Lamie and Christopher Hill

Ten

INTRODUCTION

During a 2023 press conference, following his team's elimination from the NBA basketball playoffs, Giannis Antetokounmpo, a previous champion and most valuable player for the Milwaukee Bucks, was asked about failure. The clear implication was that this past season had been a failure as his team had been eliminated from the playoffs and not repeated their ultimate victory of becoming national champions in 2021. Giannis turned the question around on the reporter and asked him, in turn, if he was promoted every year and if not, did every year then count as a failure? Giannis went on to explain that progress was what mattered, putting in the effort and getting better. He said:

> There's no failure in sports. There's good days, bad days, some days you are able to be successful, some days you are not, some days it is your turn, some days it's not. That's what sports is about. You don't always win.[1]

This is a powerful lesson to learn. How we define success is critical and must be discussed and agreed at the outset of partnership activity. TNE has traditionally been defined, in terms of success, by numbers. Number of students. Number of programmes. Number of pounds/dollars (or the currency of your choice), one clear assumption here being that the higher the numbers, the higher the returns. However, our understanding of TNE is that profit and returns are not immediate, and the value of entering into a TNE partnership arrangement must be viewed through a different lens (Hill et al., 2022).

Throughout this chapter, we reflect on what some of the practicalities might be, from the types of governance and legal procedures you might need, to how you can try to make the most of the ending and any lessons that you will have learned along the way. Unsurprisingly, structures and policies are noted as being important, but as with all things, it is also about the people and in particular about stakeholder management; remembering that stakeholder management begins at home.

Douglas Proctor: Reflections on the Lived Experience of Exiting TNE Partnerships – Saying Goodbye

Saying goodbye is the hardest thing to do... or so says the adage, but is this really the case in relation to transnational education (TNE) partnerships? Or have we reached a point in the evolution of this type of academic/commercial partnership where going our separate ways has become an easier proposition?

Several years back, I advocated for a greater understanding of the principles of stakeholder engagement among staff in higher education institutions, noting the difficulties faced by universities in implementing a strategic partnership agenda (Proctor, 2016). In so doing, I called for greater professionalism in approach, as well as a broader recognition that effective international partnerships rely just as strongly on managing internal stakeholders as they do on managing external partners. Drawing on Australian examples, I then outlined the potential scale and breadth of internal stakeholders for different types of international partnerships, noting that complex international agreements involving transnational education would, for example, touch on a much wider range of academic and professional staff within an institution than a student mobility agreement. While these reflections appear somewhat facile eight years later, I am still led to question whether institutions *effectively manage internal stakeholders* in relation to their course delivery overseas, that is, their transnational education. Personal experience indicates that we have made vast strides in this, but I still believe there is room for improvement. Two examples serve to bring this to light.

Some years back, I was working at an institution with a small set of long-standing TNE programs in Southeast Asia. Given their longevity, the webs of relationships with these partners – between academics, professional staff and senior leaders – were extensive, and many colleagues believed in the "friendship" between our university and the partners. In the early days, these TNE partnerships had been managed directly by the Faculties, but – with increasing regulatory oversight by what was then called the Australian Universities Quality Agency (AUQA) – the university had moved to establish central oversight and coordination of TNE partnerships, just as other universities had done nationwide.

Following an extensive strategic, financial and academic review of its TNE partnerships, this particular university had taken the decision to teach out one of its partnerships in Malaysia. As per university policy, that decision had been widely discussed before endorsement by both the Academic Board and the required high-level strategy/finance committee; it had the full support of the relevant Dean and the Vice-Chancellor. Given the involvement of the partner institution in the review, key staff at the partner institution also had advance notice of the review's findings and recommendation.

As such, in response to the university's decision, carefully worded correspondence was drafted (in the name of the Vice-Chancellor) to send to the partner institution recommending a teach-out plan. Naturally, this correspondence acknowledged the longevity of the partnership and the value of the relationships formed, but also pointed to the significant consideration which had been applied to the decision in the context of a shifting regulatory environment in Australia.

All good so far. In many ways, a textbook approach to the closure of a teaching partnership. But then, things took an interesting turn.

Staff in the International Office (which was managing the TNE partnership and its proposed teach-out) had done their best to ensure that all internal stakeholders were alert to the review and its recommendation. However, they had not included the Graduations Unit in their internal outreach, and had therefore overlooked an influential internal stakeholder with very close connections to the partner. As it transpired, the Manager of the Graduations Unit had accompanied the Vice-Chancellor on visits to the partner for many years in a row to oversee offshore graduations. She had established a strong personal relationship with the CEO of the partner institution, and had personally handled arrangements for the post-graduation alumni events which had been held in the CEO's private residence.

Unsurprisingly, this staff member was surprised at the university's decision to exit this partnership (as she had not been involved or consulted at any stage) and possibly saw this as a slight to her professionalism. As such, before long, staff in the International Office found that they were mounting a rearguard action against an aggrieved staff member with very close ties not only to the Vice-Chancellor but also to the partner.

The story becomes somewhat messy from here on, suffice to say that the university did end up teaching out this partnership. However, the journey to that outcome was made significantly more bumpy by way of this failure of internal stakeholder management.

Turning to the present day and my current institution, I've sought to put in place a structure and framework at Swinburne University of Technology which seeks to mitigate this particular risk through an advanced approach to stakeholder management.

Swinburne has a mature approach to transnational education, borne out of a long history of teaching partnerships, not least its longstanding branch campus in Sarawak (East Malaysia) which has been run in partnership with the Sarawak State Government since 2000. To ensure appropriate governance and management of its third-party teaching partnerships, Swinburne's TNE team is clearly structured into two areas – academic operations and partner relations. With collaborative provision (aka franchising) the most common form of TNE in the Australian context due to the requirements of our current regulatory body, the Tertiary Education Quality and Standards Agency (TEQSA), the academic operations team works closely with Schools to enable the teaching and quality assurance of units and degrees by partners.

Meanwhile, the partner relations team manages the partners and the complex sets of internal and external stakeholders involved in each partnership. This stretches from formal governance at one end of the spectrum (running Joint Management Committees and overseeing annual partner quality reviews) to day-to-day interactions and problem-solving at the other. Within the university, the partner relations team is in regular contact with each of the divisions which support TNE partners (including the graduations team, you'll be pleased to note). An extensive Wiki site provides guidance to internal stakeholders on all aspects of TNE at Swinburne, from who the partners are and what they teach, to how TNE works, to who to contact about specific academic or partnership concerns.

While I readily admit that no partnership framework based on people-to-people connections will ever be perfect, I'm confident that Swinburne – in 2024 – has the right set of structures and people to ensure that internal and external stakeholders are managed to best effect.

In parallel with the example above, Swinburne is currently teaching out some of its TNE partnerships following a cycle of review. While these decisions are never taken lightly and are always somewhat contentious (at least in the eyes of the partner), I'm pleased to confirm that we have not (as yet) seen any disruption to this intention from aggrieved internal stakeholders.

PLANNING YOUR EXIT

It may seem pessimistic, but the best time to plan an exit from a TNE partnership is right at the beginning when everyone is positive and the last thing you want is for something to end. What might arise that would cause an end to the partnership (or this project within the partnership)? What will happen to the staff and the students? What can you plan for and get in place ready for such an eventuality? You will be undertaking the planning of your exit at the beginning with the partner, as you will both need to sign up to all of the components involved, and the agreement will form part of your MOU (Memorandum of Understanding) or MOA (Agreement). It is advisable at this stage to design a generic process, not only because time will change the fine detail as you move through the partnership, but also because you will be able to use the shell of the exit plan again. Once you have designed the generic document, you can tailor it to the specific partnership context. Once again it is useful here to provide a series of scenarios.

First would be your ideal exit schedule and teach-out commitments over a short to medium-term period. It may be that you are both in agreement that the partnership is not working, but that there is no need to stop immediately, and therefore, you are looking at phasing out activity, teaching-out current students and not recruiting any more. It is vital at this point that you are still fully committed for the sake of the students and staff in particular. They must not feel as though their degree or experience has been downgraded as a result of the forthcoming exit.

Second, there may be a need to terminate the agreement more swiftly. A circumstance may have arisen that means that you have to shut down straight away. This is rare, but it does happen. Thought therefore needs to be given as to how the students will continue with their study when they may not, for example, be able to attend classes in person. One advantage of the global health crisis was that most institutions had to pivot online, and although the experience was far from ideal, it does mean that the capability is there. There are significant challenges to this scenario, not least those associated with recognition of the qualification, but it is an extreme situation and therefore would require flexibility wherever possible.

When setting up the partnership, you will hopefully have determined where your red lines are (Figure 10.1). These could fall within academic, regulatory, governance, or financial areas and will closely align with your core priorities and goals over the short, medium, and long term.

Financially, for example, it is extremely unlikely that a TNE arrangement will provide significant flow-through income for the

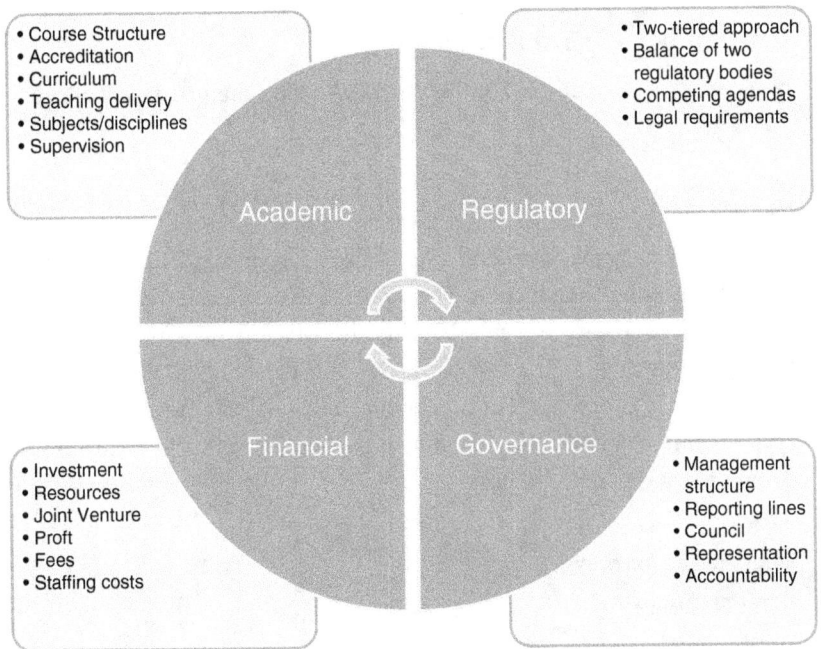

Figure 10.1 Red Lines of Partnership
Source: Authors

first few years. However, it is important to set up trigger points so that you can monitor progress and then act accordingly. Your governance and management structures should enable you to do this. It may be tempting to set meetings up less frequently once the partnership has been established, you will be busy with the actual running of the activity, but much better to have a meeting scheduled in the diary, that can finish promptly, than only discover after the event that there have been issues brewing. The advent of new technology can assist greatly here and there is no excuse for not having regular communication even when you are on the other side of the world (although staggering the timing is preferable and polite).

Once you have decided where your red lines are, you then need to determine for each what the decision-making process is. Who can make the decision? There may be legal constraints here. Do all parties need to agree? How will the decisions be recorded? What will your communication plan be – externally (to your various stakeholders) and internally? Who will do what? What will be said? What channels will be utilised? Hope for an amicable separation, but plan for one that will not be.

Case Study 10.1: YALE-NUS

https://news.yale.edu/2021/08/26/yale-nus-be-merged-new-college-2025

Context

Yale-NUS College is a liberal arts college, established in Singapore in 2011 as a partnership between Yale University and the National University of Singapore. Yale-NUS is the first liberal arts college in Singapore and Yale's first institution outside of Connecticut. The acceptance rate for admissions is between 3% and 7% from the 8,000 applications received annually, and it is therefore an elite institution occupying a distinct position and identity.

Stages in the Journey

i) The Preparation

Under the presidency of Richard Levin, Yale began developing a "internationalization" strategy that included expanding financial resources for international students and study abroad programs, founding the Yale World Fellows and the Center for the Study of Globalization, and joining the International Alliance of Research Universities. Richard Levin and National University of Singapore President Tan Chorh Chuan discussed the concept of a joint liberal arts college at the 2009 World Economic Forum in Davos, Switzerland, and less than two years later, a prospectus was presented to Yale faculty for a liberal arts college in Singapore.

ii) The Intervening Period

Yale-NUS is a four-year, fully residential undergraduate institution. The initial intake in 2013 (graduating in 2017) comprised 157 students. The full capacity of the college is 250 students per graduating class. Students select their major at the end of their second year, having by that point completed two years of the Yale-NUS Common Curriculum. Upon graduation, successful students were awarded a Bachelor of Arts degree with Honours or a Bachelor of Science degree with Honours from Yale-NUS College, conferred by NUS.

iii) The End

The decision to end this partnership was initiated by NUS President Tan Eng Chye, who communicated this to Yale President Peter Salovey in July 2021. By all accounts, this decision was unexpected on the part of Yale and was taken without input from senior representatives at Yale. Yale representatives will play no role in the oversight of the new college.

In 2021, The National University of Singapore (NUS) announced the creation of a "New College" that would, in 2025, merge Yale-NUS College with NUS's University Scholars Programme. This was presented as falling under the larger reorganisation of NUS's academic structures.

Key Themes

- **Communication and Engagement.** The partnership was created through discussion and trust building and was, in many ways, a leap for both parties – representing as it did a departure from the norm. There was reason to believe the partnership was successful and serving the needs of both parties. It appears that the decision-making process to ultimately change the nature and activity levels of the agreement was one-sided demonstrating issues of control and engagement.
- **Risk:** There is risk inherent in all international partnership activity. Even if both parties are fully and continually in agreement regarding objectives and success indicators, external factors can still conspire to halt progress or reduce activity. When partners change agendas and objectives, even more so. This example was relatively risk heavy from the beginning given the nature of the project and the previous levels of engagement in this area by both parties. This was of course mitigated, to no small degree, by the status and reputation of both institutions.
- **Control:** As a foreign partner, you are always at a slight disadvantage – despite the historical dependence of the host nation on the sending institution – as you are naturally subject to constraints and realities that differ from your home setting and reality. Regulatory guidelines; legal requirements; cultural norms all serve to create a shifting landscape that must be navigated from a distance (both literally and figuratively given patterns of cultural integration and understanding).

Lessons Learned

- Expect the unexpected. While this is of course a trite statement, there is a degree of truth to it. No partnership will last forever as new leadership, new governments, new regulations, and new realities will come to pass, and these will naturally have an impact on strategy, risk appetite, and patterns of engagement. New leadership can change policy and approach swiftly and dramatically.
- Agendas can change even if initial expectations don't. It is important to have a clear and fundamental understanding of the roles and responsibilities of both parties (or as many are in the agreement).

THE PROCESS OF TRANSITION

Engaging with Others

However amicable the separation, parting will still be a delicate process. Everyone needs to be clear on what their duties and responsibilities are as we have noted, and it is therefore wise to pose yourself a few questions as you arrive at the beginning of the end:

- What are the steps that each party needs to take during the transition process towards the final exit? What are the timelines associated with these, and how will you ensure that you are on track?
- What resources will be required? This could be financial resource as well as time, external input (will lawyers be required?) and people.
- What happens to any shared asset and is there are management plan for that asset?
- How will we manage the communication between all the relevant parties?

Strong stakeholder management, as Douglas stressed in his reflection, is important throughout the entire lifecycle of a TNE partnership, and its importance does not lessen when you are in the process of exiting. For management with the external partners due consideration needs to be given to: communication type and frequency (regular and structured can be accompanied by more informal and ad hoc); time zone differences (no one should be at a disadvantage, if there is a challenging time difference then ensure that potentially inconvenient times are spread around); and clear contact points and personnel, for both staff and students.

Externally, the management of stakeholders in-country beyond the partners, such as local and national governments and agencies, also needs to be regular and structured, but it is also important to ensure that the partner does not feel bypassed in the process. They do not have to be part of the various forms of engagement, but they do, out of courtesy at the very least, need to know that they are taking place.

> **Did You Know?**
>
> In 2018, the Chinese Ministry of Education terminated over 200 TNE programmes and partnerships due to inactivity.

Governance and Management

There will be internal processes that need to be adhered to when terminating, or not renewing, a partnership, and academic institutions will have policies that outline what these are, for example those presented by York St John University in the UK:

Either partner may initiate the termination of a partnership and/or programme. Either partner shall be entitled to terminate the arrangement by written notice to the other if either party:

- Commits a material breach of the agreement which cannot be remedied; or
- Commits a breach that can be remedied and, having been notified of such a breach, has not remedied the situation within a further period specified by the notifying party (normally 28 days).

The following identifies examples of possible concerns, which may require the University to terminate a collaborative partnership:

- Serious and repeated student complaints concerning the quality of delivery;
- Breakdown of communications between the partners;
- The process of monitoring and review indicates a decline in the standard of the operation or delivery of the programme which cannot be sufficiently rectified within an appropriate timescale;
- Extensive deviation from the agreed course and/or programme proposal;
- Either the University or the partner institution fails to meet the requirements of the agreement in other ways.

(York St John University)[2]

If the agreement is between two academic institutions in different regions or countries, then it will be unlikely that these regulations are exactly the same; this needs to be addressed in the mutually-agreed Exit Plan at the outset. It is sensible where possible to keep your regulations the same, you will have no doubt multiple agreements and you cannot have a different set for each one, but you do need to be clear what if any changes there are and that they are stated clearly in the plan and then approved through your institution's formal governance structure, up to and including any overarching governing body, such as a University Council or Board of Directors (as in the case of Regent's University London shown in Figure 10.2).

As the Australian Tertiary Education Quality and Standards Agency (TESQA, 2022: 16) states, "governance of third-party arrangements must address all activities pertaining to the partnership and ensure the institution's governing body is aware of and supports the delivery of an award with a third party". The governing body will ultimately be responsible for all activity that takes place within an institution and if all is going well, will need to be kept abreast of progress; if things are going less well they will need to know immediately, and if matters become serious then they will be the ones that will need to ensure that any activity does not compromise the overall integrity of the institution.

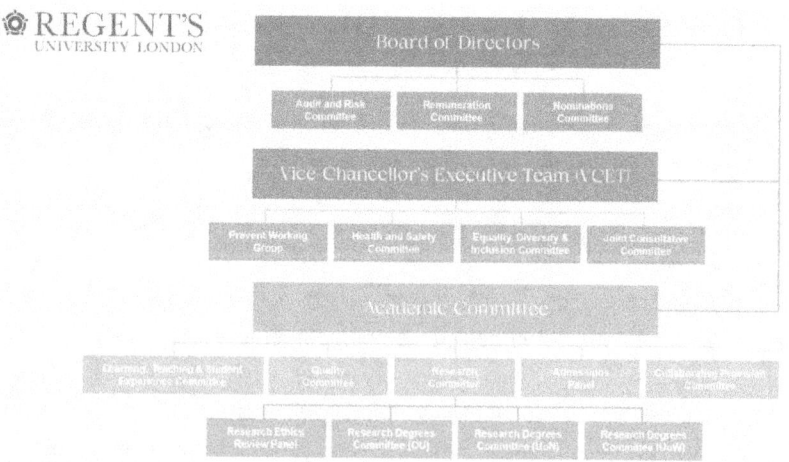

Figure 10.2 Example University Governance Structure: Regent's University London, UK[3]

PRACTICALITIES

Sometimes partnerships end before they have begun through no fault of anyone person, or institution. What seems like a good idea may not in reality be feasible. This is a reality that can stem from many factors: student recruitment; shifting mobility patterns; global pandemics; funding and so on. As the landscape changes, or governmental positions (or indeed governments themselves) change, institutions often face the need to pivot their activity. And in some cases, alter their position radically, sometimes to the point of retreat.

If and when a partnership ends, questions will arise regarding practical issues and realities, and these would be better discussed at the outset. As indicated above in Figure 10.1, there are issues of financial liability; student supervision and teaching; staffing concerns (many staff may well be foreign to the country of delivery and have visas tied to work contracts); branding and institutional reputation. Exiting without too much egg on one's face is clearly the goal, and this can be mitigated against by a thorough and transparent discussion that outlines ownership, oversight, and accountability of key elements of the partnership, day-to-day activity the fundamental student learning experience.

Case Study 10.2: Exploring the Opportunity to Establish a Campus in South Korea

Context

There are a number of branch campus hubs around the globe, the most familiar being Malaysia and Dubai. In 2007, Incheon, in South Korea, declared itself an "English City" and created the Incheon Free English Zone. The goal was to become as proficient in English as Singapore. The initiative was supported by the creation of a Free Economic Zone, with a key action being to encourage international universities to come and, with the support of the government, set up campuses in Incheon. The first campus to be established was Stony Brook University (SUNY) in 2008, followed by others including George Mason University Korea, Ghent University Global Campus, the University of Utah Asia Campus (in 2014), and the Stanford Centre in 2021.

In 2020, two universities and a private provider initiated discussions on the possibility of establishing a joint campus. The destination had yet to be determined, but after thorough market research was undertaken, and the location of South Korean was determined as the preferred choice.

Stages in the Journey

i) The Preparation

There are various subcategories that are involved in the preparation. These include (and this list is not exhaustive):

    a. Market demand and segmentation.
    b. Product development.
    c. Marketing and recruitment.
    d. Student experience and assurance.
    e. Commercial considerations.
    f. Governance arrangements.
    g. Finance.

It is also vital to consider how you are going to communicate and engage throughout the project; with the parties involved, but also with external stakeholders, both on your own campus(es) and beyond. For this project, a series of working groups were established, reporting into a Joint Steering Group. These were: an Operational group; Product Development; Student Experience and Assurance; Physical and Digital Infrastructure; and Legal (including commercial, contracting, regulatory, and compliance).

ii) The End

There was no intervening period; we went straight from the preparation to the end. It was disappointing for all involved but when the information and the guidance submitted to the Joint Steering Group is clear, then it is foolish to proceed. Better to say no and stop something before you start, rather than make a commitment and then try and extricate yourself halfway through. That is bad for the partners, the stakeholders, the students, and the local community. As long as you have been open and transparent throughout, then everyone will understand. Situations of course may also change so you may be able to pick up again in the future, or take the learnings that you have, and the trust you have developed, and transfer it to a different environment.

Key Themes

- **Communication and the importance of trust:** If multiple parties are involved then there needs to be openness and transparency from the beginning. There will be sensitive materials being exchanged, and trust needs to be developed. If you are working with established partners, this is of course easier, but still throughout the process, there needs to be a constant awareness of the need to communicate and to share all thoughts, positive, and negative.
- **Roles and responsibilities:** When there are multiple partners in a project it is essential that all know what their roles are at an early stage. If it is a project that requires delicate negotiation of financial matters, then it is more effective to have those involved in such discussions separate from those responsible for building the relationship.
- **Market insight:** The Steering Group need to ensure access to accurate, comprehensive, and timely information to enable effective and timely decision-making.
- **Capacity and capability:** The partners had a wealth of knowledge and expertise, but it was important that they recognised their own limitations and therefore gained access to appropriate external expertise when required.

Lessons Learned

- Online collaboration between partners was effective and assisted during the project by, where possible, face-to-face interactions.
- Robust market intelligence is essential, but does require updating as the project progresses as external situations and drivers may change.
- Echoing Douglas and the importance of robust internal stakeholder management engage as many people in the project across your institution as early as you can. It may be difficult initially as there could be confidentiality issues, but it is much better to bring people on board with you as you are progressing the initiative, so that they can become familiar with the goals and objectives, and indeed help shape them, before they actually need to commit to any specific actions. Finance, Legal, and Governance are a must, as are academic colleagues who may need to be involved in curriculum planning and development as well as those in educational services such as the quality team, and essentially, as you

> are developing your market insight, the marketing and recruitment teams. You may have the best and most exciting idea for programmes in the world, but if no one wants to study them, then it's a waste of time.
> - Projects need to have a clear vision of what they are trying to achieve at the outset, and all players within the project need to be signed up to and committed to that vision. A framework then needs to be wrapped around that vision so that progress can be tracked and actions taken accordingly. Structured project management from the outset is a must. It needs to be able to flex as situations change, but an overarching structure will help all those involved know what their roles are and be able to monitor the progress of the project, through the many and various workstreams.
> - Sometimes, quite frequently in the case of TNE, things don't work out as you had planned, and that is fine and perfectly normal. The most important point is to learn from the experience, whilst appreciating that all experiences will be unique, and you could undertake a virtually identical activity elsewhere and it would be a success. Therefore, don't be discouraged. Keep planning. Keep innovating. And keep learning.

An ending doesn't have to be terminal. There may be opportunities to continue the partnership in some shape or form. One of the most important things, however, is to ensure you leave on as optimistic a basis as you can. If the ending has come through any success measures simply not being achievable, then it may be that there will be other opportunities around the corner, with fewer practical obstacles, or with a more supportive external financial environment, and the positive dynamics of the relationship that has been built up over the months can be maintained and developed further.

Keeping a Lessons Learned Log is a must. There can be a temptation to just focus on the negatives. Plan A didn't work because of X, and so we aren't going to do that again. Things will never be that prosaic.

CONCLUSION

Don't adventures ever have an end? I suppose not. Someone else always has to carry on the story.

(The Fellowship of the Ring, J.R.R. Tolkein, 1954)

Gandalf was correct, it is indeed a risky, if not exactly dangerous, business going out your door, but there are things that you can do that can lessen that risk. You can be very clear in your decision-making. Develop clear guidelines setting out the decision-making process internally and externally. Involve the appropriate staff in your institution and in the partner institution. Create an action plan, that you stick too, managed by an internal project team if possible, that reviews and revises, where appropriate, the exit plan and ensures that you are on track or highlights any issues that need to be dealt with. You can prioritise communication. Communication can be both formal and informal, but should at all times be open, honest, transparent, and human. In an effort to be clear, sometimes the awareness that we are dealing with individuals can be lost. Always communicate with kindness. And you can remember that all activities will not work, whatever you may do, no matter how careful your planning and however strategic and symbiotic the endeavour. And that is ok.

There are benefits to be gained from partnerships ending. We can learn and build for future engagement. We will have had valuable experiences and be better prepared for any future collaborations. In endings, there are always new beginnings. There is always someone else to carry on the story.

Top Tips for an Amicable Academic Separation

DO

- Keep communication channels open.
- Develop an exit strategy at the beginning.
- Manage internal stakeholders effectively.
- Be aware of your regulatory responsibilities.
- Keep a Lessons Learned Log.

DON'T

- Be disheartened.
- Presume everyone knows what to do.
- Deviate from the terms of the agreement.
- Forget this is about people.

NOTES

1 https://olympics.com/en/news/success-failure-sports-giannis-viral-press-conference

2 https://www.yorksj.ac.uk/media/content-assets/registry/academic-quality-support/documents/Termination-or-Non-Renewal-of-Collaborative-Partnerships.docx
3 Academic Governance | Regent's University London

REFERENCES

Hill, C., Lamie, J. and Gore, T. (2022). *The Evolution of Transnational Education: Pathways, Globalisation and Emerging Trends.* Routledge

Proctor, D. (2016). Stakeholder Engagement for Successful International Partnerships: Faculty and Staff roles. In C. Banks, B. Siebe-Herbig, & K. Norton (Eds.), *Global Perspectives on Strategic International Partnerships: A Guide to Building Sustainable Academic Linkages* (pp. 95–108). Institute of International Education & DAAD German Academic Exchange Service.

TEQSA (2022). Transnational Education Toolkit. (Australian Government: Canberra). Found at Transnational Education (TNE) toolkit (teqsa.gov.au)

Tolkein, J.R.R. (1954). *The Fellowship of the Ring.* Allen and Unwin

Responding to the Student Voice – Reflections on Journeys in International Education – Into the Mist and Heading for the First Tree

Christopher Hill

Eleven

THE STUDENT VOICE: PANEL DISCUSSION

Introductions

Chris: Thank you for agreeing to join us to discuss your experiences in international higher education and to share your reflections on your respective journeys. First, **could you tell us a little about yourselves?**

My name is **Mohammed** AlAmeen and I'm a Bahraini national living in Bahrain. I'm currently finishing up my PhD in Educational Leadership.

My name is **Dolapo** Oguntuyi, I am from Lagos Nigeria. I currently work and reside and in the UK. I studied Construction Project Management at Robert Gordon University (2022) and Building Survey and Facilities Management at Birmingham City University in 2020. I look forward to going for a PhD in two years after gaining work experience in the construction industry.

My name is **Danielle** Wilson-Gulston and I am from Trinidad and Tobago. My programme of study is a PhD Education.

My name is **Bevin** Anandarajah and I am a former student of International Politics with French at the University of London Institute in Paris. I'm presently living in Brussels.

My name is **Tabby** Nawaz, I am originally from Manchester UK and have been living in Abu Dhabi for nearly ten years. I am married with two children, who attend an international school in Abu Dhabi. I am a full-time faculty member at Zayed University, in the College of Natural and Health Sciences. I primarily teach Psychology courses. I'm a 4th-year PhD student at the British University in Dubai. I am studying towards

DOI: 10.4324/9781003649571-12

achieving a PhD in Education. I am currently within the data collection part of my PhD and to say it's stressful is an understatement!

Origins

Chris: We began this book by thinking about journeys and starting points. We wanted to better understand experiences in international higher education through the lens of the people within it. To do this, we wanted to think about where people come from, where they think they are heading, and where they have ended up. **What did you want to be when you were young?**

Mohammed: A creative writer and an academic. I had a wild imagination when I was a child, and these ideas manifested into writing. Till today, I enjoy creating fantasy worlds and character building and coming up with plot twists that would engage readers and keep them intrigued. Another passion of mine is teaching. Because I'm the eldest of four, I used to tutor my siblings often. That's when I discovered my love for teaching; and I used to tutor my cousins and neighbours as well. This continued till university where I would help my colleagues with their coursework and revisions before exams.

Dolapo: I always wanted to be an optician as a young lady.

Danielle: To be honest, when I was growing up, I wanted be a forensic pathologist, however that changed when I realised I was no good in the sciences (Biology, Chemistry and Physics).

Bevin: My career aspirations varied greatly when I was young. Ranging from a doctor to a lawyer, librarian, social worker or teacher, my main motivator was always the human-aspect of the work; wanting to better understand and respond to a need in society.

Tabby: I didn't really have an idea of what I wanted to be when I was younger. I flitted through many ideas, but I did know I wanted to work with people - not be an office paper pusher. And I do believe I have achieved this with the different careers I have had in my adulthood (support worker, social worker, faculty member).

Where we start and where we think we are going rarely align with where we end up. However, it is often relatively straightforward to be able to trace a line back from where we are to where we started, even if the plan wasn't obvious to us as we were living it. Of course, a journey does not end once we decide on a particular job and even achieve that ambition. As Tabby illustrates, sometimes we have a goal and we might reach that goal, but then after a few years, we set another one and move on. We may not have had a specific career in mind, but rather wanted to spend our time in a certain place (outdoors, in a different country, in a social setting), or possibly were less clear about what we wanted to do and more clear about what we didn't want to do. As we conclude in Chapter 1, it's about the journey and about the people that you meet and learn from along the way.

Chris: In order to more fully understand your respective journeys in international education, we are interested to learn more about your motivations and objectives. When you reflect back on the first time you travelled for education: **where did you go, for what purpose and how long for?**

Mohammed: The first time I travelled for education was in 2010 to pursue my Bachelor degree in the UAE. It was a four-year programme, and after that, I decided to continue with my Master's degree. I always had the intention of doing my PhD, however after my Masters I decided to start working and that was when I entered the corporate world. I spent a couple of years working in Dubai in various industries until the Covid-19 pandemic. Since almost the entire educational system in the UAE at the time was online, I saw this as a chance to start the PhD programme.

Dolapo: I travelled for education in 2019 and it was for my Master's degree in Facilities Management. I came into the United Kingdom and my first postgraduate degree for was a year and the second was for about two years. To further my education was my major reason.

Danielle: The first time I travelled for education was for this PhD programme. I went to Alberta Canada to do my first semester of studies as this was an onsite course. I did three

	courses – Education Policy, Black Studies in Education and Sociology in Education.
Bevin:	Studying in Paris for three years was my first experience of travelling for education. It was perhaps a slightly unusual situation, given that I was studying at a British university overseas, but my experience felt very different to that of my friends who were studying at British universities in the UK.
Tabby:	The first time I travelled was for my BA to Leeds within the UK. This was as a young 18-year-old and I stayed in Leeds for three years to complete my undergraduate degree. It was the quintessential British experience, leave home for university, freshers, make life long best friends, learning how to budget, balancing having fun with studying and overall a great experience.

I then left home at 24 to complete my MA in Social Work at Manchester University, and despite the university being close to home, I chose to live near to university to have the "whole" university experience. As a mature student, the experience was very different as this time I was a lot more focused on my study and how to complete everything to the best of my ability and in a timely fashion.

This PhD experience I am currently in has been the most difficult and isolating of all my experiences. Being in a different country, starting during the global pandemic, online lessons and never really belonging has been a real test of my commitment and also my own wish to complete the PhD.

Chris:	Thinking a little more deeply about your experiences while studying and living away from home, can you talk about any of the **key challenges you faced and how you overcame them?**
Mohammed:	One of the most difficult things I faced studying in the UAE (besides living alone) is figuring out my career path and managing my finances. I've tackled these by setting goals, and asking for advice from friends, relatives, and teachers. Staying flexible, seeking out help from those with experience, and learning from mistakes, is what made me overcome these challenges.

Dolapo: A major challenge I faced was the culture shock and difference in the educational system in terms of research. I was an A student in my undergraduate but the method of learning and teaching was way different and there was a lot of application that I struggled to fit in and the way of writing was very different.

My first step in overcoming it was speaking to my lecturers and asking for help, and I started my essays very early so I could always show them the progress made every week. I spent an ample amount of time in the library looking at past works done and how the writing style was.

I also had some student tutors available to always assist. One major thing I did so often was ask lots of questions and spent more time in the library than anywhere else.

Danielle: One of the first challenges I faced was getting to Canada – it embarked upon a 30+ hour journey making stops in Amsterdam, Atlanta, Toronto, and then Edmonton in Alberta – it was long and tortuous. Thereafter, I had challenges in getting acquainted with the university and the documents I needed to obtain, e.g. getting my student ID, setting up a bank account, navigating the campus and transport systems (because I had to take the bus which was something I never did before). The climate was also challenging, as many days I experienced subzero temperatures – being from the Caribbean and then spending a significant amount of time in Dubai – this was unheard of – I suffered for many days.

Over the course of time and by asking questions and getting advice from students I met I was mostly able to overcome these challenges. Also getting out into the cold and just dealing with it helped a lot. One day my landlord took me to Costco to get the right snow jacket, and this was helpful.

Bevin: Well, the biggest challenge I faced during my time there was definitely the Covid-19 pandemic. Of course this challenge wasn't unique to me, but it did feel especially unusual to be overseas at a time when it was otherwise prohibited to travel.

Aside from that, there was a whole plethora of activities to undertake as a student studying overseas. From finding somewhere to live, finding a part-time job, complying with French bureaucratic and administrative requirements (with the added burden of Brexit), overcoming the language barrier, navigating a new city… the list is endless! But I would say that these challenges also made my personal growth and development over the course of my studies more rewarding. With each hurdle I overcame, my confidence grew, and it made my studies feel all the more meaningful, because I could look back and reflect on all the hoops I had to jump through to make my time studying in Paris possible.

Tabby: My BA and MA had more practical challenges, learning how to budget, balancing study with having fun etc. I was a single and young and was near home. So my family were only a phone call, car/train ride away. The PhD has been the most difficult. Not only with the higher standard of work, but the time demands as well as feeling very much on my own. I have two children who are in school and have their own very busy lives (which I am the project manager of), a husband who works in a different country and a full time job of my own.

The balancing of all my roles, the PhD demands, and the feeling of not being supported while trying to do it all has been extremely challenging. Due to starting the PhD in lockdown and primarily having online classes, I don't feel I had the opportunity to form bonds with my peers and professors. I initially didn't think this was a massive issue, but as the years have passed, it's become apparent that not having these bonds has made the whole process a solitary and dispiriting. I don't feel I have got over this challenge, as I'm still very much in the trenches!!

It is interesting to see how challenges range from the very practical (not having the correct clothes for the environment) to the pedagogical (encountering different learning systems). In all cases, these challenges forced students out of their comfort zones and required them to adapt and see the world a little differently than they had before. There are echoes of our own experiences in Malaysia and Japan; from dealing with long flights and obstinate luggage carousels, to finding that there is a wonder in a dramatically different culture, but a challenge all the same. Engaging with others, asking question, and asking at times for help is always important. No question is too silly, no problem too small, and people for the most part are there to help you and will be only too willing to take you shopping for a warm jumper or coat if nothing else. Think of yourself in this situation: you are at home, comfortable and at ease in where you are working and living, and one of your colleagues or students asks you for some advice or assistance. You are going to help. Good, kind people will always help. It is one of the truths in life that keeps you going when other things might let you down.

Chris: Having thought about the challenges you faced, could you perhaps reflect a little more on any of the key experiences you had while studying abroad? **Would you be able to talk about any lessons learned?**

Mohammed: I learned how to be more disciplined, more organized, and most importantly independent.

Dolapo: I did have a lot of experience studying abroad and one of them is Group task. There were lots of group work/activity required and understanding not everyone is a starter and finisher and the major struggle of been so quiet to listen and observe might be mistaken to be looking like not participating. I had to build confidence in starting projects and finishing as well in different scenarios.

I also had to do a lot of presentations. As a very shy individual, this was groundbreaking for me, I am soft spoken but learning how to speak really loud and understand what a professional presentation looks like came from low marks received from my first Moodle that required it.

Danielle: I think the opportunity to be in classes where there was such a wide range of opinions coming from diverse backgrounds of people at the university was a major learning experience. I think this was the first time I have been in a truly diverse setting in every sense of the word – race, religion, sexuality, ability/disability, neurodiversity, indigeneity etc.

	I think the greatest lesson learned is that sometimes you just need to be quiet and observe and absorb what you are part of. I am usually a very vocal participant in classes but at times I felt that my contributions were insignificant compared to the contributions and life experiences of others. I say this not in an insecure manner but in a manner that I am still unaware of so many circumstances and experiences of others in this world, and I do come from a place of privilege in so many ways – I think this experience made me a better listener.
Tabby:	I think because my experience is a "Covid" experience, it's hard to know if the challenges are due to the fact that I am away from my support network I had in my previous educational experiences or is it because it's a different country.
	The university is British, but the PhD system is more US. The processes are very different. And with it being a British university, I am the only British person in my cohort which was also a different experience. The main lesson I have learnt is patience; it is key to not literally losing your mind when trying to combat all the red tape and approvals in attempting to gain what you need to move on.

Identity and Communication

Chris:	A central theme of our writing, this book included, is the issue of identity and how this is shaped and changed over time. We are very much interested in how we change while we are away from home, and how to change when we get back again. **Did your sense of identity change while you were away from home and if so, how?**
Mohammed:	Definitely. Being away from home made me more independent and exposed me to new cultures and perspectives. It helped me understand who I am in a global context and made me more open-minded. This experience also challenged me to step out of my comfort zone, which was tough but rewarding. I met people from all over the world, each with different viewpoints and lifestyles. This not only broadened my worldview but also made me reevaluate my

	own values and beliefs. By the time I returned home, I felt more confident and had a clearer sense of my own identity and place in the world.
Dolapo:	I would not say it changed, I would say for a spilt second I lost it because I had to question who I was and what I capable of as this was different from where I was coming from. It was more of questioning my identity.
Danielle:	I think my sense of identity was strengthened whilst I was in Edmonton. Whilst Edmonton is a relatively small city, there are many West Indians living there and I found community and comfort in this fact. My landlord was a Jamaican, my supervisor was also Jamaican-Canadian and some of my classmates were also Jamaican. Early on in my stay the university put on a series of workshops with Jamaican laureate – Olive Senior, this brought me even closer to my culture that I had not been expose to since leaving the Caribbean in 2017.
Bevin:	I think the most interesting thing I encountered was acknowledging all the ways I was being perceived in my new environment. In some senses, the labels we ascribe to ourselves are less important than the ones people (consciously or otherwise) associate with us when they first meet us and make their assumptions.
	For example, as the daughter of an Irish mother and Sri Lankan father, my identity can be somewhat ambiguous. Growing up in London, this never felt unusual, but in France I frequently found that people assumed I was from the Maghreb region, and/or that I could speak Arabic (which unfortunately I can't). Of course, these assumptions stem in part from France's colonial relations with this region, and from the large diaspora communities now present in the country as a result. For me, it was interesting to learn about these topics in my classes, and then witness the historic and demographic specificities of France as a subject passing through this space. The experience posed an interesting reframing of how I view myself and my identity in different geographies.
Tabby:	Funnily enough, I feel more British!! The constant comparison to how things are "back home" and how they are

	here make me nostalgic. I'm sure I'm silver lining what it's actually like in the UK, but in my head I have an idea that "it's not this hard in England". I don't know if I'm right!
Chris:	In terms of the practical integration issues during your study abroad period, **how did you navigate the language and communication issues you encountered?**
Mohammed:	Since I am bilingual, I am proficient in both Arabic and English. Therefore, I did not encounter much difficulty in language and communication, especially since these two languages are the dominant ones in the UAE.
Dolapo:	I come from an English-Speaking country but pronunciations differed due to accents. The only thing I had to learn was social slang, school English registers and the use of certain grammar and vocabulary properly.
Danielle:	There was no real language or communication issues encountered since I am a native English speaker, and the university is in the English-speaking portion of Canada.
Bevin:	Fortunately, I had studied French to A-level, and my undergraduate course included a minor in French. I also worked in French families, and I befriended a neighbour who I would meet weekly for a spoken language exchange, so I continued to work on and improve my level of French over the course of my time in Paris. Being in a large, cosmopolitan city, many people were very proficient in English and so I was also very fortunate that I could revert to my mother tongue if I got stuck without it being too much of a problem.
Tabby:	By practising patience, it's literally the only way to combat the changes and systems. Most of my cohort are of an Aran descent, so speak Arabic a lot to each other. Even in the WhatsApp group which is supposed to be for all of us, a lot of the time I have to take myself out of the conversation because I just do not understand. My supervisor is also of Arab descent and even in the communication group they have set up, Arabic is the main language used, so I just don't engage.
Chris:	Taking this a step further, once you had navigated the communication issues, **how did you engage with others while studying abroad?**

Mohammed: While studying abroad, I actively sought out ways to connect with others by joining clubs and attending university events. After university, I would spend my time with work colleagues mostly during my lunch break and getting to know more about their culture. Moreover, spending time with friends, whether eating out or exploring the city, helped me bond with them. I stayed open and curious, which led to meaningful friendships and a deeper understanding of my surroundings.

Dolapo: It was a little difficult for me as I was a very shy individual but luckily for me, I just had five people on my course and I made friends with four of them who invited for social gatherings, coffee and lunch and from there I started to network with different people. I got opportunities to attend industry seminars and conference and that was my ticket to engage with different individuals and I joined the university student buddy scheme and became one and through volunteering programmes as well.

Danielle: To be honest, I went to Canada with the mentality that I am not here to make friends – especially since I expected to be a minority in this situation. However, this quickly changed as I realised the need for a community if I wanted this experience to be positive. I met some great people along the way from various heritages.

Tabby: It's been difficult due to the pandemic situation, the language constraints and distance factors. The university is in Dubai, most of my cohort is in Dubai and I live and work in Abu Dhabi. There hasn't been a lot of engagement, and this has been a real loss for me.

There are interesting reflections here on identity, culture and communication and on how being overseas, or at least away from your usual home, can reinforce your national identity and in some ways your pride in your country and culture. This could in part be a protective reaction, if you feel that you may lose your sense of identity, or it may simply be that things that you hadn't really thought of before are brought to the surface by a situation that is different from the one that you have been used to.

> **Did You Know?**
>
> In a UK International Student Survey[1] of over 11,000 prospective students in 2022, the top five things most important to students were:
>
> High-quality teaching
> A welcoming environment
> An appealing culture and lifestyle
> A good reputation
> The opportunity to build a network of connections

There and Back Again: Home

Chris: We fully understand that, while being away from home can be exciting and rewarding, there is often a part of us that misses home. **What reminded you of home when you were away?**

Mohammed: Thankfully, the culture of UAE is very identical to Bahrain's, so most of the time, I did not feel like I was away from home. I used to get homesick at times, but after living away from home for almost ten years, I got used to it (it also helps that the UAE is only an hour away from Bahrain by plane) so I used to make frequent weekend trips back home.

Dolapo: It was the restaurants and shops as I enjoy cooking a lot. Seeing the shops that sell certain ingredients brings nostalgia feeling to me or the aroma of Nigerian meals. Sometimes walking on the road and hearing someone speak the Yoruba language brings smile to my face.

Danielle: Mostly the Jamaicans I met along the way.

Bevin: Studying in a British university in Paris, I never really felt that removed from home. Coming into our university building and meeting other students there in the library or common areas was enough to remind me of home because of our shared language and culture. We existed as a British bubble in the heart of Paris, which perhaps accelerated the process of feeling at home in the city, because we had each other, and we could also share our knowledge, experiences and recommendations for making the most of the city.

Tabby:	The way things didn't work the way they should- Ha!
Chris:	Having successfully navigated your study abroad, with all the challenges and rewards it involved, we are curious to know **what did it feel like when you got back home again? Had you changed?**
Mohammed:	Yes, as I previously mentioned earlier. I became more open-minded, more independent, and felt like I had a totally new perspective on life. I believe I changed in a lot of good ways which I'm proud of.
Dolapo:	I am yet to return home for vacation but hopefully I can answer this later this year.
Danielle:	To be honest when I got back to Dubai it was bittersweet because whilst I was happy to be out of the cold and with family, however, I felt I was now getting accustomed to university life. I was beginning to enjoy the activities associated with being a PhD student.
Bevin:	Returning home felt similar to visiting your old school after you've left. Somehow things feel smaller than how you remembered them when you used to be there. Coming back to London, I felt so much more confident in the city, and I also had a desire to explore more of the city, as though I was seeing it through new eyes. The familiarity of home will always be comforting, but I also found I was missing some of the "challenges" of life away, like the opportunity to converse in French.
Tabby:	Not sure where home is! We've bought a house in Dubai, we're moving to Dubai this summer and committing our future to the UAE for at least the next 12 years (when the kids are done with school).
	Ask me this question when I finish the PhD (inshallah).
Chris:	If you could reflect back over your whole experience, what would you say is **the value of study abroad?**
Mohammed:	Studying abroad has really broadened my outlook. It's exposed me to new cultures and helped me grow more independent. Having this experience has also improved my resume and allowed me to make connections with people from different parts of the world (I even keep in touch with them on social media). Overall, it's been a game changer for both my personal and professional life.

Dolapo:	I would say it was of great value as my major intention was to learn from a developed country who already started using BIM in the construction industry and I could learn and adopt to my developing county as well.
Danielle:	I think being exposed to different educational delivery styles has been particularly impactful for me. It has shown me that teaching can be impactful even though delivered in different ways. It has had a great impact on how I now teach and the perspectives I how have on teaching and learning.
Bevin:	The value of studying abroad is immeasurable, and I would recommend it to anyone. Prior to my studies, I had been working in London for a number of years on policy and project development in regional government, and I had (naively) assumed that studying would simply aid in my career progression when I returned to the UK. However, the opportunity to study abroad exposed me to the possibility of new horizons, and really made me re-evaluate my ambitions.

My newfound appreciation for life in Europe has led me to my current role working in Brussels, and this is all thanks to my decision to study outside the UK. Studying abroad really gave me a new appreciation for what it means to find and build a community. My international network has expanded, and I love being exposed to new ways of viewing the world and our place in it through the people I meet and the cultures and contexts they come from. |
| **Tabby:** | Despite all the things above, I truly believe my experience is not everyone's experience. It's a unique case due to the pandemic etc. etc.

Study abroad should and is a rich and diverse experience whereby you learn and immerse yourself in the different cultures and people you encounter. I'm sad I didn't get this opportunity |
| **Chris:** | Any finally, **what advice would you give to a student about to embark on study abroad? Any top tips?** |
| **Mohammed:** | As cliché as this advice would sound, you really only live once. So don't be afraid of trying new things. Make mistakes. It's okay. Because these mistakes will make you grow stronger, and with time, wiser. Be bold. Be fearless. |

	Your 20s are all about self-discovery, so it's the perfect time to take risks, take on new challenges, and explore new things.
Dolapo:	Consider if the university is one of the best in that field and look at their success rate in research as well. Look at the standards in the industry as well. Affordability and cost of living is important to look at. What opportunities are available to international students is another factor to look at.
Danielle:	I think one must give themselves enough time and grace when acclimatizing to new situations – everything would not be perfect, but perfection is not the goal.
Bevin:	Keep an open mind and an open attitude. There will be so many things to see and do, which might feel overwhelming at first, but you will get the hang of it! Be prepared that there will always be hiccups or unforeseen obstacles, but in the end these things are always manageable, and you'll feel so much more confident with every hurdle you overcome.
Tabby:	GO! Open yourself up the wonder of the worlds. Be patient, be you but learn to adapt as you go through things day by day. It will one of the best things you ever do.

Top Tips from Our Panel on Studying Abroad

- Do your research
- Pick the best institution for you
- Ask questions
- Make mistakes
- Step outside your comfort zone
- Don't strive for perfection
- Give yourself time
- Be patient
- Have fun!

CONCLUSION

The students were, as always, honest and reflective. Travel and study abroad is not without its challenges and hardships but the ultimate value cannot be ignored. Students were overwhelmingly in favour of studying abroad and felt that it was something others should try. They were fully aware of the need to prepare and be ready to adapt. It will be an adventure, but you can always try to be ready for it.

APPENDIX 12.1: PANEL PARTICIPANTS

Mohammed Adnan AlAmeen is a Bahraini national living in Bahrain. He works in strategic management in F&B industry and has just submitted his PhD thesis in Educational Leadership at the British University in Dubai.

Dolapo Oguntuyi is from Lagos Nigeria and is currently working and residing in the UK. She studied Construction project management at Robert Gordon university (2022) and Building Survey& facilities management from Birmingham City University in 2020.

Danielle Wilson-Gulston is from Trinidad and Tobago. My programme of study is PhD Education.

Bevin Anandarajah is a former student of International Politics with French at the University of London Institute in Paris. She is currently living in Brussels.

Tabby Nawaz is from Manchester UK and now living in Abu Dhabi. She is a student at British University in Dubai, studying towards a PhD in Education with a concentration in Special and Inclusive Education.

Tabby Nawaz is originally from Manchester UK and has been living in Abu Dhabi for nearly ten years. She is a full-time faculty member at Zayed University, in the College of Natural and Health Sciences. She is a fourth-year PHD student at the British University in Dubai.

APPENDIX 12.2: PANEL QUESTIONS

1.	Tell us a little about yourself – i.e. your name, where you are from, what you are studying
2.	What did you want to be when you were young?
3.	Please tell us a little about the first time you travelled for education: where did you go, purpose, how long for?
4.	Can you talk about any of the key challenges you faced and how you overcame them?
5.	Can you talk about any of the experiences you had while studying abroad? Any lessons learned?
6.	Did your sense of identity change while you were away from home and if so, how?

7.	How did you navigate the language and communication issues you encountered?
8.	How did you engage with others while studying abroad?
9.	What reminded you of home when you were away?
10.	What did it feel like when you got back home again? Had you changed?
11.	What is the value of studying abroad?
12.	What advice would you give to a student about to embark on study abroad? Any top tips?

NOTE

1 https://www.qs.com/reports-whitepapers/international-student-survey-2022-uk-edition/

Conclusion

Christopher Hill and Judith Lamie

In chapter one, we entered the wonderful world of transnational higher education through its many and varied routes. We ponder the different motivations that place us along this pathway and discuss the extent to which they are by luck, or by design, and what we expect to find and to achieve? As the authors delve into the reasons why they may have ended up where they are, this chapter introduces the recurrent themes presented throughout the book of communication, engagement, management styles, and culture.

In chapter two, we began our journey in earnest. We thought about what to pack and how to approach the process of international travel. We included tips and advice from seasoned international travellers about what to pack, what not to pack, and what to be aware of.

In chapter three, we traced journeys back to their origins and talked to colleagues about student mobility and exchange – a common entry point for a subsequent career in international higher education. We talked about language and the importance of communication. The chapter included examples and experiences of a Chinese student studying in the UK, and English students studying in France and Germany. At the heart of this chapter is the human experience of being somewhere different – often far from their comfort zone – and needing to find ways to talk to people and to communicate.

In chapter four, we turned our focus back to the practical and personal and discussed what actually goes into an international work trip, from the planning to the "joys" of travel itself, to the balancing of work at home while away. Drawing on case studies from Taiwan, the Balkans, China, and Uzbekistan, this chapter pulled back the curtain to show the inner workings of international trips.

In chapter five, we began the conversation about partnerships and reflected on how to engage with this process – how to decide the where, who, and why. The chapter drew upon market research to examine the approaches to strategic development, regulatory environment, and

DOI: 10.4324/9781003649571-13

introduced several case studies related to branch campus development and strategic alliances.

In chapter six, Stephanie Martin addressed the issues of diversity and equity in transnational higher education and asked the question whether TNE partnerships can ever truly be equitable, and does it even matter if they are? This chapter talked about the value of travelling abroad and suggested ways in which we can use the lessons of travel to help students integrate into their new community whilst celebrating their own culture and heritage. It also explored the difference between diversity and decolonisation and how simply including multicultural examples in our teaching is a good start but more must be done to critically address issues and discuss varying perspectives.

In chapter seven, a range of female international higher education professionals from around the world reflected on the topic of women in leadership in transnational education. They shared their thoughts and reflections on a number of aspects, from systemic barriers and training opportunities to mentoring and celebrating success, as well as sharing stories from their own personal journeys.

In chapter eight, the authors further examine culture, community, and communication in international travel. With any journey in TNE comes the need to be open to new experiences, and this chapter stressed the need to pay it forward, that we are part of a community with the opportunity to learn from each other and seek greater understanding through engagement. The chapter, including case studies of travel and study in Japan and China, firmly acknowledged that it is not always easy and there are lots of opportunities for misunderstandings.

In chapter nine, Nigel Healey and Rob Hickey provided a reflective account of managing transnational education partnerships. The chapter draws upon data and expert insight to talk about the challenges of managing partnerships from the perspective of staff, local and international students, teaching, research, the home campus, and the host government. This chapter is a comprehensive review of all facets of the process.

In chapter ten, the authors addressed the issue of success and impact – and perhaps more importantly, how you measure it and how you know when to walk away. The chapter draws upon recent case studies to discuss the importance of planning, communication, and the very real need for an exit strategy.

In chapter eleven, the authors incorporated the views of international students to determine what the future might hold for them as individuals as they embark on their journeys and what the weird and wonderful world of international higher education might have in store next. The chapter provided students with a reflective point of engagement to discuss their experiences in international education; what they learned along the way; challenges they faced; and advice they have.

Index

Note: Page numbers in *italics* refer to figures and page numbers in **bold** refer to tables.

A-level 31–32, 153, 218
Abache, Melissa 123, 125
Abu Dhabi 179, 209, 219, 224
academic 4, 6, 15, 21, 46–47, 50–51, 62–63, 65, 69, 79, 86–87, 91, 96, 103, 105, 109–113, 116, 118, 125, 130–132, 134, 136, 139–140, 142, 157–158, 161, 168–171, 172–174, 176–178, 181–183, 193–*197*, 199, 201–202, 205, 207, 210
Academic Registrar 136
academic staff 111, 167, **167**, 170, 172, 175, 181–182, 186
Academy of Social Sciences in Australia 38
Achampong, Joyce 123, 125–126, 128, 130, 134, 136, 139, 142
Adams, Douglas 54
Adams, William 8
Adaptability *39*, 158
Additional Learning Needs – ALN 51
Afghanistan 126–127
Africa 2, 35, 107–108, 125, 154
Afrikaans 105
Agencies 61–62, 64, 66, 80, 86, 131, 168, 201
Akkas (elder sisters) 33–34
AlAmeen, Mohammed 209–212, 215–216, 218–222, 224
Alberta 211, 213
Allen, Charlene 124, 143
alliance 87–89, 92, 96, 165, 198, 227
alumni 60, 63–64, 66, 69, 71–72, 80, 90–92, 125, 194

alumni networks 90
American Academy of Arts and Sciences 38
Amsterdam 213
Anandarajah, Bevin 209–210, 212–213, 217–218, 220–224
Anglophone 68, 106, 108, 161, 163, 176, 187–188
Annie 148
Antetokounmpo, Giannis 192
Apartheid 105
Arab 113, 116–117, 218
Arabic 100, 102, 104, 106–107, 109, 111–112, 217–218
Argentina 47–49, 52
Artificial Intelligence (AI) 55, 166
Asian financial crisis 165
Assistant Language Teachers (ALTs) 8
Atlanta 213
Austen, Jane 115
Australia 9, 38, 42–43, 68, 100–101, 103–108, 111–113, 116, 124–125, 129, 134, 162, 163, **163**, 164–165, 178, *180*, 182, 187, 193–195, 202
Australian Universities Quality Agency (AUQA) 193

Babakhodjaeva, Lobar 123, 125, 127, 128, 131–132, 135–136, 141, 143
Babel Fish 54
Bacon, Roger 39
Bad Homburg 31–32
Bahrain 102, 209, 220, 224

Balkans 61, 226
Baron Victor Frankenstein 31
Barry, Stephen 45
Basketball 14, 192; NBA 192
Bavaria 48
behaviour 11, 19, 51, 110, 129, 133, 144
Beijing 69–70, 155
Belgium 43, 51
Berra, Yogi 25
bias 133, 141
Birmingham City University 209, 224
Blackboard 21
bookkeeper 6
Bournemouth 124
Bournemouth University 128
brand enhancement 80
branding 17, 26–27, **167**, 168, 174, 203
Brexit 50, 61, 214
British Academy 38
British Council 44, 61–63, 69–71, 81, 124, 155, 168
British Council Going Global Conference 71
British Embassy 62, 69
British University in Dubai (BUiD) 87, 209, 224
Bruges 51
Brummie 44
Brussels 209, 222, 224
Buddhist Vesak Festival 33
Bulgaria 61–63

Calais 43
campus 15–19, 21–22, 27–28, 35–36, 40, 46, 48, 59, 67–68, 72, 80–81, 85–86, 106, 134, 140, 153–154, 156–157, 161, 165–179, *180*, 181–185, 187–188, 195, 203–204, 213, 227
Canada 2, 9, 38, 106, 125, 134, 163, **163–164**, *180*, 211, 213, 218–219
careers 4–5, 134, 169, 171, 182, 210
Caribbean 213
cashier 6
Celtic 41

challenge 2, 6–7, 10–12, 14, 17, 20–21, 26, 38, 41–42, 47–48, 50–51, 59, 62, 68, 70, 72–73, 77, 79–80, 82, 87, 89, 93, 97, 101, 110–111, 113, 124, 126–127, 132, 135, 137–138, 140–141, 143, 159–161, 169–172, 174–175, 178, 180–181, 184–185, 187, 196, 212–216, 221, 223, 224, 227–228
change 11–18, 20, 22, 25, 27–30, 37–38, 61, 72, 77, 82, 85, 88–89, 98, 123–124, 128, 132, 142, 154, 157–158, 166, 175–177, 180–182, 186–187, 196, 199–200, 202–206, 210, 216–219, 221, 224
Cheshire 5
Chicago 60
China 9, 31, 40, 67–72, 92, 134, 151–156, 158, 163, 166, 174, 180, *180*, 183–185, 187, 226–227
China Beacons Institute 184
China Education Association of International Exchange (CEAIE) 70
Chinese Taipei Comparative Education Society 123, 126
Chinese Ministry of Education 70, 177, 183, 201
cholera 35
Christian 116–117
Christmas 51; markets 51; trees 51
classics 14, 115
classroom 10–11, 13, 19–20, 41–42, 47–49, 55–56, 86, 103–104, 106, 110, 113, 115–119, 144, 159
cockroaches 32
colleagues 1–2, 9, 11, 16–18, 21, 24, 27–28, 36, 53, 59, 66–67, 71, 73–74, 76, 98, 104, 123, 127, 133–134, 136, 139–141, 143, 145, 150, 155, 157, 175, 193, 205, 210, 215, 219, 226
Colombo 32
Communication 8, 10, 12, 16–17, 19–20, 27, 30, 37, *39*, 40, 42, 49, 51–52, 72, 75, 81, 89, 98–99, 104, 106–107, 129, 150–151, 155–156,

183, 185, 197, 199–201, 205, 207, 216, 218–219, 225–227
communities 4, 13, 18, 21, 77, 87, 124, 217
compassion 34–35, 52–53, 129
Connecticut 198
Consul-General Residence 71
consultant 123–124
control 2, 13, 167–169, 174, 187, 199
cooperative education 46–47
Coordinators for International Relations (CIRs) 8
Costco 213
COVID-19 46, 163, 211, 213, 216
cross cultural relationships 40, 102, 151; skills 7
cultural 7, 13, 17, 23, 38, 41, 46, 49, 51–52, 56, 59, 71, 76, 78–80, 86–87, 96–97, 100, 103–104, 106–107, 109–112, 114–119, 132, 137, 140–141, 144, 147, 151–152, 154, 156, 158, 165, 171–174, 181–182, 185, 199
cultural networks 13
Cultural Revolution 152, 154
culture 1, 2, 4, 7, 9–11, 13, 14, 16–21, **26**, 31, 34, 37–38, 44, 48–52, 54, 56, 65, 75, 79, 81–82, 97, 101, 103, 107, 109–111, 113–115, 117–119, 124, 127, 129, 131, 137–142, 144, 147, 150, 158–159, 161, 170, 173–174, 176, 181, 184, 187, 213, 215–217, 219–222, 226–227; shock 36
curriculum 8, 11, 42–43, 87, 97, 101–108, 110–119, 166, **167**, 168, 172–174, 176–177, 183, *197*–198; reform 11

data 55, 81–82, 91, 149, 162–164, 166, 173, 180–182, 186, 210, 227
Davies-Smith, Sharon 144–145, 150
Dean of Faculty 125
decision making 70, 78, 82, 187–188, 197, 205, 207
Deputy Vice Chancellor 181, 188
De Liefde trading ship 8
Dictaphone 32

diplomacy 10, 14, 51–52
diplomat 14, 170
Directorate for Academic Recognition 62
diversity 18, 46, 100–103, 108, 111, 114, 116, 118–119, 130, 158, 176, 185, 227
doctor 35–36, 210
doctorate 96, 97, 126, 129, 175, 184; doctoral degree see doctorate
Dracula 67
Dubai 87, 124, 182, 203, 209, 211, 213, 219, 221, 224
Dutch Burgher 32

Ecctis 63–64
Edinburgh 71, 88
Edmonton 213, 217
education hubs 182
Education Insight 62–63
Edvance Consultants 123–124
Elizabethan 115
Ellie 51
Emirati 87, 113
employment 14, 46, 100, 106, 131, 161, 170, 173–174, 182
empowerment 126–127
EMSAT 111
engagement 2, 4, 21–22, 28, 36, 49, 58, 61, 64, 69, 71–73, 75, 81–82, 84, 87–90, 92–93, 98, 115, 124–125, 150–151, 156, 158–159, 162, 170, 185, 193, 199–201, 207, 219, 226–228
English 7–8, 10–11, 33, 38, 40–43, 47–48, 86, 100, 102–113, 115–116, 118, 146, 148, 154–155, 157, 161, 172, 203, 218, 226; Baccalaureate 42; Second Language 113, 165; enterprise 4, 97, 187
environment 1, 7, 9–10, 12–13, 21, 24, 55, 70, 78–80, 84–86, 100, 102–107, 112–114, 119, 125, 138, 147, 150, 158, 175, 177, 179, 181, 194, 204, 206, 214, 217, 220, 226

equity 80, 85, 100–101, 103, 105–108, 111, 113, 116, 118–119, 227
Erasmus 45–50
Euripidean 1
Eurocentric 105, 114
Europe 41, 43, 67, 107, 141, 146–147, 222
European 45, 48, 50, 61, 67, 108; Union 61; universities 46
evolving nature of universities 4
Executive Board 181
exit plan 196, 202, 207

faculty 6, 65, 79, 86, 91, 125, 171, 187, 198, 209–210, 224
failure 1–2, 35, 42, 49, 89, 113, 150, 175, 192, 195
Falklands War 155
female leader 124, 129, 132–133, 137–139; leadership 129
Flanders 51
flexibility 19, 58, 119, 157, 159, 196
flying faculty 80, 171
food 1, 11, 17, 23, 34, 54, 59, 65, 144, 151, 153
footballer, professional 5, 14
Foreign Language Education 8–9
Forensic Pathologist 210
France 7, 9, 41, 43, 45, 96, 124, 152–153, 155, *180*, 217, 226
France, Alan 137
franchise 28, 80, 167–168, 177–178, 186
Frankfurt 31
French 9, 41, 43, 45–46, 110, 151–153, 209, 214, 218, 221, 224; Embassy 96
Fudan University 151, 155

Gaijin Sensei 10
GAMSAT 111
Gandalf 207
General Certificate of Secondary Education (GCSE) 41–42
Gross Domestic Product (GDP) 81
Gender Equality Office 140

geography 9, 42
George Mason University Korea 203
Germany 9, 31–32, 43, 47–50, 124, *180*, 226
Ghent University Global Campus 203
global enrolments **164**
global health pandemic 39, 68
global north 127, 161, 170, 185
global south 127, 131, 180, 185
Global Regional Engagement Groups 89, 92
Goh, Jazreel 78, 81, 84
Google 9, 147, 149, 166
governance 2, 126, 174, 178, 188, 192, 195–197, *197*, 201–202, 204–205
government 8–9, 21, 38, 42–43, 50–51, 56, *56*, 61–62, 65, 79, 81–82, 86–87, 91, 96, 111, 130–131, 155, 165–166, 168, 174, 176–179, 183–185, 188, 195, 200–210, 203, 222, 227
graduate school 15
guidebooks 27, 150
gulf region 87, 101–102, 110

Hakkone 147
Healey, Nigel 227
Heathrow Airport 32
HH Sheikh Rashid Bin Saeed Al Maktoum 87
Hickey, Rob 227
Higher Education Institution (HEI) 68, 82, 124, 130, 168, 193
Higher Education Statistics Agency (HESA) 81, 166–167, 180
Hill, Christopher 14, 30, 58, 74, 209–212, 215–216, 218, 220–222
Hindi 40
Hiroshima 147
history 9, 11, 41–42, 61, 65, 108, 117, 176, 195
home campus 16–19, 22, 27–29, 35–36, 106, 167–177, 179, 181–184, 187–188, 227
homesick 54, 220; homesickness 10, 12

Hong Kong 153, 179
Hou, Angela Yung Chi 123, 126, 128, 132, 134, 136, 140, 142

IC Global Partnership 123–125, 127, 130, 133
IELTS 111
impact 4, 11, 17, 19, 27–28, 38, 52, 58, 60, 62, 65, 77, 84–85, 97, 125, 136, 142, 151, 169, 200, 222, 227
Incheon 203; Free English Zone 203
inclusion 85, 102–103, 113, 118–119, 130, 176
income generation 80
India 85–87, 131, 163, 180, 185, 187
indigenous 41, 108
INSEAD 179
integration 2, 114, 156, 174, 186, 199, 218
integrity 17, 27, 108, 173, 202
intercultural 42–44, 46–47, 103
International Branch Campus (IBC) 21, 86, 161, 166–168, 170, 172, 175, 178–182, *180*, 184–186 188
International Higher Education 1–2, 4, 6, 18, 24–26, 28, 30–31, 36, 38–39, 58, 60, 65, 75, 123, 125, 128, 144–145, 150, 181, 209–210, 226–228
International Relations 8, 14
International Women's Day (IWD) 126–127
internationalisation 8, 46, 59, 65, 72, 80, 102, 124, 130, 133–134, 143, 162, 171
Ireland 9, 46, 48–49, **163–164**, *180*
Istanbul 125
Italy 147
Italian 41, 52, 152
itinerary 29, 58

Japan 7–11, 145–149, *180*, 215, 227
Japan Exchange and Teaching Programme (JET)
Japanese 8, 11, 13, 46, 145–148, 152; Embassy 7; Language Proficiency Tests; 11; Ministry of Education 8; Parliament 8
Jed 5
jetlag 10
Jew 116–117
Jewish 117
Jihu 5
joint steering group 204
joint venture (JV) 168, 177–178, 186, *197*
Joosten, Jan 8
Joseph Fourier Universite 96
journey 1–4, 7, 9, 15, 22, 26–27, 30–32, 35, 37, 40, 47, 53–54, 57, 62, 69–70, 77, 88, 96, 100–101, 110, 116, 119, 123, 137, 144–148, 152–153, 155, 194, 198, 204, 209–211, 213, 226–228

Kansas 27
Keats, John 115
Kenya 35
Kipling, Rudyard 115
Kuala Lumpur (KL) 30
Kyoto 147
Kyushu 8

laboratories 39, 71, 86
Lamie, Judith 5, 7, 35, 124, 126, 128, 132, 135, 137, 141, 143
language 1–2, 7–9, 11–14, 20, 38–50, 52–56, 62, 65, 75, 80, 86, 100, 102, 104–116, 118–119, 125, 143, 144, 146–147, 149, 152, 154, 157, 159, 161, 165, 170, 172, 176, 214, 218–220, 225–226
Language Opportunities Programme 46
Latin 41, 152
Latin America 125
Leeds 212
Levin, Richard 198
Lewis, Vicky 31, 35, 52, 123–124, 126, 128, 132, 135, 138, 142
library 213, 220
Lincoln, Abraham 27

London 7, 34, 147, 153, 166, 179, 182, 202, 209, 217, 221–222, 224
Luxembourg 43, 56

Madrid 14
Makwabarara, Jason 4
Malaysia 15–17, 165, 168, 176–178, 181, 188, 194–195, 203, 215
Malaysian Qualifications Agency 168, 177, 183
Malta 147
Malvinas Islands 155
manager 6, 53, 65, 123, 125, 128–130, 135, 137, 141, 169–179, 181, 184–186, 188, 194, 214
Manchester 209, 224
Mandarin 40
Mandela, Nelson 53
marginalised groups 105
market intelligence 72, 81–82, 90, 205
Martin, Stephanie 123–124, 126–129, 132–133, 135, 138, 141, 142, 227
Mason 5
mathematics 8, 42
Memorandum of Understanding (MOU) 196
mental health 13
mentors 2, 124, 135–137, 142
Michigan College and Innovation Centre 70
Middle East 31, 100, 103–104, 108–110, 112–113, 116, 179, 186
Middle East North Africa (MENA) 105
Milwaukee Bucks 192
mobility 2, 25, 38, 43–46, 50, 56, 70, 91–92, 97, 101, 110, 161, 193, 203, 226
motivation 2, 4, 6–7, 127, 150, 174, 211, 226
Mount Fuji 148
MS Teams 183, 185
Muslim 179
Myles, Sirin 123–124, 127–129, 133, 135, 138, 142

Naha 7
Nara 147
narrative 1, 55
National Centre for Recognition and Equivalency of Diplomas (CNRED) 63
National Chengchi University 123, 126
National Council of Rectors (NCoR) 63
National Education Policy (NEP) 85–86
National Science Foundation of China (NSFC) 70
National University of Singapore (NUS) 198–199
navigation 8
Nawaz, Tabby 209–212, 214, 216–219, 221–224
network 6–7, 10, 13, 36, 47, 62, 64, 66, 69–70, 73–74, 84, 90, 102, 142–143, 151, 216, 219–220, 222
networking 62, 64, 66, 69–70, 73, 90
neurodiversity 215
New York University Abu Dhabi (NYU) 179
New Zealand 9, 113, 155, 163, **163–164**
Nigeria 31, 209, 220, 224
Norma Conquest 41
North America 125
nurse 6

Office for Students (OfS) 62
Oguntuyi, Dolapo 209–211, 213, 215, 217–224
Okinawa 7, 10–11
Oktoberfest 48
Open University 166
operations 79, 84, 161, 165, 170–171, 177, 179–180, 182–183, 186, 195
optician 210
origin stories 2
overseas campus **167**
Oxford Suzhou Centre for Advanced Research (OSCAR) 71

packing 1, 29, 59, 148
Paris 45, 209, 212, 214, 218, 220, 224
partnership 1, 25, 51, 61, 63–64, 67–72, 77–83, 85–99, 94, 110–111,

123–124, 136, 161, 169–175, 177–179, 181–188, 192–197, 199–203, 206–207, 226–227
pedagogy 114–117, 174, 182–183
Physical and Digital Infrastructure 204
Pivot Education Consulting Group 123
Poetry 107–108
policeman 5
policymaker 6, 69, 103
Portfield School 51
practitioner 4, 6, 20, 23, 131
prioritisation 98
Prithipura Infant Home 32–34
Pro Vice Chancellor 130, 181, 188
Proctor, Douglas 193, 200, 205
Professional 4–5, 10–11, 14, 17, 20, 24–25, 27, 42, 60, 65, 74, 78, 100, 102, 111, 123–126, 128–129, 132, 136, 138, 140, 142, 144, 151–152, 157–159, 161, 170, 180, 193, 215, 221, 227
profile raising 90
programme development 4

Qatar 102, 179, 181; Foundation 179
qualifications 11, 19, 85, 100, 103, 134, 142, 166, 177, 183
quality assurance 17, 19, 26–27, 63, 79–80, 84–85, 87–88, 108, 111–113, 116, 126, 158, 168, 170, 173, 183, 195
Quality Assurance Agency (QAA) 62–64, 183
Queensland 100; Curriculum and Assessment Authority 108
Quinn 5

Rabies 35
Rector 63, 132, 143
Regent's University London 202
Regulations 64, 79–80, 86, 140, 158, 176, 200, 202
regulatory compliance 72, 86
regulatory environment 78–79, 84–86, 194, 226
regulatory frameworks 62, 64, 72, 85, 86

reputation building 90
research 4, 6, 12, 40, 52, 63, 68–72, 79–81, 86, 87, 90–92, 96–97, 101, 105, 117–118, 124–128, 130–131, 133, 136–138, 140, 142–143, 162, 169–171, 175, 179–182, 184, 187–188, 198, 204, 213, 223, 226–227; culture 173–174, 184
resources 6, 55, 69, 73, 86, 88, 90, 98, 101, 103, 105, 107, 140, *167*, 170, 173, 176–177, 186, *197*, 198, 200
risk 69, 72, 82–85, 88, 93, 95, 106, 131, 152, 154, 161, 169–170, 183, 195, 199, 200, 207, 223; management 2, 140
Robert Gordon University 209, 224
Rollercoaster 14
Romania 60–64, 67–68
Romanian Agency for Quality Assurance in Higher Education 63
Royal Society of Canada 38
Rugg, Evelyn 136

salesperson 6
Samurai 8
Sarawak 195
school 4–6, 8–15, 31, 34–35, 38, 40–45, 48–49, 51–52, 56, 64–65, 68–70, 86, 104, 111–112, 124, 126, 128–129, 139, 145, 148, 152–153, 162–163, 171, 195, 209, 214, 218, 221
school exchanges 43–44
Science and Innovation Network 62
secretary 6, 31–32
Semaine Culturelle 45
Senate 88, 131, 187
senior academic 169, 175, 181
Shakespeare, William 105, 107, 114–116; The Merchant of Venice 115–116; Shylock 116–117
Shanghai 69–70, 151, 153; Jiao Tong University 70; Theatre Academy 71
shipbuilding 8
Shogun 8

Singapore 179–181, 183, 187, 198–199, 203
Sinhalese New Year 33
Sino-foreign universities 177, 184
skills 5, 7–8, 39–40, 44–49, 51–52, 55–56, 96–97, 106, 116, 133–134, 141, 151, 157, 172
Soba 11
society 8, 101, 114, 117, 126, 135, 140, 147, 154, 184, 210
South Africa 100, 105, 109, 124
South Korea 203–204
Southeast Asia 125, 179, 186–187, 193
Spain 14, 134, 147
Spanish 40–41, 46, 48–49, 152
Sprout 5
Sri Lanka 31–33, 35, 52, 173, *180*, 217
stakeholder 6, 69–71, 79, 87, 111, 125, 142, 174, 188, 193–195, 197, 200–201, 204–205, 207
Stanford Centre 203
stolen generation 108
Stony Brook University 203
strategic direction 72, 79, 84, 88, 98
student recruitment 21, 68, 72, 77, 80, 87, 90, 125, 131, 165, *167*, 203
student voice 2, 80, 209
Sub-Saharan Africa 125
success 1–2, 21–22, 26, 77–80, 84–85, 88, 91, 93, 95, 97–99, 107, 113–114, 123, 135, 141, 179, 192, 199, 206, 223, 227
Sunway University 178
Suzhou 69
Swansea 4, 97; University 23, 50, 95, 144–145
Sweden 51, 56
Swinburne University of Technology 195

Taith 50–51
Taiwan 2, 58–59, 74, 126, 226
Taliban 126
Targets 97–98, 183
Taylor's University 178, 188

teacher 6–8, 10–11, 13–14, 20, 40, 42–44, 48, 52, 54, 100, 104, 106, 112, 115, 124, 126, 128, 145, 153–155, 157–158, 172, 210, 212
television 5, 13
tertiary education 162–164
Tertiary Education Quality and Standards Agency (TEQSA) 195, 202
tertiary enrolment *162*
tetanus 35
Thatcher, Margaret 155
Think Education podcast 1
time difference 16, 19, 28, 30, 75, 200
TOEFL 111
Tokugawa Ieyasu 8
Tokyo 7, 10, 146–147; Haneda Airport 146
Tolkien, J.R.R. 7, 22
Toronto 213
tourist 11, 28, 148, 163
training 11, 18–20, 22, 42–43, 45–46, 63, 85–86, 92, 97, 123, 134, 136, 170, 227
Transnational Education (TNE) 4, 6, 18, 20–21, 23–24, 26–28, 30, 61, 63–64, 68, 70, 72, 78–79, 80, 81–82, *83*, 84, 85, *85*, 100–103, 105–108, 110–119, 123–124, 138, 141–142, 158, 161, 164–188, 192–196, 200–210, 227
trilogy 1
Trinidad and Tobago 209, 224
Turing 50–51
Türkiye 2, 124, 130–131, 134, 140, *180*
Tutor 53, 145, 170, 210, 213

UAE 87–88, 101–105, 110–111, 113, 116, 124, 131, 177, 181, 211–212, 218, 220–221
UK-China Creative Industries Research and Innovation Hub 71
UK-China Higher Education Mission 67–70
United Kingdom 9, *163*, **163–164**, *180*, **180**, 211
Université de Caen Normandie 152
Université Grenoble Alpes 95–97

Universities UK International (UUKi) 62, 168, 181
University Grants Commission (UGC) 86
University of Bolton Academic Centre Ras Al Khaimah 168
University of Cambridge 123, 125, 182
University of Edinburgh 88
University of Glasgow 88
University of Leeds 151, 156
University of Limerick 46–47, 57
University of Limerick Global Lounge 46
University of Limerick Language Learning Hub 46
University of London Institute in Paris 209, 224
University of Manchester 88, 212
University of Nottingham Ningbo 174, 184
University of Utah Asia Campus 203
University of Wales 178
University of Warwick 7, 187
University of Westminster (UoW) 136
Uppsala 51
USA 106–107, **163–164**, *180*
Uzbekistan 2, 74, 123, 125, 131, 132, 226

Validation 15, 53, 80, 95, 168, 186
Venezuela 2, 125, 136
Vice Chancellor 128–130, 184, 187, 194, 202
Volunteer 31–33, 51, 56, 157, 219

Wales 51, 60, 124
Welsh government 51, 96, 178
West Africa 182, 187
Western International College 168
Westminster International University Tashkent (WIUT) 74, 123, 125
Wild Atlantic Gateway 46
Wilson-Gulston, Danielle 209–211, 213, 215, 217–224
Women 2, 123–124, 126–134, 136–141, 179, 227

Xhosa 105
Xi-an Jiaotong Liverpool University 174

Yale – NUS College 198–199
Yale University 198–199
Yasai tempura 11
Yu, Cheryl 40, 53

Zayed University 209, 224
Zoom 10, 21, 26, 183, 185
Zulu 105

For Product Safety Concerns and Information please contact our EU representative GPSR@taylorandfrancis.com
Taylor & Francis Verlag GmbH, Kaufingerstraße 24, 80331 München, Germany

www.ingramcontent.com/pod-product-compliance
Lightning Source LLC
Chambersburg PA
CBHW061711300426
44115CB00014B/2644